MINISTER of RELIEF

MINISTER of RELIEF

Harry Hopkins and the Depression

SEARLE F.
CHARLES

GREENWOOD PRESS, PUBLISHERS
WESTPORT, CONNECTICUT

Library of Congress Cataloging in Publication Data

Charles, Searle F
Minister of relief: Harry Hopkins and the depression.

Reprint of the ed. published by Syracuse University Press, Syracuse, N. Y.
Bibliography: p.
1. Hopkins, Harry Lloyd, 1890-1946. 2. Depressions --1933--United States. 3. Work relief--United States. I. Title.
[HV28.H66C47 1974] 362.5'092'4 [B] 74-2585
ISBN 0-8371-7407-4

This book has been published
with the assistance of a
Ford Foundation grant.

Originally published in 1963 by Syracuse University Press, Syracuse, New York

Reprinted with the permission of Syracuse University Press

Reprinted in 1974 by Greenwood Press,
a division of Williamhouse-Regency Inc.

Library of Congress Catalog Card Number 74-2585

ISBN 0-8371-7407-4

Printed in the United States of America

TO

BARBARA,
DON, LYN ELLEN,
JUDITH, JANNE

Foreword

Federal relief to the unemployed and needy was a major program of the New Deal. Within three months after Franklin D. Roosevelt became President, the federal government launched our nation's first federal relief system. As administered by Harry L. Hopkins under Roosevelt's leadership, federal relief brought about a marked change in this nation's concept of aiding the unemployed and needy. The beliefs and convictions of people shifted, making possible more extensive relief programs at all levels of government. Work relief rather than the dole became characteristic of relief for the able-bodied unemployed. In addition, the belief in adequate rather than minimum assistance gained momentum and became an integral part of most state and local relief programs.

Although there is no undisputable answer to the question whether there should or should not have been federal relief, research has convinced this author that a federal relief program can be more efficient than a conglomeration of unrelated local and state relief efforts, that federal relief need not be "cold and distant," that political interference exists at all levels of government because of the nature of our society, and that the convictions of the chief administrator of such programs are of fundamental importance in defining the nature of activities. Emphasis is placed on the three most important federal relief agencies during the years 1933 to 1938. The Federal Emergency Relief Administration (FERA), the Civil Works Administration (CWA), and the Works Progress (Projects) Administration (WPA) comprise this trio. The formation, administration, and relation to politics of each are described and analyzed. The impact of a dynamic personality in administration is stressed.

I am indebted to several individuals for their assistance in bringing this book to completion. Professor Frank Freidel gave considerable counsel and advice. Arthur Schlesinger, Jr., worked a reading of an earlier draft into his busy schedule. Professional colleagues John Appel and William Koehnline read portions of the manuscript and suggested worthwhile changes in style and content. Dr. Rexford G. Tugwell and Benjamin V. Cohen read appropriate chapters. Dr. Eugene Smith, historian-administrator and president of Willimantic State College, read the manuscript, made a detailed analysis of it, provided many valuable ideas, and gave encouragement during the trying and difficult moments. Aubrey Williams, closely affiliated with Harry L. Hopkins and second in command in the administration of the federal relief agencies, read parts of the manuscript and answered many questions with a frankness appreciated by the author. Mrs. Eleanor Roosevelt, Miss Lorena Hickok, and Benjamin V. Cohen were interviewed and responded candidly to questions.

The staff of the Franklin D. Roosevelt Library was extremely helpful. Herman Kahn and Elizabeth B. Drewry were ever thoughtful and productive in ideas. William F. Stickle, William Nichols, and George Roach made many valuable suggestions, and produced on many occasions the documents needed to answer questions. The staffs at the New York State Library, the National Archives, the Oral History Research Office, Yale University libraries, and the Indiana State Library rendered excellent assistance.

Miss Maxine Corbin and Mrs. Elizabeth Duryea, typist-proofreaders, worked patiently and effectively with the author in making the final copy. My wife, Barbara Yount Charles, typed, proofread, criticized, and exhibited the patience necessary on the part of a wife who contributes actively to the professional career of her husband.

SEARLE F. CHARLES

Willimantic, Conn.
Spring, 1963

Contents

Foreword vii

Abbreviations xi

Introduction 1

I. The Die Is Cast 5

II. Meeting Immediate Needs 23

III. Trial Balloon: The Civil Works Administration 44

IV. Mattresses, Safety Pins, and Politics . . . 66

V. A Variety of Interests 82

VI. Angling, Planning, and Wrangling . . . 94

VII. The Works Progress Administration . . . 128

VIII. Fluctuating WPA Rolls 159

IX. Politics Galore! 174

X. Presidential Aspirations 206

XI. The Task: Well Done? 220

XII. Hopkins' Imprint 237

Notes 249

Bibliography 269

Index 277

Abbreviations

AAA	Agricultural Adjustment Administration
CCC	Civilian Conservation Corps
CWA	Civil Works Administration
DAI	Division of Application and Information
FERA	Federal Emergency Relief Administration
FSRC	Federal Surplus Relief Corporation
NRA	National Recovery Administration
NYA	National Youth Administration
PWA	Public Works Administration
RA	Resettlement Administration
RFC	Reconstruction Finance Corporation
TVA	Tennessee Valley Authority
USES	United States Employment Service
WPA	Works Progress (Projects) Administration

MINISTER of RELIEF

Introduction

The Great Depression of the thirties is one of the most important events in the history of the United States. Striking in dramatic fashion in October, 1929, with the big stock market crash, it halted the prosperity of the twenties. No longer were just a few industries "sick," having failed to recuperate from postwar ailments. By 1930, most industrial establishments in the United States were curtailing production. The number of unemployed industrial workers increased at a rapid pace from 1929 through 1933. Agriculture, already in economic difficulty, reached new levels of stagnation for the next three years. The prosperity of the twenties, with its frills, its social idiosyncrasies, and its nineteenth-century liberalism, ceased to dominate the economic and social pattern of our society.

Our leaders floundered. It made little difference in which endeavor they were engaged; they could produce no solutions which were acceptable to the public. In turn, millions of Americans lost faith in their leaders. For many, faith in American democracy and capitalism was severely shaken. They sought desperately for new leadership which would produce prosperity and security.

The Republicans, in power in Washington when the crash occurred, could not reverse the downward spiral. Thus, in 1932, the American people chose their new leaders; the Democrats gained an important victory. When Franklin D. Roosevelt took the oath of office as President of the United States on that cold, blustery day of March 4, 1933, he and the Democratic party had the overwhelming support of the people. Expressing concern for the "forgotten man," the new President promised action. The people were relieved. Recovery would soon be underway. A surge of confidence swept through the nation.

President Roosevelt moved on several fronts. Banking, currency, agriculture, business, and industry received immediate attention. Federal relief to the unemployed and needy became an important phase of these endeavors. In maintaining the health and skills of millions of people, in supporting public education, and in renewing faith in the American democratic system, the relief program was as important as any other one program of the New Deal; it was a fundamental phase of this nation's life in the middle and late nineteen thirties.

Direct grants to the needy, work relief, federal funds to students and teachers—these were provided in response to the Great Depression. If economic blight, that killer of men's achievements, hopes, and dreams, had been less extensive and prolonged, federal relief would not have existed at all. Because the depression was both severe and widespread, it became the challenge of leadership to respond to the needs of the country.

There were no precedents in the area of federal relief to guide the new leaders. Harry L. Hopkins, chief administrator for the relief agencies, and his staff often felt their way. Their activities became a part of Roosevelt's experimentation, a reflection of his belief that the government had a responsibility to every group within it and that therefore it was better to try something than to do nothing.

There can be no definitive answer to the value of these relief programs. Where one relief project seemed to miss the mark for one group, it hit the mark for another. Federal relief, like aid for agriculture, favorable legislation for labor, and sympathetic programs for business, was an attempt by the federal government to demonstrate an interest in the welfare of the people. Certainly the reasons for aiding the unemployed were not solely political. A response to the need of these unemployed was extremely important during the discouraging days of the thirties when millions in Europe and Asia turned to fascists and communists for leadership. Here in the United States a responsive federal government actively assisted state and local governments in meeting the needs of the times in a manner which encouraged the citizenry to adhere to most of their democratic and capitalistic traditions.

> I hold that the maintenance of the sense of individual and personal responsibility of men to their neighbors and the proper separation of functions of the Federal and local governments requires the maintenance of the fundamental principle that the obligation of distress rests upon the individuals, upon the communities and upon the States.
>
> —HERBERT HOOVER

> It is common sense to take a method and try it; if it fails, admit it frankly and try another. But above all, try something.
>
> —FRANKLIN D. ROOSEVELT

I. The Die Is Cast

President Franklin D. Roosevelt and the 73rd Congress originated, passed, and implemented fifteen major legislative acts during the famous Hundred Days of Roosevelt's first term. The Federal Emergency Relief Act providing $500,000,000 for relief was the fifth act in the series. Passed May 12, 1933, its implementation began on May 22 when Roosevelt gave the oath of office to Harry L. Hopkins, who left his position as director of the New York state relief agencies in order to accept this new post. After swearing Hopkins into office, Roosevelt told him to give adequate relief without paying attention to politics and politicians. In less than an hour Hopkins was in his office headquarters. Surrounded by boxes, unpacked files and typewriters, workers arranging furniture, and without organized clerical help, he initiated within twenty-four hours formation of a staff, a notice to governors to form state relief organizations, and disbursement of over $5,000,000 of federal relief money to seven different states.

The task Hopkins undertook was at that time in many ways second in importance only to the work of the President of the United States. Between four and five million heads of families were in need of financial assistance. Seventeen to eighteen million people were dependent upon someone other than themselves for cash, food, and clothing. Bread lines, occasional riots, acts of force by farmers to keep farm products off the market or to prevent foreclosures on farms, all were becoming common in our society. Unrest—real, not imagined—was present in sections of the nation. What to do was not clear because all kinds of forces were at work pulling in many different directions. Anything done would be both condemned and praised in the press, on the radio, and by members of Congress. As Hopkins began his work, the echoes of the Hoover administration were resounding across the land. What was its heritage for Hopkins? What had Roosevelt experienced as governor of New York that would be helpful? Were the people really ready to accept a federal relief program?

Herbert Hoover was at the zenith of his political career when he took the office of President in March, 1929. Four years later he left the White House at the nadir of his popularity. Within these four years financial loss, a lower standard of living, personal frustrations, and a fading belief in the American way of life became dominant in our society. With each additional year of depression, despair, doubt, and hopelessness increased until bitterness and spitefulness toward Hoover became rampant in the hearts and minds of millions of Americans. In addition to difficult economic and social conditions, Hoover had to face hostile psychological forces.

During his years as President, Hoover diligently sought suitable answers to the dilemma. Within two weeks after the stock market crash in October, 1929, Hoover had taken action to curb the impact of the depression which exceeded considerably any ever taken by previous presidents. He looked upon this latest depression as a great war, in that it was not a battle upon a single front but upon many fronts.

On this premise, Hoover held a series of conferences with government, labor, and industrial leaders during November of 1929. His goals were to step up federal expenditures for public works, speed up private construction, liquidate inflated debts and prices, and maintain current wage levels. He believed profits, not wages, should absorb the first and worst blows of the depression. He asked labor to avoid strikes and to make no demands for higher wages. Hoover received considerable support in his approach from industry and labor.

Having the comprehensive and detailed information available to the President of the United States, Hoover realized within a few weeks the seriousness of the crash of October, 1929. He hoped an upward spiral in the nation's economic life would soon occur, but each month new national and international situations developed which prevented systematic recovery. Hoover feared that the people would become too pessimistic during the first several months of the depression. He issued short statements of encouragement; for example, in March, 1930, he stated that all the evidence indicated the worst unemployment would be over in sixty days, and in June, 1930, he told the United States Chamber of Commerce that the worst was over and with unified effort recovery would come rapidly. While President Hoover needed to take the leading hand in lending encouragement in the disheartening days of 1930 and 1931, it seems in retrospect that he believed too much in his optimistic comments and could not shake himself loose from his traditional concepts of government's role in society. Fortunately, however, he was able to do this better than many other prominent American leaders, many of whom attempted to prevent Hoover from breaking with tradition as much as he did.

The initial impact and first responses to the economic crash were barely over when, in the spring and summer of 1930, a severe drought developed in the Midwest and South. This eventually affected an estimated one million farm families and twenty million animals, as well as resources of seeds and feed. Here was catastrophe and suffering such as Hoover had handled successfully during World War I and immediately after. Here was a chance for Hoover to dramatize himself and his humanitarian qualities. He did take certain steps quickly. He induced railroad owners to have their companies haul feed to these drought sufferers at a 50 per cent reduction in rates. He held conferences with governors and Red Cross officials in an effort to coordinate relief efforts. He directed the funneling of highway construction funds into drought areas as a means of providing employment for distressed farmers. He ordered that flood control and waterway projects be built sooner than originally planned. And in addition, he directed the Federal Land Banks and the Federal Farm Board to expand credit facilities.[1]

In all of this Hoover overlooked what proved to be most essential—money, food, and clothing for the farmers and their families. Many farmers became bitter when they learned they could get money for hay for their cattle but no money for food for their families. True, the Red Cross had been mobilized, but many claimed the task was so extensive that the agency could not handle the need. In a few instances Red Cross depots ran out of relief. Senators Caraway and Robinson of Arkansas, the state most affected by the drought, took the cause of the farmers to Congress. They asked for direct money grants to help feed and clothe the farmer and his family. Immediately Republican House Leader Tilson called any such relief a "dole." Debate in the Senate began to wax hot. The insurgent Republican from Idaho, Senator William E. Borah, did not want the term "dole" attached to the needs of the American farmer. In a colorful and fiery speech in the Senate, fighting for "principle," he declared:

> So far as the drouth regions are concerned no new principle is presented to the American people. . . . Everyone concedes that the conditions in the South are due to what we are prone to call an Act of God. The people . . . have been visited by a drouth which has been as devastating, as cruel

> and as remorseless as a flood or an earthquake. . . . We are simply proposing to deal with a condition which has again and again been presented to the Congress of the United States. . . . When before . . . there has been a fire or a flood or an earthquake, has there been talk about establishing a *dole?* In no sense does the dole system apply. . . . We will either feed these people, or we will stay here and tell the American people why we do not feed them! [2]

After many more bitter words, but also with quick acceptance of slight changes in phraseology, the Senate and House passed a bill which allowed the farmers to secure direct aid if they could prove they needed it.

Out of it all Hoover lost prestige. Many a farmer seemed to feel as did one of the Senate's outstanding Republican senators, George Norris of Nebraska, who wrote this epitaph to the bill:

> Blessed are they who starve while the asses and the mules are fed, for they shall be buried at public expense.
>
> Blessed are they who hunger in the land of Drought, for they shall be told that a great Government feeds the starving in foreign lands.
>
> Blessed are the little children who shiver in the cold, for their suffering shall receive "sympathetic consideration." [3]

Many Americans believed that Hoover had lost sight of the human being in this episode of giving relief. Bitter over the attacks made upon him and what he had done, he struck back in this ringing statement of his beliefs:

> This is not an issue as to whether people shall go hungry or cold in the United States. It is solely a question of the best method by which hunger and cold shall be prevented. It is a question as to whether the American people on one

hand will maintain the spirit of charity and mutual self-help through voluntary giving and the responsibility of local government as distinguished on the other hand from appropriations of the Federal Treasury for such purposes. . . . The basis of successful relief in national distress is to mobilize and organize the infinite number of agencies of self-help in the community. That has been the American way of relieving distress among our own people and the country is successfully meeting its problem in the American way today. . . . I am willing to pledge myself that if the time should ever come that the voluntary agencies of the country together with the local and state governments are unable to find resources with which to prevent hunger and suffering in my country, I will ask the aid of every resource of the Federal Government because I would no more see starvation amongst our countrymen than would any senator or congressman.[4]

Concurrent with his actions to secure cooperation from industrial and labor leaders and to aid farmers, President Hoover took important steps aimed at preventing excessive hunger and cold for those people in honest difficulties. In 1930 he established the President's Emergency Relief Organization which came to be called the Woods Committee, after its chairman, Colonel Arthur Woods. The committee sought to assist state and local relief efforts by encouraging public works, by working with industry to maintain employment, by encouraging those not in need to carry on projects which would give part-time jobs, and by publicizing the needs of the unemployed workers. It was a coordinating, fact-finding agency of service, but clearly not one to engage in relief work itself.

The Woods Committee had considerable success for a voluntary organization. Within a year it formed 3,000 or more state and local committees to aid in the relief program.

Relief organizations were functioning, in varying degrees of efficiency, in every state, 227 large cities, some 2,000 smaller cities, and over 1,000 counties. Colonel Woods reported to the President in August, 1931, that up to that time actual suffering from want of food, shelter, or clothing had not occurred on any large scale.

The world and national economic situation became worse during the spring of 1931. Fears that unemployment would be worse instead of better during the coming winter continued to increase. Fred Croxton, acting chairman of the President's Emergency Employment Committee, which replaced the Woods Committee when Col. Woods and several other members returned to private employment, informed the President that "for every thousand families restored to economic independence" there would be "another thousand whose resources would become exhausted." In many cities, reported Croxton, the number of dependent families would be double that of the previous winter. Croxton saw the need for "social statesmanship." He believed private philanthropy could not possibly raise all the funds needed. Boston was carrying 95 per cent of the relief load out of city funds. In Cleveland, Philadelphia, and New York all the funds raised had already been spent before the year was half gone. Local and state public works projects were declining, cutting employment, although federal expenditures for public work offset this to some extent.[5]

Disturbing information about unemployment and the need for relief poured into the White House from other sources. Governor Gifford Pinchot of Pennsylvania wrote, "Wages are decreasing. Distress is acute. . . . You have yourself asked for appropriations by Congress for relief of the needy in distant parts of the world. It would seem to be most opportune that you should do no less for our own needy here at home." Republican Senator Reed Smoot of Utah expressed concern by saying, "We should raise sufficient funds to feed the hungry, even if we have to issue bonds to do it." [6] And a few weeks later William Green of the American Federation of Labor stated the issue more sharply:

> Some of us have been wondering whether the present industrial order is to be a success or a failure. No social order is secure where wealth flows at such a rate into the hands of the few away from the many. . . . We will be in favor of having the United States Government take it away through taxation and distribute it to the masses. . . . The right to work is a sacred right that every government, no matter what it's for, must guarantee if it is to endure. What shall we say of a system that relegates men at the prime of life to the human scrap heap and that knows no remedy for the situation other than a reduction in the standard of living? I warn the people who are exploiting the workers that they can only drive them so far before they will turn on them and destroy them! They are taking no account of the history of nations in which governments have been overturned. Revolutions grow out of the depths of hunger.[7]

On the credit side Hoover learned that $300,000,000 more of public works would start before winter set in. The United States Employment Bureau informed him jobs had been found for 281,769 persons during the previous four months. The Department of Public Health told him the health of the nation had actually been better in the winter of 1930–31 than in the winter of 1928–29. Hoover probably took comfort when he heard such men as Silas Strawn, newly elected president of the United States Chamber of Commerce, state publicly: "It would be deplorable if this country ever voted a dole. When we do that, we've hit the toboggan as a nation." [8]

Other factors tended to offset pessimistic information reaching Hoover. In August, 1931, the President received answers from many of the governors of key states that they could take care of their own unemployed. The governor of

Michigan telegraphed, "The people of Michigan will take care of their own problems." Telegrams implying no need for federal aid came also from the governors of California, Connecticut, Delaware, and New York.[9]

Hoover believed a special session of Congress unnecessary to meet the challenge of the new conditions. He took executive action. He set forth the debt moratorium plan as a world business stimulant. He asked community chest groups to estimate the relief load for the winter of 1931–32. He formed the President's Organization on Unemployment Relief. Walter S. Gifford, president of the American Telephone and Telegraph Company, headed this new network of committees. Fred Croxton directed the administrative activities. Several subcommittees, each headed by a prominent American, were organized in an effort to give more attention to specific phases of providing relief. Owen D. Young's committee attempted to stimulate state and local agencies by fund-raising campaigns. Another subcommittee encouraged employment by such devices as "spread-the-work." James R. Garfield and his group had the task of increasing employment through increased public works—all to be financed in the traditional manner. Although many people worked conscientiously doing much good for thousands of people, still need increased more rapidly than did aid. As for the spread-the-work concept, which involved the principle of giving part-time work in the factories to more workers rather than full-time work to fewer workers, it fell by the wayside in the summer of 1932, when more manufacturers dismissed workers or cut wages. It was too high a penalty for the men who did work. Dr. R. A. Stevenson, director at the time of the Employment Stabilization Research Institute of the University of Minnesota, summarized the problem by pointing out that a contribution of 25 to 50 per cent in time and wages was too much for most workers, particularly when fund-raising campaigns were calling for a 5 or 10 per cent donation.[10]

In his presidential messages of December, 1931, and 1932, President Hoover outlined to Congress measures he thought would aid recovery. Congress was indecisive. The Democrats, who controlled the House by 1932, opposed much of his program. Some action eventually was taken, but usually many months after it would have been most effective. For example, the Home Loan Bank Bill (weakened by several amendments) passed its last congressional hurdle eight months after Hoover requested its passage. During that time thousands of homes were lost by owners to mortgage-holders. Action came more quickly on means to aid business, finance, and transportation. The Reconstruction Finance Corporation was authorized in late January, 1932. But even here, as Hoover pointed out later, the delay in its establishment cost the public $465,000,000 in lost bank holdings and investments. Several of Hoover's suggestions never received serious consideration by Congress prior to his leaving office.

The Democrats, for their part, did not present any coherent program better than the ideas of President Hoover. It is true that several of the Democratic congressional leaders were willing to spend several hundred millions, even several billion dollars, for federally stimulated public works. Senators Robert Wagner, Joseph Robinson, and John Nance Garner presented bills which, if enacted, would have given money to the unemployed with no return of any great consequence to the government. In short, it would have involved the federal government in deficit financing, thereby increasing the national debt. For example, Senator John Nance Garner of Texas introduced a bill calling for a $2,300,000,000 non–self-liquidating public works program. Hoover was strongly opposed to increasing the national debt. He was fighting for a balanced budget; therefore, he condemned Garner's bill. Said Hoover, "Never before has so dangerous a suggestion been seriously made to our country." [11]

Meanwhile the unemployment figures continued to rise,

the bread and soup lines increased in length and number, and "Hoovervilles" with their dirt and squalor and feeling of despair became more common in many areas of the nation. In March, 1932, at least ten million American workers were unemployed. Hoover knew further steps must be taken. He called a meeting of important congressional leaders of both major parties and put these questions to them:

1. Should we continue to administer "direct relief" through our organization of committees?
2. Should the federal government make grants to the states for the committees' support, conditioned upon regular state and municipal participation also?
3. Should the federal government appropriate funds for direct doles and also take over the administration of them?
4. Should we expand appropriations from the Federal Treasury for public works beyond the programs I proposed?

Hoover later recorded that both Democrats and Republicans agreed:

1. There should be no federal doles.
2. Grants-in-aid to the state governments should be made if doles did become necessary.
3. There should be no expansion of non-liquidating public works for relief.[12]

In the spring of 1932, Senator Robinson renewed with great vigor his efforts to get more done for the unemployed. He received support for a $2,000,000,000 bond issue for self-liquidating public works from such men as Bernard Baruch, Owen D. Young, and Al Smith. Hoover could not ignore this proposal or the men who backed it. It was a self-paying proposal. Still, if he accepted the proposal he would involve the federal government directly and actively in helping to provide jobs in a pattern for which there was no major precedent. As an alternative he could rely on the effort of American industry combined with moderate help to the states for relief. He chose to do the latter, for this approach, he believed, would not directly increase the national debt or force the government into a direct relief program.

Later, as the unemployment and relief situation became more acute, Hoover agreed the states needed assistance. He approved and supported the passage of the Emergency and Reconstruction Relief Act of July, 1932, which provided $300,000,000 to be loaned by the Reconstruction Finance Corporation to the states for relief purposes. Loans could also be made by the RFC to the states up to a total of $1,500,000,000 for public works of the self-liquidating type. For localities already in debt and unable to borrow, the latter amount was of no value. But further than this Hoover could not go, for he believed that "a cold and distant charity which puts out its sympathy only through the tax collector yields a very meager dole of unloving and perfunctory relief." In the last analysis, Hoover the humanitarian was trapped by the Hoover who believed that "the sole function of government is to bring about a condition of affairs favorable to the beneficial development of private enterprise." In 1932, Senator Wagner was far closer to a majority of the people when he said: "We shall help the railroad; we shall help the financial institutions; and I agree that we should. But is there any reason why we should not likewise extend a helping hand to the forlorn American, in every village and every city of the United States, who has been without wages since 1929; must he alone carry the cross of individual responsibility?" [13]

As economic conditions grew progressively worse, Hoover became the butt of bitter jokes. The majority of the people became hostile toward him and he lost the public esteem he had when he first took office. No longer was he viewed as the great humanitarian. In addition to the grim realities of increased unemployment and decreased industrial and construction activity, came the episode of the Anacostia Flats and the presidential campaign of 1932.

In his handling of the veterans camped on Anacostia Flats, Hoover missed an opportunity to show the nation a warm heart and a friendly hand. Fifteen to twenty thousand of these men were in and about Washington for approximately two months before a small group finally maneuvered an incident which resulted in need for police action. During this two-month period Hoover did not find it advisable to confer with any of the duly selected leaders. When, in the midst of their stay on the Anacostia Flats, the veterans learned that the Senate had rejected their request for immediate payment of a bonus, they did not riot or stampede the Capitol Building as many had expected. Although Hoover encouraged passage of a bill providing money to pay their way home, the money was to be deducted from the bonus due them in 1945. This was no answer to the immediate needs of their families. Finally, a unit of the United States Army drove the veterans, some with their families, from the Flats into Maryland or else put them on trains for home. General Douglas MacArthur summed up the attitude of the administration when he said that the "mob" was about to seize control of the government and the whole thing was animated by the "essence of revolution." Later, Hoover lost another chance to show his concern for the unemployed veterans when he refused to see Sherwood Anderson and Waldo Frank, vocal intellectuals, who went to Washington to protest the use of troops against unarmed civilians.[14]

The Veterans Bonus March to Washington was symptomatic of the increasing concern of the people about the severe social and physical effects of the depression. People began to talk and write more boldly about the need for a change in the pattern of our national government. Apathy turned to demands for action as men stood in the bread and soup lines more frequently and for longer periods of time. The more militant farmers began to withhold milk and crops from the market and in instances forced other farmers to do likewise. The radical Holiday Farm movement spread rapidly in the Midwest. The Farm Bureau organization selected a man of action, Ed O'Neal, to lead it. Local mob pressure for food and clothing increased, particularly in the coal mining regions. Cuts in wages and the number of hours worked increased tensions. Farm, labor, and industrial leaders, as well as social and literary figures, talked kindly of Russian communism or of the need for a Mussolini for the United States, and often made clear that they thought American capitalism was doomed.

Hoover, now busy with campaigning for reelection, took no further action to provide direct relief. Surrounded by men more conservative than himself, opposed to the insurgent-liberal Republicans, hateful of Democratic leadership in Congress for its own shortsighted political moves, he drifted through his last painful months in office unable to bring himself to demonstrate to the people that the federal government would aid them *directly* by grants of money with which to buy food and clothing. Thus he left office amidst further economic decline without extending a sizable amount of aid directly to the laborer and the farmer. Both organized labor and organized agriculture were for many years to picture Hoover as the friend of business and the enemy of the common man.

Despite the shortcomings of the Hoover administration in providing aid to the unemployed and needy, an objective appraisal would include the observation that Hoover, in first stressing local government, state government, and private charity groups as the agencies to provide relief, took the attitude acceptable to the majority of the American public. Social welfare agencies were for the first two and a half years generally in favor of this. As the need for aid increased, Hoover not only tried to aid state and local agencies through national coordination and expanded public works but also moved finally to direct loans to states by the Reconstruction Finance Corporation. There is no real evidence to prove that Hoover would not have gone further had he remained in office.

Contemporary with Hoover's efforts to combat the depression on a national scale were those of Governor Franklin D. Roosevelt of New York. As governor of the wealthiest and most populous state, Roosevelt responded to the early effects of the depression in much the same manner as had President Hoover. Local efforts—public and private—were Roosevelt's first answer for the care of the needy. After observing the situation during the first winter of the depression, 1929–30, he appointed a Committee on Stabilization of Industry. This committee scratched the surface. In a rather meager way it finally reported that public works could be expanded in bad economic times and that the bulk of any immediate aid should be carried out by the local government and business leaders.

During the winter of 1930–31, the state of New York, under the direction of the governor, did make available for use cots and blankets kept at national guard and naval military armories. But these were available only after the ordinary facilities of each locality had been exhausted. Roosevelt encouraged the expansion of public works, and in the fiscal years 1930 and 1931, New York increased public works. But Roosevelt, like Hoover, found that unpaid taxes and other limitations in taxing forced a reduction in public works for 1932.

In January, 1931, the Governor's Committee on Unemployment reported to Roosevelt that nearly half of the cities in the state had inadequate relief facilities; that there was a great variety in the quality of relief being given; that the administration of local relief was inefficient; that physical health, mental health, earning power, and morale were beginning to deteriorate. The committee suggested that more work relief be given rather than home relief. It also recommended increased expenditures for public works.

In the summer of 1931, the State Board of Social Welfare and the State Charities Aid Association in a joint report pointed out that individual savings and credit and assistance from relatives had been almost exhausted. Their reports showed that in almost every city in the state as much money or more had been spent for relief in the first half of 1931 as in the entire year of 1930. With this and other evidence indicating the gravity of the situation before him, Governor Roosevelt called a special session of the State Assembly.

In his address to the New York legislature, Roosevelt made his philosophy of relief clear. He made three points. One, the giving of relief under ordinary circumstances was primarily a local function. Two, in emergencies the state needed to supplement local aid by a method of granting funds which in turn would stimulate local giving. Three, the state would attempt to handle relief on a pay-as-you-go basis. To carry out his third point, Roosevelt asked for a tax increase of $20,000,000. After bickering over the organization for providing state aid and the handling of the funds, the state legislature approved the sum requested.

Roosevelt had hardly completed his organization of the New York Temporary Relief Commission on October, 1931, when it became evident that the state and the nation were having such a severe economic decline that further state aid would become necessary. Therefore, he called for approval of a $30,000,000 bond issue. New York voters supported this proposal. Thus, the state of New York turned to deficit financing not because it was a pet idea of Roosevelt or of anyone else, but because private and local public relief efforts were inadequate for the actual need existing.[15]

Roosevelt's ideas regarding the necessity for active state and federal relief programs changed during the spring and summer of 1932. In his famous Forgotten Man address of April, 1932, Roosevelt said:

> People suggest that a huge expenditure of public funds by the Federal Government and by state and local government will completely solve the unemployment problem. But it is clear that even if we could raise many billions of dollars and find definitely useful public works to spend these billions on, even all that money would not give employment to the seven million or ten million of people who are out of work. Let us admit frankly that it would be only a stop-gap. A real economic cure must go to the killing of the bacteria of the system rather than to the treatment of external symptoms.[16]

But shortly thereafter in another talk the future President left the door open for some type of action when he told an audience at Oglethorpe University: "The country needs, and unless I mistake its temper, the country demands, bold, persistent experimentation. It is common sense to take a method and try it; if it fails, admit it frankly and try another. But above all, try something." [17]

When Hopkins became relief administrator, Hoover's experiences provided a frame of reference from which Hopkins could operate, and added to it were those experiences and ideas of Roosevelt in the unemployment situation in New York State. Roosevelt had not, as governor, gone out and crusaded for the unemployed and the rights they might claim for themselves. He approached the problem of unemployment very gingerly, feeling his way just as Hoover was doing on the national level. He hoped local relief efforts would do the job. They proved to be inadequate for the times. He hoped a reasonable increase in taxes would provide the necessary financial aid for relief, but this proved a less than adequate solution. Following his conviction that the state was the servant of the people and observing that the people of his state needed additional aid, Roosevelt turned to bonding for the necessary financing. Thus, Roosevelt and Hoover were both pushed further and further from their own original concepts of how to deal with both the unemployed employables and the unemployables. The people in all areas of the nation were by this time ready for a new approach. The majority hoped that Roosevelt and Hopkins would carry out the provisions of the FERA act with vigor and without undue delay.

The primary need of the unemployed was the lack of money, not lack of character, employability, or adequate adjustment to community life. —E. WIGHT BAKKE

II. Meeting Immediate Needs

The dynamic personality behind the development of the Federal Emergency Relief Administration and other major relief agencies of the New Deal was Harry L. Hopkins. Many of his concepts governed the development of the relief activities carried on by the New Deal. He inspired his fellow administrators. He contended with a great deal of perseverance for the procurement of funds. He fought off his critics with skill, sometimes with a scathing counterattack. Above all, he learned the importance of loyalty to his chief, the President.

A native of Iowa, Hopkins left Grinnell College upon graduation for New York City, where he became a prominent social worker. By the end of the 1920's Hopkins headed several social welfare agencies. The best known of these was the New York Tuberculosis Association. His main interest was in health, but he spent many days and weeks of each year working with groups aiding the unemployed and their families. In 1931, Jesse Isador Straus, president of R. H. Macy and Company and chairman of Governor Roosevelt's New York Temporary Relief Administration, selected Hopkins as deputy administrator for the state relief program. When Straus resigned in 1932, Roosevelt selected Hopkins to head the agency. As administrator of the state relief program Hopkins did his work well, stressed work relief, and learned the importance of power. It was logical that Roosevelt, thus acquainted with Hopkins and his work, should select him to direct the federal relief program.[1]

When reporters interviewed Hopkins during his first few

weeks in office, they found a man with a restless, gangling body and a sardonic, good-natured face whose intent, suspicious eyes gave the impression he was watching all with the utmost caution. They observed that he worked with quick, nervous motions, taking time only for "quick cigarettes," "brief sarcasm," and "cynical statements," giving the impression of being one impatient of petty detail. He obviously did not care about the trimmings while on the job. Gadgets, fancy decorations, expensive furniture—none of these surrounded him in his bare office with its unshined desk, peeled, clockless walls, and overflowing ashtrays.

Two of Hopkins' traits were quickly revealed to reporters. After a few press conferences his tendency to be cynical and caustic in dealing with certain subjects and individuals was clearly evident. Reporters liked this; it made his comments better copy. It made the politicians dislike him, for a time at least, for he questioned their motives. Possessing these traits, Hopkins vigorously challenged the sincerity of his critics, and thus often countered their criticisms with sarcasm, as when he said of Governor Eugene Talmadge, "He doesn't contribute a dime but he's always yapping." And later, when Governor Talmadge complained of the high CWA wage rates, Hopkins retorted, "Some people just can't stand seeing others make a decent living." His cynicism, however, prevented him from being too idealistic. Joseph E. Davies once remarked of Hopkins, "He had the purity of St. Francis of Assisi combined with the sharp shrewdness of a race track tout." Yet Harry Hopkins' sincerity and straightforwardness impressed reporters and congressional leaders. In fact, *Time* magazine reported in February, 1934, that Hopkins had so impressed Congress with his sincerity that one senator remarked, "If Roosevelt ever becomes Jesus Christ, he should have Harry Hopkins as his prophet." [2]

A vivid account of Hopkins in the early Washington years occurs in Ernie Pyle's newspaper column for October 26, 1935.

And you Mr. Hopkins, I like you because you look like common people. I don't mean any slur by that either, because they don't come any commoner than I am, but you sit there so easy swinging back and forth in your swivel chair, in your blue suit and blue shirt, and your neck is sort of skinny, like poor people's necks, and you act honest, too.

And you answer the reporters' questions as tho you were talking to them personally, instead of being a big official. It tickled me the way you would say, "I can't answer that," in a tone that almost says out loud, "Now you knew damn well when you asked me that I couldn't answer that. . . ."

And that old office of yours, Mr. Hopkins, good Lord, it's terrible. It's so little in the first place, and the walls are faded and water pipes run up the walls and your desk doesn't even shine. But I guess you don't care. Maybe it wouldn't look right for you to have a nice office anyway, when you're dealing in misery all the time.

One nice thing about your office being so little, tho, the reporters all have to pack close up around your desk, and they can see and hear you and it's sort of like talking to you in your home, except there they'd be sitting down, I hope.

The reporters tell me, Mr. Hopkins, that you're about the fastest thinker of any of the big men who hold press conferences. Ickes is fast too, and so is Farley they say, but you always come back right now with something pretty good. And you've got a pleasant, clean cut face, too, and they say you never try to lie out of anything.[3]

In administering federal relief, Hopkins found both assets and drawbacks in the state and local public relief agencies throughout the land. They had done and were doing much valuable work. Conscientious Americans manned most of these agencies, but their method of operation was outmoded. The "poor laws" and work tests of the preceding century were not adequate for the demands of depression years. In addition, most public relief agencies lacked the funds to be effective even if they did have the necessary attitudes and knowledge.

All forty-eight states had laws providing for relief by the time Hopkins went to Washington. But only ten states had old-age assistance laws, and many of the aged were in dire straits by 1933. A greater number of states provided assistance to the blind. Most had laws which outlined steps for the care of dependent children, maintaining institutions for their care. In most other areas of relief activities, the localities bore the costs and controlled the programs.

Local and state relief agencies had expanded during the Hoover administration. Too many, however, were still restricted in operation by tight regulations which prevented many persons in legitimate need from receiving assistance. Work tests were still used by many agencies. Residence requirements were often very restrictive. Many social workers still believed every case should be thoroughly investigated before any type of relief should be provided. These requirements were too confining, particularly in cities where the individuals needing relief numbered in the thousands in contrast with the hundreds of two or three years earlier.

The complexities of establishing and maintaining an adequate relief program for eighteen million people appeared even more of a challenge to Hopkins and his staff when they evaluated these facts:

1. More than half the families on unemployment relief were in eight states and more than a third in four states—Pennsylvania, New York, Ohio, and Illinois.

2. In some states one-fourth of the population was receiving relief. At the other extreme seven states had only one-twentieth of their population on unemployment relief.

3. Negroes were on relief in almost twice as great propor-

tion to their numbers in the population as were whites. Almost 18 per cent of the Negroes were on relief in October, 1933, compared with 9.5 per cent of whites on relief.

4. The percentage of urban Negro population on relief was three times that of the urban white population. The rural population, Negro and white, ran about the same.

5. Six states possessed one-half of the total urban relief families.

6. Principal cities had a higher percentage on relief than the nation as a whole.

7. Large families were more frequently on the relief lists than small families.

8. Children formed a disproportionately large part of the relief groups as compared to the general population. Forty-two per cent of the persons on relief were children under 16.

9. Slightly more males than females were on relief lists. (This was not true during the time CWA and WPA existed, but, of course, those under these programs were receiving federal, state, and local relief funds.) [4]

It was plain enough that no planned system, such as that based on population or property within a state, could serve as the sole determining factor in the distribution of relief funds. Need had to be the final criterion used.

What was need? How was it defined? Basically, it was not having sufficient goods and services to maintain adequate health and job stability. An inherent problem faced by the administrator of any relief program is to judge need accurately. Then he must convince others that people in need are not necessarily lazy or shiftless. Further progress occurs when administrators of relief agencies convince the public that merely keeping the relief recipients alive is not nearly so beneficial to the public as rehabilitation, helping individuals to become economically productive. By 1933 the task of implementing a federal relief program was made easier because very great numbers of the population were in actual need of legitimate goods and services. A majority of our people across the nation knew the real problem of the unemployed "was the lack of money, not lack of character, employability, or adequate adjustment to community life."

Hopkins had a basic faith in the integrity of the great majority of the unemployed. He believed the nation should take action to avoid suffering and to eliminate the general feeling of insecurity. Through his years of social work Hopkins knew of the hurt, the despair, the hopelessness that grew within men and women as months passed with no jobs and no income. Among his experiences was the case of a boy shot to death while stealing milk so his baby sister could be fed. Hopkins also knew the tragedy of fifteen hundred people evicted from their homes and sent to live in basements in a river bottom. Three hundred died of various diseases because of dampness and cold, and the survivors stood in line for their one meal a day consisting of half a loaf of bread and a cup of slumgullion served from big garbage cans transformed into soup containers. Hopkins knew what poverty was. He had observed first-hand the strains and tensions of those able and willing to work when no work was to be had. Certainly Hopkins' experiences during these years marked his thinking about social and economic problems. There can be no wonder, really, at Hopkins' tendency to be caustic with those who knew little and sometimes cared less about the unemployed and their families.

The first few months of the FERA were hectic. Selection of personnel, problems carried over from the Emergency Relief Division of the RFC, and demands by state and local agencies that FERA take over their organizations plagued Hopkins. He immediately assured the states that they could count on money through the end of July, 1933, thus allowing him time to make readjustments and to plan new procedures. Hopkins then proceeded to select additional personnel, including several men from the RFC who had intimate knowledge of what had been done by that agency's Emergency Relief Division. One of these men, Pierce Williams, had been director of the National Bureau of Economic Research and the author of studies on problems related to welfare work before working for the RFC and as a field representative with FERA. Robert Kelso, also formerly with the RFC, had been director of the St. Louis Community Fund and the Boston Council of Social Agencies and a state commissioner of public welfare for Massachusetts. C. M. Bookman came to FERA on leave of absence from Cincinnati, where he was director of the Community Chest and Council of Social Agencies. Bookman was past president of the National Conference of Social Work, dean of the Community Chest directors, and member of the board of directors of Survey Associates.

One of Harry Hopkins' most loyal lieutenants was Aubrey Williams, a hard-working, sincere man, who occasionally became involved in controversies because of lack of tact. From a poor Alabama family, Williams pushed his way up the ladder of success by his ability and effort. He worked his way through college, fought in World War I, stayed in France after the war, and returned to the United States with a doctorate from the University of Bordeaux. By 1932 he was a highly respected social work administrator in the Midwest, where he worked with Frank Bane and others of the American Welfare Association.

Corrington Gill, in charge of statistics, majored in economics and statistics at the University of Wisconsin. In 1932 he began work as a reporter for the Washington Press Service, feeding news to forty cities in the United States; later he became business manager of this press service. In 1931 he organized the statistical work for President Hoover's new Federal Employment Stabilization Board. Hopkins drafted him for FERA when Gill came over one day to see if he could be of any help. Like Aubrey Williams, he remained with Hopkins the entire time Hopkins was administrator of relief, although Gill could have earned much more as a private consultant than he ever did working as an administrator for FERA, CWA, and WPA. This was true of most of Hopkins' top aides.

Jacob Baker, a thick-set, amiable fellow, handled the work division for Hopkins during the existence of FERA. Before joining FERA, Baker taught science and agriculture in rural high schools. Later he became a superintendent of ranges and mines in Mexico, a personnel expert for Bethlehem Steel Building Corporation and the San Joaquin Light and Power Company of California, and a consultant engineer for other large firms. In 1926, he organized what became known as the Vanguard Press.

One of Hopkins' best field representatives, who later joined the inner circle of FERA and WPA administrators in Washington, was Alan Johnstone of South Carolina. A graduate of Harvard Law School, Johnstone spent much of his time during the depression as head of various social organizations. In 1932–33, for example, he was director for the South Carolina Relief Administration.

Other members of Hopkins' staff with notable experience were Sherrard Ewing, formerly director of the National Association of Travelers' Aid Societies; Rowland Haynes, director of the Cleveland Welfare Federation at one time and secretary of the University of Chicago; Frank Bane, of the American Welfare Association, an adviser during the early months; and Howard O. Hunter, who became one of Hopkins' trusted field representatives and a close friend.

Harry Hopkins and his staff provided the three immediate objectives and guiding principles for the FERA program. First, adequate relief must be given—all in need should have enough food, shelter, and clothing if at all possible. Second, work relief rather than dole relief must be given the employables. (Employables were defined as citizens fit for employment but unable to find jobs, thereby being unemployed on private jobs.) Third, the work relief program should be diversified so as to allow opportunity for those in the program to perform activities related directly or indirectly to their ordinary occupations.

Administrator Hopkins created four main divisions within FERA. The first was the Division of Research, Statistics, and Finance. Its tasks were to collect information pertaining to all phases of relief work, federal, state, and local; to put the information into meaningful form; to analyze each state and local unit for its ability to contribute toward relief; and to account for the expenditures of FERA.

The establishment of the Works Division reflected Hopkins' strong belief in work relief in preference to the dole. It tried to develop suitable work programs. The projects were not originated or sponsored by the FERA, except for federal projects. The Works Division's main task was to raise the caliber of work projects already in existence. Only after the Civil Works Administration was curtailed in the spring of 1934 did it give most of its attention to the direct sponsorship and development of new federal work relief projects.

The Division of Rural Rehabilitation had the responsibility of aiding farm people in restoring their own economic well-being, removing families from submarginal land, and establishing them on land from which a profitable livelihood could be obtained. It also aided in the establishment of joint rural-industrial communities.

In the day-to-day operations of FERA, the Division of Relations with States was of primary importance. It supervised indirectly the direct relief program of the states; hence, it contacted the states' offices concerning major points of policy. Hopkins' chief assistant, Aubrey Williams, was head of this division during most of the time FERA existed.

Important adjuncts to these main divisions were the field

representatives. These men coordinated the state FERA programs with Washington FERA offices. Their power depended partly upon their abilities; however, the scope of power and activities each had, with no reference to individual ability, increased considerably after May, 1934, when regional offices were established. The field representatives supervised the regional offices in their areas except for a few roving representatives who moved about from region to region investigating special problems. Hopkins organized in most regional offices four divisions similar to the divisions in the federal office. The state and local offices were generally organized in a similar manner. The Washington staff usually sent material concerning a particular area or locality through the field representative to the regional office and then to the pertinent state and local offices. Most of the field representatives selected by Hopkins proved to be men of excellent ability.[5]

Amid the confusion of the first weeks of FERA there emerged by August, 1933, definite patterns and regulations which guided FERA throughout its existence. First, Hopkins and his staff decided the unemployed must apply to a public agency for relief. In order that private charity workers with skill and experience could be used to advantage, FERA suggested they be hired, either full-time or part-time, by local and state relief agencies. Second, the FERA staff stipulated that federal relief funds could not be used for rental of buildings for offices, for salaries of regularly employed public officials except those working directly on emergency relief, or for salaries of relief workers not working directly under the supervision of the unemployment relief authorities. Autos and equipment could not be purchased with federal relief funds. Third, FERA decided the unemployable unemployed could receive the benefits of federal relief funds. This interpretation of rules and regulations meant the national government could legally share the financial burden of caring not only for those who were now unemployed but also for the sick, crippled, and blind. Evidence soon indicated the states and localities usually could not care properly for all these unemployables. The results of investigation of each family seeking relief determined the amount it should receive. FERA provided the difference between the need and the income. This became known as the budgetary deficiency standard.

Federal emergency relief funds could be expended in two ways. First, $250,000,000 could be given to the states on the basis of one dollar for every three dollars they appropriated and used for relief. Second, $250,000,000 could be used by the administrator of FERA for direct grants to states when each state's governor could prove his state no longer had financial means for necessary relief. Of these two methods the second became the more important after the first $500,000,000 was spent. Later appropriations allowed the funds to be distributed by the federal relief agency on a direct rather than a matching basis.

Although there is precedent for the grant-in-aid system dating back to federal grants of land in the late eighteenth century, the grant-in-aid system is really a product of the present century. Perhaps the Morrill Act of 1862, supplemented in 1890 with additional legislation, is the best precedent for the grant-in-aid system which developed after 1900. Since 1890 the federal government has usually stipulated that certain requirements be met before funds are transferred to the states. Hence, the federal government before the time of the New Deal did have means to secure state acquiescence in practically every grant-in-aid program. This was true in the fields of public roads, vocational education and rehabilitation, distribution of nursery stock, and agricultural experiment stations and extension work in agriculture, and in home economics.

By the thirties these three main conditions governed the

federal grant-in-aid system. First, the state legislature accepted the federal act and created a state agency with power adequate to execute the work involved. Second, the agency created by the state drafted and submitted a plan which met federal approval. The state was responsible for the actual execution of the plan, but it conformed to minimum standards set by the federal government. And third, the state matched funds. FERA held the states to all three points for a time. Throughout all of its existence, it stressed the matching of funds, even in arranging direct grants, for it insisted that states and localities contribute funds whenever possible.[6]

Members of Congress differed as to the best method of distributing FERA funds. Those who ordinarily opposed federal grants for relief opposed also the method of discretionary disbursement by a federal administrator. Those who ordinarily supported federal grants-in-aid to states for relief supported the methods eventually used by Hopkins. The small states and the less wealthy states particularly favored discretionary action by the administrator. They paid federal taxes, as did the wealthy states, but once their citizens had done this individually they did not have sufficient money left to contribute heavily to the state treasury. Therefore, the matching dollar system proved of no real benefit to them. On a discretionary basis these states could appeal directly to the administrator, prove their need, and receive federal money.

In cases where states could not raise money for matching grants, Hopkins used the discretionary basis for distribution of FERA funds. He made only small grants on this basis. In fact, during May, June, July, and August of 1933 he allotted only $37,000,000. During this same time he granted $138,-000,000 on a matching basis. But the inauguration of the Civil Works Program soon brought a change of emphasis. It would have been possible, under the laws involved, for the wealthier states to request undue proportions of both FERA and CWA funds. If wealthy states having matching funds available had so desired, they could have used most of the relief funds appropriated by Congress. In the fall of 1933, therefore, Hopkins obtained President Roosevelt's approval for expanding the discretionary basis for approving grants to the states.

This change in granting of funds was very important. It assured a fairer distribution of relief funds by providing more support for the poor states. Of equal importance were the enlarged discretionary powers of the administrator. Now he had considerable control over where FERA money went. Under the matching dollar plan he did not control, in actual practice, the size or timing of the grants. The federal administrator could now *force* states to establish better relief organizations and he could *influence the content* of the relief program of any given state by the threat of refusing to grant money unless certain conditions were met by the state.

Use of the discretionary basis created two new problems for Hopkins' staff. It was necessary first to ascertain the total relief requirements or needs of each state, and second, to determine the sums states and localities could raise to meet these total requirements. The FERA staff planned to use federal funds to meet the difference between the needs of the states and their ability to supply money to meet those needs.

The first step used to determine need was the examination of basic documents submitted by the governor of each state. The governor first signed a sworn statement showing funds needed for the period of one month, the amount his state could provide, and in what manner its funds would be provided. He also agreed to spend money according to the general rules and regulations of the federal relief administrator. Statistical information was given to support the governor's statement, and accompanying briefs provided in narrative form an account of factors in the state affecting relief problems and funds. The FERA staff in Washington reviewed these briefs and statements, making recommendations for action to Hopkins.

Although careful consideration was given to the requests of the governors, the reports of the field representatives and the personal observations of the assistant administrator were more influential in determining the financial contributions of FERA to the states. The field representatives were familiar with the relief activities in each state within their assigned area. More than that, they made it a business to check the entire economic activity and condition of their territory. They talked with bankers, lawyers, businessmen, financiers, agricultural leaders, farmers, and staffs in the state relief offices. They testified before state legislative committees, providing them with much information not available at that time from any other source. Further, the assistant administrator visited various sections of the country often enough to obtain first-hand information relative to relief grants.

Sums granted the states were often below what the governor requested. The governor might purposely list more than the state needed, or the state might have more taxing power or bonding power than it had yet been willing to use. If so, FERA would ask that it use it. Sometimes FERA questioned the statistical information presented by the states. The reports of the field representatives served as a check on the requests of the governors. So influential were these men and women—as several governors realized—that the state administrator of FERA, who usually prepared the application for funds for the governor, would check with the field representative before submitting it. Occasionally, FERA had to force states to ask for enough money so they could give adequate care to those on relief. Several southern states and occasionally a northern state sought money but made no effort to feed, clothe, and shelter relief recipients adequately. One of the purposes of FERA was to encourage the giving of *ade-*

quate relief. This Hopkins sought to do at all times for he firmly believed the "conservation of our human resources should be our guiding principle." This was to him of "greater importance, even, than the conservation of our physical resources." [7]

From the very first Hopkins stressed the importance of having states and localities give all they could toward financing relief. Neither he nor President Roosevelt wanted the federal government to assume increasing responsibility for those on relief. On June 14, 1933, President Roosevelt told governors and state administrators the Federal Emergency Relief Act of 1933 was:

> an expression of the Federal Government's determination to cooperate with the states and local communities with regard to financing emergency relief work. It means just that. It is essential that the states and local units of government do their fair share. They must not expect the Federal Government to finance more than a reasonable proportion of the total.[8]

On July 20, 1933, Hopkins wrote the state administrators, "Every department of Government that has any taxing power left has a direct responsibility to help those in distress." [9] In his direct, personal contacts with state governors and state officials, Hopkins made it even clearer that the states and localities must put up funds to get funds. He wrote the governor of Texas:

> In making these funds available to Texas, I wish to point out that it is going to be possible to carry only a part of the cost of unemployment relief in the state of Texas out of federal funds. I understand there is pending a proposal to amend the State Constitution so as to permit the legislature to bond the State up to twenty million for relief of the unemployed. What I wish to make clear is that funds

must be available by the State and/or its political subdivision, by this or some other means if we are to continue to make grants from the federal funds.[10]

On July 12, 1933, Hopkins telegraphed Governor Laffoon of Kentucky that his state must appropriate additional money for relief to match federal dollars if his state wanted relief after August 15. In the case of New York, where it seemed sometimes that the governor and others thought they should receive special consideration, President Roosevelt, after Hopkins had apparently failed to convince Governor Herbert Lehman, wrote the governor that federal aid was given on two prerequisites: first, that the municipalities within a state do their full share toward raising and distributing relief funds; and second, that the state supplement these funds to the extent of its ability to do so. When both of these had been done the federal government would assist.[11]

Ohio refused to make additional sums available for a time during the summer of 1933. Hopkins told a group of Cleveland officials he would make no more money available until the state legislature came across with suitable contributions. When questioned about the Ohio situation, Hopkins spoke frankly: "One of the reasons the Legislature did nothing was that they thought I was bluffing. I am glad to have the issue drawn. . . . If the Ohio Legislature decided the unemployed of Ohio are not important to them, I do not see why we should lose any sleep about it here." [12]

Several states refused to make any real contribution. Thus, Hopkins reported to Senator Carter Glass of Virginia in reference to FERA expenditures:

> Unfortunately, in some instances, State authorities . . . have taken an attitude in complete reversal to that assumed by Congress in passing the Act. These authorities

> have assumed that it was the obligation of the federal government to bear all or substantially all of the relief burden and accordingly, have resented insistence by the Relief Administrator that their States contribute a fair proportion of relief expenses even when the determination of that portion was based upon consideration of economic conditions, total amount of relief required, existing revenue systems, attitude towards relief and other factors that might affect a State's proper contribution.[13]

In the fall of 1934, Hopkins and his staff began to move from the system of considering the ability of each state to contribute to a general formula for determining the amount the federal relief agency should provide. Hopkins had tired, apparently, of arguing with each state over amounts it could or could not provide. At least, he hoped to obtain more information on which to base his arguments in seeking state and local financial contributions. Of equal importance in suggesting to him and his staff the need for a better system was the fact that in the late winter and early spring of 1935, forty-four state legislatures were to meet. Here lay the best opportunity, and indeed in most of these forty-four states the only opportunity, to secure the financial cooperation of the states. New bond issues, new taxes, new appropriations—all had to be approved by the state legislatures. It seemed the best time to use the full weight of the federal relief administration to secure proper state support for both state and federal relief.

The Municipal Finance Section of the Washington FERA headquarters made the most thorough study ever conducted prior to 1934 of the economic resources of the states in an effort to determine where federal money should go. All phases of a state's tax resources, income, and economic activity served as a basis for judging its economic capacity. The Municipal Finance Section set four different quotas for each state. Manufacturing, mining, agricultural production, and related factors served as the basis for quota one. Population statistics formed quota two. Quota three consisted mostly of federal tax collection statistics. State government financial activity and value of property made up quota four. Balancing these four quotas, FERA obtained a fifth quota. This was a weighted and adjusted quota which showed the economic wealth of the states. To this set of statistics FERA applied a national uniform tax scale, and the results served as the basis for deciding how much each state, in reference to other states, could contribute toward relief funds.

Certain imponderables limited the role played by the final results obtained by the Municipal Finance Section. Short-term factors such as floods, droughts, and seasonal shifts of employment interfered with detailed, projected planning. Further, the economic ability of a state to pay and its immediate ability to raise funds were not identical. Constitutional and statutory limitations, restrictions on taxing powers, tax systems already in use, and the attitude of the people toward relief in each state were important factors. Considering all of the above, as well as the economic capacity of the states, the FERA staff concluded that for the year 1935 the states could provide $509,480,000 for relief purposes. In setting this amount, FERA did not expect that a state would have to stop its own needed functions or tax its citizens to the point where the state would be in an unsound financial situation.

In actual practice FERA did not stick with quotas based solely on the $500,000,000 total. It worked out additional quotas based on securing sums of $400,000,000 and $300,000,000. If a state had poor economic resources and was suffering from damages by drought or flood, the $300,000,000 quota was used. If a state was basically wealthy and suffered no hardship, an amount consistent with the $500,000,000 quota was assigned it. The remainder of the states had the $400,000,000 quota level. Within each level thus established, the information secured through the work of the Municipal Finance Section determined the amount a state would contribute and the amount to be granted by the FERA.

In the last analysis, *need,* not facts and figures, determined the amount of aid Hopkins and his staff were willing to give except as limited by the total amount available to FERA from federal funds. Hopkins never reconciled himself to letting figures dominate the giving of relief.

It is to the credit of the Municipal Finance Section that there proved to be a strong correlation between sums asked for and those subsequently obtained. The total amount secured from all states in 1935 was $468,000,000. In only fifteen instances were there more than five places difference in the rank order of states as they were listed on quotas and the rank order of states on actual performance. This in itself indicates that Hopkins and his staff had succeeded in two ways. First, they had increased state contributions. And second, they had estimated accurately the contributions the various states could make.

During this period, as well as later, Hopkins and his staff were under fire from critics of the relief program for not awarding relief grants on the basis of population. Nevertheless, there was actually a high correlation between the amount states were allotted and their population.

Supported by all kinds of facts, figures, statements, and the desire to get all he could out of the states and localities, Hopkins went forth in the spring of 1935 to meet and challenge reluctant states. On March 4, 1935, he told Governor Olson of Minnesota that his state must put up its fair share or get no more money. Minnesota contributed the amount asked. In Maryland, Hopkins helped force the passage of a 1 per cent gross sales tax, the returns of which were to be used for relief. On March 26, Hopkins told Governor Earle of

Pennsylvania that his state must give $5,000,000 a month if FERA was to give it additional amounts. He got this rate of contribution.[14]

In a few states the struggle between Hopkins and the state over financing of relief was bitter and long. It made no difference, apparently, whether Republicans or Democrats controlled the state government. In Illinois, controlled by Democrats, Hopkins had one of his hottest battles. In April, after he had already told Illinois to contribute more if the state wanted more, he refused to give money for May until the state legislature made funds available at the rate of $3,000,000 per month. President Roosevelt backed Hopkins on his stand. On May 3, 1935, Hopkins did divert $1,288,767 to Illinois from the rehabilitation fund, but this did not change his basic policy. Finally Governor Henry Horner succeeded in securing the passage of a sales tax bill to raise money. On May 25, he and Hopkins met at Cleveland. Hopkins made $5,000,000 immediately available.[15]

Meanwhile much hardship for those on relief occurred in Illinois. Several newspapers severely criticized Hopkins for his actions, which had forced numerous relief offices to close their doors for lack of funds.

> We accuse Harry L. Hopkins . . . of an attempt to coerce Illinois into doing his will, by provoking hunger and perhaps even violence in this state. . . . We accuse him of a deliberate effort to usurp the constitutional prerogatives of the Illinois legislature in the matter of state taxes.[16]

In this accusation the Chicago *News* raised a crucial point. On the other hand, Hopkins had no way of making a state contribute if it really did not want to. If Illinois wanted to look after her own without federal money, it could do so. Events proved that Illinois, a wealthy state, could contribute more to relief than it had in the past.

Whether Hopkins was right or wrong in bringing pressure

against states to contribute is debatable. The fact that he increased state and local contributions cannot be denied. While some southern states still contributed practically nothing, most states increased their quotas noticeably. Thus, contrary to the arguments that federal participation would lessen the amounts localities and states would give to relief, in actual practice it increased the total amounts. This was a real victory for Hopkins.

Hopkins' tactics were in part responsible for the levying of additional sales or income taxes in several states. Critics of Hopkins questioned the wisdom of this. If it occurred with no improvement in the quality and quantity of relief, obviously it was not justified; however, his staff did force several states providing inadequate relief to raise their weekly grants to needy families. Hopkins, with his conviction that relief must be adequate to be really valuable, succeeded in nearly doubling the amount given to each needy family. In addition, he and his staff encouraged state relief agencies to extend coverage to types of cases usually ignored in the past. These were the most important achievements in the FERA and state relief programs in their first two years of operation.

I believe firmly that able-bodied people should work for their existence. —HARRY L. HOPKINS

III. Trial Balloon: The Civil Works Administration

The famous Hundred Days of Roosevelt's first term established a new atmosphere in Washington. The tones of defeat and hopelessness were gone. With each new administrative and legislative act, confidence surged forth. From February, 1933, when Walter Lippmann believed the nation was not much more than "a congeries of disorderly panic stricken mobs and factions," the nation became in the fall of 1933 a people once again full of vitality and ideas. It began demonstrating the self-assurance necessary to combat the depression even though millions were still unemployed.

This return of confidence did not mean everyone knew where this country was heading. Winston Churchill observed at the time that Roosevelt was an explorer who had embarked on a voyage as uncertain as that of Columbus. Some severe critics of the President in these early weeks claimed to be sure of this. Psychologically, however, for most people, where Roosevelt was heading in relation to economic and social theories seemed less important than the fact that he was active. Presidential fireside chats, legislation passed, men heading agencies that were doing something to help the people—these brought comfort to many. The unemployed noted passage of acts to provide relief and stimulate economic recovery; a large mass of Americans who had lost faith in banks had their faith restored; homeowners appreciated action to preserve the ownership of their homes; many farmers benefited from new farm credit arrangements and the efforts to raise farm prices.

Roosevelt seemed to be trying to do something for everyone. As Richard Hofstadter has observed, "If the state was believed neutral in the days of T. R. [Theodore Roosevelt] because its leaders claimed to sanction favors to no one, the state under F. D. R. could be called neutral only in the sense that it offered favors to everyone." [1] Roosevelt was taking seriously his own words of 1932; he was experimenting. He was the quarterback of a team of government leaders working with experts in various fields. Some of the more radical of these experts believed the best thing to do was to toss out completely the old approaches and techniques. Roosevelt kept many of these extremists in the background. Thus, he did not establish a national banking system, but chose to work with the bankers he seemed to have condemned in his inaugural address. He chose the larger, more conservative agricultural groups and their ideas in preparing legislation aimed at aiding agriculture. The National Industrial Recovery Act providing for a system of industrial self-government was, in construction and in operation, dominated more by conservatives than liberals.

The main goal the Roosevelt administration had to achieve, if it was to remain politically acceptable to the people, was that of recovery. The giving of relief was important, but the administrative leaders themselves recognized relief as a supporting measure only. Many believed sweeping reforms were essential, but they were in the minority and even several of these realized that recovery would have to be well underway before fundamental reforms could be written into satisfactory legislation. The basic question which Roosevelt faced during the spring and summer of 1933 was whether the approach to recovery should be limited to the various possible actions conducted within the United States or coordinated with efforts to restore recovery in the other major industrial nations of the world. The answer for the first year and a half of the New Deal was to lick the depression at home by concentrating on what seemed to be needed here. Roosevelt sought to raise prices, increase purchasing power, shorten hours and raise wages, and to limit production to levels closely correlated with consumption.

In the early fall of 1933 it became increasingly clear to leaders of the Roosevelt Administration that the recovery experienced from March through August was due more to restored confidence than to fundamental improvements in economic organization. Actually, during August and September the production of manufactured goods declined. This trend, if continued, would result in serious repercussions for the nation, and also for the Democratic party. These facts were evident in early October. The summer of 1933 had brought practically no improvement in agriculture. Industry was not hiring workers rapidly enough to offset new available workers (high school and college graduates). Purchasing power of the consumer was increasing very slowly. The PWA, established to conduct construction programs to stimulate heavy industry through government loans to public agencies, would not be in full operation until the spring of 1934. Roosevelt's ditching of the London Economic Conference in the summer of 1933 was proving to be unpopular in several quarters, although hailed as a wise decision in others. In summary, Roosevelt faced the possibilities of a winter (1933–34) as dismal and bleak as any during President Hoover's tenure in office.

Hopkins, fully aware of the plight of the New Deal, had a keen concept of the task Roosevelt faced. Evidence indicates Hopkins gave much thought to the nation's economic ills, although he was certainly not an economic theorist. His analysis of the situation was enriched by the ideas of Louis Brownlow, Director of the Public Administration Clearing House, and Frank Bane, organizer of the American Public Welfare Association. Hopkins had important discussions with these men on the weekend of October 28, 1934, while visiting the president of the University of Chicago, Robert Hutchins.

Leaving Chicago, Hopkins went on to Kansas City, Missouri, to participate in a conference. As he traveled, Hopkins had time to reflect on the facts, figures, and ideas presented to him by Bane and Brownlow. While in Kansas City Hopkins talked with Harry S. Truman, then Federal Unemployment Director for Missouri, and with J. F. McElroy, who urged Hopkins to develop more work projects. Aubrey Williams made an important contribution to the planning when he called Hopkins from Chicago to tell him that Dr. John R. Commons, the famous expert on labor, said Samuel Gompers, the great American labor leader, had recommended a work program for the unemployed in 1898. This was what Hopkins needed to make headway with his historically oriented boss. He called the White House for a luncheon appointment with Roosevelt on the day of his return to Washington.

Hopkins sold his plan. He and his staff would initiate federally sponsored work projects across the nation. These projects would be of the type on which the unskilled and semiskilled could work with the guidance and assistance of skilled workers. Street repairs and construction of new roads, repair of public buildings, development of playgrounds, grading and asphalting of country roads were the major projects for such an agency. This work would be valuable; people needed work, and needed money for the necessities of life. Since these projects were each small in scope and were not major construction projects, they could be started quickly and also terminated on short notice. Perhaps four million persons could be placed on jobs by this means during the winter of 1933–34.

President Roosevelt knew Harold Ickes could not develop the PWA work program with sufficient speed to put nearly four million people to work during the winter of 1933–34, perhaps not even two million by the fall of 1934. While the quick shot in the arm to aid recovery would not be of much benefit to heavy industries, it was quite apparent it would boost morale and stimulate purchasing of perishables and low-cost semidurable goods. Having nothing better available to consider, and hoping Hopkins and his staff could do the job, Roosevelt gave the go-ahead signal.

When Hopkins left the White House following this conference with the President, he "fairly walked on air." Putting through a telephone call to Aubrey Williams, he insisted Williams interrupt a speech he was delivering long enough to hear the news. Hopkins then called his aides into action. He asked Williams, Brownlow, and Bane to come to Washington. These three men, aided by Hopkins, Howard Hunter, Jacob Baker, Julius F. Stone, Corrington Gill, Pierce Williams, and T. S. Edmonds, worked Saturday night and Sunday. A few days later Hopkins told Roosevelt his crew was ready to launch a new work program. On November 9, nine days after Hopkins had decided to present the idea of such a program to the President, Roosevelt announced the creation of this new agency which was to operate under Title II of the National Industrial Recovery Act. Thus the Civil Works Administration was born.[2]

The CWA hit a responsive note in most sections of the nation. Governors and mayors of the larger cities who attended a briefing session in Washington returned to their localities with enthusiasm. In the Midwest, where agricultural conditions were bad, the people were quick to seize it as a means of alleviating the distressing economic situation. In New England, where for two hundred years self-help had been the dominant philosophy, mayors of towns and cities were quick to initiate CWA projects. In Massachusetts, for example, Joseph W. Bartlett, newly appointed by the governor to check CWA as well as PWA projects, held a meeting for local officials in which he explained the types of projects that could be carried through to completion under CWA regulations. Then, finishing his talk, he announced he would receive applications for projects. The mayor of Worcester immediately stepped out into the aisle and came forward. The mayor of Lowell followed him. They both returned home that evening with approved plans.[3]

Officials in other sections of the nation felt CWA was "a godsend." Reports from Hopkins' field representatives and the Press Intelligence Division of the United States government indicated popularity, although there was some grumbling because projects were not always immediately available. Many more people wanted to work on CWA projects than could be employed. When men started to work in Sioux City, Iowa, the city engineer commented, "You just can't believe that these are the same men who were listlessly and unwillingly doing their time a week ago on work relief projects to get their grocery orders." The Republican *State Journal* in Wisconsin observed that the "click of pick and clink of shovel are Christmas bells to many at this time." [4]

Several prominent business and political leaders opposed CWA from the beginning. Al Smith, who was soon identified with the anti-Roosevelt American Liberty League, attacked CWA sharply, calling it a "cover up" for the failure of Harold Ickes to get PWA started on a large scale. Rather than admit PWA's failure, said Smith, Roosevelt had created another of his "alphabetical soup" agencies. While he admitted he had not studied the matter thoroughly, Smith believed the CWA to be illegal. CWA could not, he thought, lead to anything but confusion, could not benefit heavy industry, and could not produce much of value in three or four months. On the other hand, CWA would cause localities to dump more of their relief problems on the federal government, would discourage private building, would certainly dislocate wages in thousands of communities, and would cause men to loaf more rather than less. "Half way between a lemon and an orange is a grapefruit," wrote Al Smith, and "half way between a public work and a relief work is a civil work." To this Harry Hopkins promptly retorted, "If putting 4,000,000 men back to work means going into the grapefruit business, then I'm delighted to be in it." [5]

The organization of CWA was fundamentally different from FERA. CWA administration was entirely federal, while the FERA was a federal, state, and local cooperative venture. Hopkins, not the governors, appointed state CWA administrators. The state CWA administrators helped select local personnel. Both officials and workers were responsible to the federal government. FERA officials were given dual appointments where feasible to avoid creation of an entirely new group of personnel.

The funds for the CWA program came from several sources. The federal government provided 90 per cent of the total. The President transferred $400,000,000 from PWA to CWA. Hopkins made an additional $88,960,000 available by taking back unused FERA grants to states. By a special act of February 15, 1934, Congress provided an amount of $345,000,000 for CWA. The states and local governments contributed approximately 10 per cent, which amounted to nearly $90,000,000. Eventually the CWA program cost slightly over $900,000,000.

Several factors determined where this $900,000,000 was spent, the number of workers a state could place on the rolls being the most important. (At least half of those placed on CWA payrolls were already on relief, and the rest, unemployed but not on relief, were selected largely by the United States Employment Service.) Another factor was the balance of urban-rural population in each state, urban relief loads being much higher than rural relief loads. Local wage rates, cost of materials, and types of projects also affected the total amount a state received.

Many Congressmen objected to the fact that eleven states received 57 per cent of the total spent by CWA. However, this seeming disproportion is explained by figures which show that 39 per cent of the total went to 93 large cities with the highest density of unemployment, and these cities were in the eleven states of New York, Illinois, Ohio, Pennsylvania, Michigan, California, Indiana, Massachusetts, New Jersey, Texas, and Wisconsin.

Harry Hopkins tried to keep CWA decentralized. Only through decentralization could the program come into existence with the speed desired, but decentralization meant also that dishonesty and graft increased. Many kinds of irregularities existed. The contract system, not used by CWA, might have prevented some of this, but the major difficulty was the dishonesty of people at the local level. Many local supervisors lacked originality and resourcefulness. Had all of Hopkins' directives been followed, leaf-raking would never have occurred. Corrington Gill summed up the situation correctly: "In communities where plans were not drawn up [prior to CWA] and where local public imagination was at a low ebb, the projects left much to be desired."

Local projects had to receive the approval of the state CWA officials. Only when the project was federally sponsored was it approved or disapproved by the Washington staff. Because of the magnitude of the task and the shortness of time, state CWA officials spent very little time checking projects sponsored by local and state agencies. Brief attention to events in the medium-sized state of Indiana will illustrate this.[6]

After attending the conference of mayors, governors, and other interested officials at Washington on November 15, 1933, Paul McNutt, governor of Indiana, started that state's program rolling. Fred Hoke, chairman of the governor's relief commission, called a meeting of FERA and state relief officials of the state that same week. Applications for projects appeared immediately. By November 20, 122 projects were approved. On the following day 109 more received approval. By the evening of November 21, Indiana had at least 30,000 men at work on CWA projects. On November 26, 1933, eleven days after the conference in Washington, this state had approved 910 projects and over 48,500 men were listed as employed on CWA payrolls.[7]

The types of projects approved by CWA administrators varied considerably; however, over 80 per cent of CWA expenditures were for completion of projects involving improvements on public property including street and road repairs, sewage and water works, repair and construction of buildings, and development of recreational facilities. Hopkins and his staff authorized several research and administrative projects, but these took only 15 per cent of the funds. The remainder of the appropriation was used for administrative expenses, accident compensation, and similar items.

The wage-rate policy of CWA proved to be one of the major targets for criticism. The wage scale used by CWA in the beginning was the one used by PWA. The minimum hourly rates were:

	Southern Zone	Central Zone	Northern Zone
Skilled	$1.00	$1.10	$1.20
Unskilled	.40	.45	.50

Special rates were established for semi-skilled, clerical, and general white-collar workers at approximately $18.00, $15,00, and $12.00 per week for the northern, central, and southern zones.

These rates were in keeping with the suggested new "floors" under wages established by the blanket code set forth under the National Industrial Recovery Act. The contents of the blanket code stipulated minimum wages of 30 or 40 cents per hour. Since the blanket code wages were subjected to considerable criticism during 1933 and 1934, it is easily understandable that similar rates for work relief would be attacked.

Under the original plan each person, clerical workers aside, could work up to 30 hours per week with the eight-hour day as maximum. Clerical and professional workers could work as much as 39 hours a week. Hopkins and his staff believed this would provide enough for most workers to live on but not enough to destroy the incentive for private employment. In actual practice this did not work, however, and in the South particularly, the wages proved to be too high. Thousands of men working for CWA received more money per week than they had ever received in their lives, and they passed up opportunities for private employment. This was partly the fault of local administrators who classified too many semi-skilled workers as skilled, permitting them to earn $30.00 per week. A second basic difficulty lay in the fact that traditional southern wage scales were very low for poor white and Negro workers. Farmers in 1932 and 1933 paid five cents an hour for hired help. Women could be employed for even less.[8]

CWA changed its wage scale in January, 1934. This change was not entirely caused by protests against the level of the wage scale. Lack of money to carry the program through the winter was the most important factor. Expenditures of funds moved much more rapidly and extensively than had been contemplated. The system of staggering work hours was first set forth in January. Hours were limited to 24 per week in cities over 2,500 and to 15 hours per week in rural areas. This cut the average weekly pay from $15.04 to $11.52. Although it extended the length of time CWA could continue its program, it resulted in many families' once again seeking direct relief to supplement CWA pay checks. On March 2, CWA dropped its PWA wage scale completely and reverted to the 30 cents per hour minimum wage scale used on FERA work relief projects. Again, if the prevailing wage was above 30 cents, it was to be paid.

Hopkins disliked the PWA wage scale from the beginning but was convinced that it had to be used. It proved to be a serious mistake in view of reaction from southern leaders. No doubt the wage earners in the South did benefit from it, perhaps as much after it was abandoned as while it existed. Nevertheless, the wage scale of CWA was a sore spot which contributed to its unpopularity among many private employers. Later many CWA workers complained when reductions were made. Al Smith's claim that CWA would dislocate wages was true for the South.[9]

Harry Hopkins selected personnel for FERA and CWA with little regard to politics. His main concern was the zeal and competence of his staff. As noted previously, he hired several men who had worked for the RFC relief division while Hoover was President. He chose hundreds of other men and women solely on the basis of their ability, experience, and knowledge of the problems of social work and relief. As mentioned earlier, President Roosevelt had told Hopkins, when he began his job in May, 1933, not to play politics. Evidence that he did not do this the first few years in office is plentiful in the Roosevelt and Hopkins papers. An example is a comment by Governor Gifford Pinchot of Pennsylvania dated November 2, 1934: "I have never seen the slightest indication of a desire on his [Hopkins'] part to play politics with relief."

Numerous letters were written about politics in CWA by Democrats who complained that CWA was a tool of the local Republican machine. For instance, Ed Dolan, collector of internal revenue of Hartford, Connecticut, wrote James Farley, "It [the CWA] is entirely in the hands of the Republican Party and they are building up a beautiful machine to the detriment of our group."[10]

Letters such as Dolan's had little influence on Hopkins. He was perfectly willing to select a Democrat for a typist in preference to a Republican if they were both properly qualified. But he would not let Farley, state governors, or senators tell him whom to select for his staff or for positions as state administrators. Senator Edward P. Costigan asked: "Is it too much to ask that names considered for important official administrative posts here be referred to me in advance for advice?" [11] This was a very sensitive point with the senators, who were used to playing a major role in dealing out political patronage.

One of the biggest political squabbles involving CWA was in California, where United States Senator William G. McAdoo attacked Ray Branion, state FERA and CWA administrator. Hopkins had Pierce Williams, field representative for the area, check McAdoo's charges. Williams reported that selfish political considerations were behind the senator's complaints concerning Branion's work. Meanwhile Hopkins received several reports favorable to Branion.

Williams later reported further investigation showed practically all complaints came from politicians. McAdoo told him personally that a clause in the Federal Emergency Relief Act of 1933, which authorized the appointment of a federal relief administrator for each state, was put there largely through his effort to make sure the Democrats could have more political appointments available. Williams reported that McAdoo seemed very disappointed when he learned that only under certain conditions did the federal administrator appoint state FERA personnel. On this same day McAdoo telegraphed James Farley, "I want a nonpartisan administration of these funds. A Democratic state administration can bring that about." [12]

Hopkins discussed the Branion situation with his staff. On the basis of facts they analyzed, Hopkins relieved Branion of the CWA post. Several staff members apparently believed that Branion had too many responsibilities holding both positions.

A large amount of the difficulty in this particular case was that Senator McAdoo was well along in years; therefore, younger Democrats were fighting for key positions in an attempt to align themselves for a possible nomination for United States senator or for governor of the state. George

Creel was one of these. There were others, such as John B. Elliott and P. M. Hall. Hall, the United States district attorney for the area, indicted Ray Branion and Pierce Williams on charges of conspiracy to defraud the government. Hall had at one time applied for Branion's job. Furthermore, Hall had written to Richard F. Roper, executive secretary of the Democratic National Committee, asking that Branion not be appointed (presumably as head of CWA) against the wishes of McAdoo and other Democratic leaders. His charges were made for a time period between December 15, 1933, and March 15, 1934. Branion was neither actively nor officially head of CWA during that time. Alan Johnstone reported to Hopkins, after checking the case, that the indictment was "full of holes."

Hopkins concluded that Branion was at least honest and trustworthy, even if not as efficient as some administrators. Therefore, he asked the attorney general's office in Washington to investigate. He also reported the incident to President Roosevelt. Roosevelt gave his consent to have the indictment quashed if the Justice Department would agree. The attorney general sent Joseph Keenan, assistant United States attorney general, to California to investigate. On November 12, 1934, Keenan told the court there was not sufficient evidence against the two men. He asked that the case against the defendants be dismissed. This was done. McAdoo and his associates were defeated on their first political clash with Hopkins. Branion and Williams were later shifted from California to other areas. They rendered valuable and trustworthy service to Hopkins for several years.[13]

Politics and graft were vexing problems for Hopkins and his staff. Starting the program of CWA, keeping it going, and terminating it were challenging to the skill and imagination of the top administrators. Inefficiency and lack of ability on the part of lesser officials, state and local, were understandable. Various means could be devised to make corrections. In the case of political interference, graft, and misuse of funds, the moral fiber of individuals was involved. It was most difficult to try to reform dishonest but respectable businessmen using questionable means to acquire a few extra hundred dollars. Some local and state officials were glad to obtain federal money and spend it as they saw fit. As one of Hopkins' field representatives wrote him on one occasion, someone should invent the phrase "socially approved dishonesty." The Kelly-Nash group in Chicago kept insisting that various odd jobs which were not approved by CWA be done with CWA (and FERA) money. In Chicago it became necessary, as it did in several cities and states, to place an engineer in each main CWA office, and to use army engineers as CWA state administrators, since they were relatively free from the need to play politics.

Misuse of CWA involved more than just misuse of funds by local officials. In some areas union officials told CWA workers they must join a union before they would be accepted for CWA work. CWA officials stopped this practice when they became aware of it. Some local chapters of the American Legion sought to increase their membership by telling workers they must join if they wanted CWA jobs. Men were told that membership in the American Legion would "at least help chances" in securing approval for employment on CWA projects. From the workers' viewpoint this way of depriving them of money honestly earned was as dishonest as a city mayor or private contractor taking a kickback on material purchased.

Quite a few businessmen made contractual arrangements whereby they received more money than that agreed to for goods delivered. Materials, especially tools, could be delivered and then returned to the company, to be sold again. Artificial raising of prices proved a convenient way to make the percentage of profit increase tremendously. Hopkins and his staff learned that government is as honest as private citizens who surround it and work with it. In the case of CWA too many private individuals rather than government officials were dishonest.

As one way to combat graft, Hopkins ordered all books and records of payrolls and purchase of supplies opened to the public. He hired investigators to check charges of graft. The Department of Justice took control of cases involving criminal violation of the laws. In one of his major radio addresses explaining to the public the purposes of CWA, Hopkins said: "It is unthinkable that anybody would use any part of these funds for any private profit or gain or for political purposes. We shall not tolerate any such connivance in this program." [14]

Later Hopkins wrote Presidential Secretary Marvin H. McIntyre, in reference to the Census Bureau going into the political record of people referred to them by the reemployment bureau, "I simply want you to know I have no intention of tolerating this kind of political interference with Civil Works. It is in direct violation of the President's instructions and I intend to go down the line with it." On November 23, 1933, Hopkins threatened to withhold CWA funds from Florida and from Youngstown, Ohio, because of reports of graft and chiseling.[15]

Hopkins reported to a Congressional committee in January, 1934, that "political interference has been a difficulty." He said he had "quit getting mad about it," although he was still "amazed at the number of people who are trying to horn in on making a little money." In view of the size of the operation the graft was small; but it loomed large in the public mind. "It may be my own fault. . . . I may have made a mistake in kicking a lot of this stuff outdoors. But I don't like it when people . . . finagle around the back door." Then a few days later Hopkins commented, "I find you can control this thing about so far down all right, but when you spread this thing over the United States they beat you." [16]

Time magazine reported on February 19, 1934, that Hopkins had 130 investigators checking CWA and PWA frauds. A staff of accountants were kept busy going over books of the state relief funds and CWA projects. All state expenditures were reported to Hopkins' staff. Seven hundred and fifty-one charges of a serious nature eventually were made concerning CWA projects and activities. By April 1, 1935, 639 investigations were completed. Charges proved to be true in 240 cases. Of these, 163 were cases of irregularities that did not involve criminal violations. Dismissals and restitution took care of the 163 cases. The 77 cases involving criminal violations resulted in 17 convictions. Considering the expenditure of nearly one billion dollars on over 180,000 projects in which over four million persons were working, this was a commendable record rather than a poor one.

Other than organization and administration of the program, graft, and politicians, the major worry Hopkins had was trying to make the public, including hundreds of state and local officials, understand the intent and purpose of CWA. CWA had been in progress only a few weeks when the Washington office received complaints to the effect that CWA workers were spending all their money and were not saving any of it. Actually, many families on CWA income had no choice but to spend all their weekly income for food and shelter alone. In many families CWA income did not meet all basic expenses. Other families had members who spent the money unwisely, something not always done solely by the poorer element of society. Hopkins did not like to see money wasted. He was, however, one who believed that a glass of beer probably tasted as good to a man who handled a shovel all day as a cocktail did to those of the local country club set. He never seriously concerned himself with expenditure of CWA income by families receiving it.

The most constructive attack on CWA, and also a typical one, was made by Fred L. Cramford, a well-known construction contractor of New York City. He said: "Money paid out in wages for work done without materials leaves little trace behind it. In the first place, it is converted into consumable goods—that is, food and clothing. On the other hand, if you employ materials in your projects you convert your money into capital goods industries which are in desperate need of aid." He referred to CWA as only 2.5 per cent efficient because of its lack of emphasis on capital goods.[17]

The intent of the CWA program was precisely that which Cramford had criticized, i.e., to put money quickly into the hands of the many who worked for it and would have to spend it on the basic needs of life. The government desired it to be spent as quickly as possible, thereby adding a boom to certain economic activities until the winter was over and seasonal employment increased. CWA did not exist to do what PWA eventually did. It is doubtful if Hopkins ever succeeded in getting the critical segment of the public to appreciate the basic reason for CWA's existence.

In January, 1934, Hopkins and President Roosevelt asked Congress to appropriate more money for the CWA and FERA programs. This led to a discussion concerning the scope of CWA. Many Republican senators opposed its extension, but most administration supporters, including some Republican members of Congress, voted for the $950,000,000 appropriation. A few senators demanded a greater amount and wished CWA to continue for an indefinite period. Senator Bronson Cutting presented a measure calling for an appropriation of $2,500,000,000 for CWA and related activities. Senator Robert La Follette suggested a sum of $1,500,000,000 for CWA. Senator Robert Wagner said he thought Hopkins was asking for too little. Wagner pointed out that Hopkins would only have $22.00 per month for each worker for the next ten months, or roughly $4.00 per person per month for a five-member family. Senator Wagner asked: How much food, clothing, shelter, and medical care could this sum provide? But more conservative influences prevailed; Vice President John Nance Garner, Lewis Douglas of the Bureau of the Budget, and others won their point with President Roosevelt. The latter, and even Hopkins, announced opposition to the extension of CWA beyond the May 1, 1934, deadline.

The announcement signaling the curtailment of CWA caused many of its supporters to speak out in its favor. Governor Lehman of New York said that stopping CWA might bring "grave social and economic consequences." The American Association of Social Workers at their annual national meeting noted that curtailment of CWA created a new feeling—a "serious feeling of insecurity." They suggested it be continued. In February and March, when Hopkins effected a major curtailment in CWA operations, the White House and Hopkins' office received over 50,000 letters and 7,000 telegrams opposing his action. The content of many of these letters and telegrams made it clear that thousands upon thousands of Americans preferred work relief to the dole. In many places across the nation small riots occurred. A few of these were sponsored by Communists, but most were spontaneous expressions of feeling by those who feared the future once CWA ceased.[18]

The reasons for ending CWA were simple and few in number. First, it was a makeshift work program developed for use during the winter of 1933–34, and was never intended for a longer period. Hopkins and other leading administration officials opposed the suggested expansion of CWA. Hopkins wished to continue the work program, to be sure, but not necessarily under the title of CWA. He was able to continue it under the FERA in a modified form. Second, CWA was expensive. Therefore, as quickly as it served its prime purpose, it was discarded or curtailed, in the South first and later in the North. The termination of CWA was partly an economy measure by Roosevelt. There was hope that business would increase its activities in the spring of 1934, and with the help of the RFC and PWA, the President anticipated that industrial production would move steadily upward. The real task of Hopkins' agency was once again relief, not stimulation of economic activity.[19]

A third reason for replacing CWA with another program involved politics and graft. Hopkins and his staff in Washington hated political interference and graft all the more because of the inordinate demands imposed upon their time.

It is impossible to give an evaluation of CWA which would suit all persons and even all authorities on the subject. The question of the necessity of the program is usually raised. Many groups, such as the United States Chamber of Commerce, advocated strict use of dole relief. Even those who preferred work relief to dole relief legitimately asked whether CWA was the right type of work relief program. Perhaps a program better planned to go into effect in the spring of 1934, using dole relief during the winter for the unemployables on FERA and an expanded FERA work program, would have given more effective results. It is obvious that CWA extended the influence of the federal government in the field of relief for the unemployed and needy. A federal work program had now superseded state relief programs. What would be the eventual ramifications of this development? Taken by itself it was an important development; when linked to centralization occurring in other New Deal programs it was even more important. The real battle concerning the extent of work relief sponsored by the federal government came later, however, with the establishment of the Works Progress Administration.

The CWA did have in its origin and administration certain basic defects. First, it was put into operation too rapidly for efficient administration. Confusion existed between CWA and the United States Employment Service in hiring the two million unemployed not on relief roles. Selection of projects was poorer than it would have been with sufficient time for planning. Lack of tools in many instances lowered the caliber of work. The element of time also meant that projects must be the type which could be finished in a few months. Whether Hopkins, as administrator of relief, made a serious blunder in trying for a short-term works program in CWA is an unanswerable question. Economic and social conditions throughout the nation were extremely critical during the winter of 1933–34. CWA did have a tremendous psychological influence among men who had the opportunity to work for money rather than stand in line for it, and some say this in itself made CWA worth the cost. Despite what its critics say, much material improvement throughout the nation did result from CWA.

The second basic weakness of CWA, and now one can turn to more concrete aspects of the problem, was the obtaining of $400,000,000 from PWA to help run the work relief program. This made it a necessity, as previously noted, to use the PWA wage scale. This resulted in increased opposition to CWA in the South and in some sections of the North. It also made the cost of CWA more than Hopkins had originally estimated.

The third basic defect was the poor quality of many projects and the inadequate supervision of the projects. As noted earlier, local and state groups sponsored most of the projects. Some of these local men and women were able to provide sound leadership. Most of them were honest, but some were not. Others had little capability. Many were honest and had ability, but lacked the imagination to see what really could be done for their communities. There was no need for leaf-raking and similar projects. The vigor with which men worked depended, of course, not on the Washington office or even state CWA officials, but on the leadership ability of local leaders, plus their own vitality, mental attitude, and capabilities. Strong supporters of CWA point out that it is little wonder that out of 180,000 projects of CWA a few local politicians got away with some questionable activities.

On occasion, when approval for logical projects was slow in coming, some local leaders were hard put to keep men busy, but did not want to dismiss them outright. The number of persons involved in CWA was over six times the employment of all steelworkers in 1952. The very magnitude of the program meant, actually, that even 1 per cent inefficiency in local planning would provide a lot of newspaper columns for news-hungry reporters. However, many projects should have had better planning and supervision to assure that tax money was used for work relief in a worthwhile manner.

Most of the published laudatory comments, like the criticisms, were made with little study or evaluation. However, the Hopkins manuscripts contain an unpublished statement concerning CWA which is interesting in view of its source, a man who, at that time, was relatively free from political pressures of any kind. Lieutenant Colonel John C. H. Lee of the Army Corps of Engineers made a study of CWA for the army. This was done for any help it might be in mobilizing a vast number of men and activities in a short period of time. Part of his analysis and summary is given below.

> The accomplishments of the C.W.A. were possible through the arduous efforts of the young Administrator and the group of able young assistants which he has assembled and inspired. They have worked daily long into the night with a morale easily comparable to that of a war emergency. These assistants address Mr. Hopkins fondly as "Harry." There is no rigidity or formality in their staff conferences with him, yet he holds their respect, confidence, and seemingly whole-souled cooperation. Practically all have had active experience in social welfare or other work of a relief nature. Insofar as such a class of workers was available, Mr. Hopkins has assembled a corps of professionals for the fulfillment of the President's relief program.
>
> On the whole, it is apparent that the mission of the Civil

Works Administrator had been accomplished by 15 February 1934. His program had put over four million persons to work, thereby directly benefiting probably twelve million people otherwise dependent upon direct relief. The program put some seven hundred million dollars into general circulation. Such losses as occurred were negligible, on a percentage basis, and even those losses were probably added to the purchasing power of the country. Thus, Mr. Hopkins' loose fluidity of organization was justified by the results achieved. It enabled him to engage for employment in two months nearly as many persons as were enlisted and called to the colors during our year and a half of World War mobilization, and to disburse to them, weekly, a higher average rate of wages than Army or Navy pay.[20]

The lift in morale cannot be measured. CWA improved the lives of over sixteen million Americans for a period of time. CWA built and repaired over 40,000 schools and 255,000 miles of roads and streets; built 469 airports and improved 529 others; laid 12,000,000 feet of sewer pipe; and employed 50,000 teachers so that many rural schools could remain open. Adults were taught new trades and skills as well as the usual literacy subjects, and children reaped the benefit of over 3,500 playgrounds and athletic fields. The quality of work done on these projects and others would have been better if CWA had not started on short notice and if it had existed for a longer period of time. Hardships, at the beginning and at the end, for thousands going on and off its rolls could have been lessened. Local officials could have made the program more successful if they had avoided chiseling and politics. Despite these weaknesses, CWA stands out in all American history as one of the greatest peacetime administrative feats ever completed. For this Hopkins and his staff must be given credit.

I do not believe . . . that society owes every man a living, but . . . every man shall have access to the opportunity to provide for himself and his family a decent and American way of living. —HARRY L. HOPKINS

IV. Mattresses, Safety Pins, and Politics

Harry L. Hopkins and his staff stood on solid ground in extending work relief within the FERA as they curtailed the CWA. Experience had shown that many people in need came to relief stations only when work relief was available. The serious troubles in FERA before the spring of 1934 sprang from direct relief rather than work relief. The American Association of Social Workers supported work relief, as did the mayors of medium-sized and large cities. Delegations at the rate of one or more a day came to Hopkins' office to demand work relief rather than dole relief.

In the spring of 1934, various divisions of the FERA arranged projects, assigned eligible employees, and conducted related activities in connection with the expanding work relief program. Many projects not completed when CWA ceased operations were continued under FERA sponsorship, but most of the projects were new. They were still largely locally sponsored and managed. This new work program of the FERA was much improved over that of 1933. For one thing, FERA and the sponsoring agencies initiated and completed more large construction projects. The majority of the new projects were further removed from the leaf-raking of 1933. Officials set aside more money for materials; they also bought better equipment.

To provide a more diversified program to meet the needs of the unemployed, the federal office of FERA encouraged, and sometimes sponsored, projects for skilled or professionally trained unemployed. One of the most important of these activities was that of planning the new FERA work program. This required, at all levels, a staff of architects, engineers, technicians, and other men and women with special skills. At the state, district, and local levels, the FERA selected men for this type of work from relief roles. About 1 per cent of FERA employees were engaged in these planning activities.

Work on public property provided the bulk of employment for FERA. FERA emphasized construction projects of all types: repair and building of schools and state, local, and federal buildings, recreational facilities, conservation projects, highway construction and repair, airports, sewers, and waterworks. Such projects accounted for approximately 77 per cent of the work relief activities of FERA for the period April, 1934, to July, 1935. Lesser areas of activity in the FERA program included housing projects of various kinds, such as rural rehabilitation and resettlement, production and distribution of goods needed for the unemployed, and various white collar projects designated as health and recreation, education, arts, and research. Of those on work relief, 22 per cent were employed in these areas.[1]

When the work program of FERA came to a halt in the late summer of 1935, it had completed nearly 240,000 projects representing an expenditure of $1,300,000,000. FERA gave employment to a monthly average of two million men and women. The high point was reached in January, 1935, when 2,446,000 were employed. During 1934 and 1935 FERA also aided farmers suffering losses from droughts.

FERA workers in 1934–35 built 5,000 new public buildings; every three out of ten were school buildings. They repaired 200,000 miles of roads and rebuilt completely, or built new, 44,000 miles of highways. They constructed 7,000 bridges. They laid 2,700 miles of sanitary and storm sewers; dug over 9,000 miles of drainage, irrigation, and other ditches; built over 2,000 miles of levees; laid 1,000 miles of new water mains;

and constructed over 400 pumping stations. They provided Americans with 2,000 more playgrounds, 800 new small and large parks, over 350 new swimming pools, and over 4,000 new athletic fields.

In production-for-use activities, done in behalf of farmers and relief personnel, the men and women working on FERA processed 195,000,000 pounds of meat and preserved over 60,000,000 pounds of fruits and vegetables. They made over 1,000,000 articles of infant wear, over 3,500,000 women's and girls' dresses, and over 1,000,000 men's and boys' shirts. Also, 1,250,000 mattresses were made, 5,000,000 pillow cases, and 4,000,000 sheets. The FERA and related agencies distributed these goods to families on relief.

In the field of health and education those employed on white-collar projects made notable contributions. Over 1,000,000 typhoid, smallpox, diphtheria, and scarlet fever immunizations were given to children. Teachers taught over one and a half million adults reading and writing plus, for some, various trades and skills. In April, 1935, 290,000 persons attended literacy classes. In the one year, the spring of 1934 to the spring of 1935, teachers employed by FERA taught over 500,000 adults to read and write. Granted that much of this work was not efficiently or well done, it does explain why Hopkins and Roosevelt could consistently defend work relief. The knowledge that socially constructive projects were being carried out must have dulled the point of many a critic's sharp thrust.[2]

Work relief cost more than direct cash relief. It was also more expensive than the grocery basket method of giving relief. In fact, three systems of relief were less expensive than work relief, if considered solely from the point of money spent. Lowest in cost was quantity buying of foodstuffs and clothing from wholesalers at discount prices and distribution of the necessities through commissaries. Hopkins thought this to be the "most degrading." Next least expensive was to give people on relief slips which were used to select groceries at the stores designated by relief authorities. Very little freedom of choice in spending existed under this system. More expensive than these two, but still less expensive than work relief, was the direct cash payment. Hopkins preferred the direct cash relief method if work relief was not used. This gave more freedom and a certain amount of independence. Hopkins believed, however, the additional 15 per cent in cost for work relief was of more benefit to the people and the nation.

The two aspects of the work relief program of FERA severely criticized during 1934 and 1935 were the production-for-use activities and the white-collar projects. The most controversial of the production-for-use schemes was mattress-making. Hopkins learned through his work with the Federal Surplus Relief Corporation that the Department of Agriculture possessed great quantities of surplus cotton. He wanted to combine the cotton with surplus labor. Neither FERA nor the people on relief had money to purchase the goods which could be made from the raw cotton. Mattresses and quilts had not been purchased to any great extent by FERA or by local relief agencies due to lack of funds. Many people on relief needed mattresses. It seemed logical to take the 250,000 bales of cotton available through the Agriculture Adjustment Administration and, using unemployed workers, turn it into needed products. Women working in abandoned factories did the work, mostly by hand. FERA purchased the ticking and other needed items through regular trade channels, stimulating economic activity in that area. The mattresses were distributed to those who were absolutely destitute. Such a system made FERA funds go further than if the mattresses were purchased and FERA not only had to pay for the mattresses but still provide the same number of women with the same amount of relief money as it would have with the work performed by them.[3]

Providing mattresses to the needy by such means was condemned by some people and groups as being socialistic. Letters of protest concerning mattress-making arrived at the White House and at Hopkins' office in fairly large quantities. The National Association of Manufacturers denounced the activity as contrary to individual enterprise, stating that "entrance of the Government into the manufacturing business in competition with its own citizens, even to supply relief for the unemployed, constitutes an extravagant use of the taxpayers' money." Hopkins indicated in press conferences that FERA had to provide mattresses and related items in this way or not at all. The only alternative was to increase the amount FERA could spend for relief. He pointed out that the type of activity under criticism in this particular case had saved FERA $200,000,000 during the previous 12 months.[4]

It was the white-collar projects, particularly those relating to the arts and sciences, which provided the most publicity and opportunity for critical and sometimes unrealistic statements. The term boondoggling was revived to describe many of these projects. Those white-collar projects that had to do with the betterment of public schools were fairly popular with a large portion of the public, but the painting of murals, the copying of art work created by past masters, and the research of scientists, all provided material for interesting and often critical newspaper stories. For example, in the spring of 1935, newspapers in New York City carried the account of a project for research scientists investigating the making of safety pins. The following excerpt from a press conference explains Hopkins' attitude on the subject of white-collar projects. It also reveals the explosive nature of his personality.

Q. Are you contemplating any Federal investigation of any kind of the general situation in New York City?

A. (Hopkins). No. You mean apropos of this stuff in the paper a day or two ago?

Q. Apropos of the project for safety pins.

A. Sure, I have something to say about that.

Q. I asked first, have you contemplated making an investigation?

A. Why should I? There is nothing the matter with that. They are damn good projects—excellent projects. That goes for all the projects up there. You know some people make fun of people who speak a foreign language, and dumb people criticize something they do not understand, and that is what is going on up there—God damn it! Here are a lot of people broke and we are putting them to work making researches of one kind or another, running big recreational projects where the whole material costs 3%, and practically all the money goes for relief. As soon as you begin doing anything for white collar people, there is a certain group of people who begin to throw bricks. I have no apologies to make. As a matter of fact, we have not done enough. The plain fact of the matter is that there are people writing and talking about these things in New York who know nothing about research projects. They haven't taken the trouble to really look into it. I have a pile of letters from businessmen, if that is important, saying that these projects are damn good projects. These fellows can make fun and shoot at white collar people, if they want to. I notice somebody says facetiously, repair all streets. That is all they think about—money to repair streets. I think there are things in life besides that. We have projects up there to make Jewish dictionaries. There are rabbis who are broke and on the relief rolls. One hundred and fifty projects up there deal with pure science. What of it? I think those things are good in life. They are important in life. We are not backing down on any of those projects. They can make fun of these white collar and professional people if they want to. I am not going to do it. They can say, let them use a pick and shovel to repair streets, when the city ought to be doing that. I believe every one of these research projects are good projects. We don't need any apologies!

Q. In that connection, I am not trying to argue with you.

A. I am not really mad. . . .

Q. About this white collar—there are 300 million for white collar relief. Would it be your idea in administering 300 million, that might just as well continue?

A. The best of them will be continued, sure. Those are research projects that they are jumping on.

Q. As a matter of fact, don't you think there are a lot of research projects that would be more valuable to mankind in general than the classic example of ancient safety pins?

A. That is a matter of opinion. You may be interested in washing machines—somebody else in safety pins. Every one of those projects are worked out by technical people. In the field of medical science, we have doctors, in physical, we have physicists; in the social, social research people. You can make fun of anything; that is easy to do. A lot of people are opposed to the whole business. Let these white collar professional fellows sit home and get a basket of groceries, that is what a lot of people want.

Q. You say that people don't want to work?

A. No, these fellows want to work, but there are a lot of people who don't believe in the work program and want people to go back to direct relief. These people who want direct relief will always kick about these technical projects. Anything that from their point of view isn't utilitarian.[5]

The Washington *Post* referred to Hopkins' defense of white-collar projects with a caustic editorial.

Of all the unmitigated tripe dished out by members of the Administration in two highly loquacious years, this blurb by Harry, in favor of the farcical New York "white collar" work relief projects, is about the most ridiculous. That it could be seriously uttered by a responsible official of any but a comic opera government would seem incredible. It sounds more like a cue for Vice President Throttlebottom to take the stage.[6]

Hopkins never did change his mind about the necessity for white-collar projects. He believed there was a basic difference in human abilities and interests. The best relief program would recognize such differences. Allow these people, he said, to use the tools they know how to use and they can more quickly earn their way back to a better level of existence. FERA faced the fact that slightly over 10 per cent of the persons on relief were by occupation members of the white-collar group. The census of 1930, Hopkins reminded his critics, showed that 30 per cent of the gainfully employed were of this group. He believed that if it were preferable to have an unemployed bricklayer work on construction projects, a violin player should earn his relief money with a symphony orchestra and not by trying to lay sewer pipes.[7]

The federal, state, and local governments incurred a total obligation of $4,119,005,000 for public relief from January, 1933, through December, 1935. This amount included all general and special relief activities in the continental United States. Of the total obligated during this period, the special emergency relief programs to help the farmers, transients, teachers, and youth accounted for 5 per cent, or a total of $209,192,000. General relief, both direct and work relief, accounted for 78 per cent, or $3,211,807,000. Earnings of nonrelief persons performing skilled and supervisory work on emergency work relief projects accounted for $109,673,000. Combining this with the $138,218,000 spent on purchases of materials, supplies and equipment, another 6 per cent of the total is accounted for. Eleven per cent ($450,114,000) involved rental of equipment, such as trucks and teams, and also administrative costs and other miscellaneous items. These figures show that the bulk of the expenditures went for regular types of direct and work relief; that only a small part of the total amount was used for the controversial aspects of the program; and that the administration of the entire program, although inefficient in several states, was fairly efficient in the nation as a whole. No programs on the scale of FERA and CWA, other than conduct of war, started and operated on such a short timetable, had ever been attempted within the United States. There are no precedents that can be used for comparisons.

During the winter and spring of 1934–35, Hopkins continued to battle the politicians. Political pressure was heavy from both top and bottom. Local Democratic leaders continued to write James Farley about Republicans controlling relief. Often a congressman or United States senator would complain to Farley and to President Roosevelt. Senator Theodore Bilbo of Mississippi, for example, protested Hopkins' selection of personnel used in the Mississippi relief organization. Sometimes factional groups of the Democratic party caused trouble for Hopkins. Several Democrats in Indiana complained that the Democrats in their state were not profiting from FERA. Yet, the administrators of FERA in Indiana were mostly Democrats; they simply belonged to a different faction within the Democratic party in Indiana. Senator Joseph Guffey of Pennsylvania sent to Farley's office a newspaper clipping which indicated that some relief officials were not friends of the Roosevelt administration. The Senator advised that Hopkins had best "consult with the President's friends and not his enemies henceforth." Farley kept sending these letters with little political notations on various situations to Hopkins, who apparently paid scant attention to them.[8]

Hopkins was usually quite blunt in rejecting complaints

of state and local politicians. To those higher up he may have been circumspect, but he was still very frank. To Marvin McIntyre, White House secretary, he wrote on one occasion:

> This is to let you know that I am probably about to have a head-on collision with Senator McCarran . . . of Nevada. It is true that our Relief Administrator in Nevada is friendly to Senator Pittman, but Mr. Upman is not in politics, and in my opinion is doing a very good job. Further, it is my opinion that the Senator wants to dominate the relief show politically, and I have no intention of allowing him to do it.[9]

On another occasion Hopkins wrote Aubrey Williams, "When you get to Murray's state [Senator James E. Murray of Montana] . . . will you take a good look at the qualifications of Neil Gardner, Washita County, and Grover Hope, Frederick County. They are both politicians and so far as I know have no qualifications to run the show." [10]

In the case of Vice President John Nance Garner, Hopkins' battle to keep politics out of FERA was extremely difficult. Farley instructed Hopkins:

> In order to be certain that the interests of the Democratic Party is protected at all times, I am desirous that, on every appointment made in or from the State of Texas, you secure the approval of the Honorable John N. Garner, Vice President of the United States. Texas is his State and it is only fitting and proper that he be thoroughly advised on all recommendations and definitely approve all appointments before they are made. In other words, be certain to consult with him at all times. This is in accordance with the wishes of the President.[11]

Hopkins had some of his men investigate several complaints about which Garner had consulted Farley and the

President. He wrote Aubrey Williams a few weeks later that the President should see the report he had on Texas, for it would eliminate certain difficulties. A week later, he wrote again, "I will take occasion soon to get over to the President what I think of the Texas setup." [12] Garner and political activity in Texas hampered Hopkins, however, all the time he was administrator of relief.

In several other states Hopkins had trouble keeping FERA from being tossed wholesale into the political arena. In Minnesota, Governor Floyd Olson resigned as head of the relief organization because of political accusations, which seemed justified by evidence available. Hopkins was quick to accept his resignation, but this did not help much, as the man Olson appointed engaged in political pressures to the point of forcing social workers to give more aid to certain families than to others. This Hopkins stopped quickly, once he learned of it. In the neighboring state of North Dakota, Governor William Langer became so involved in politics that legal charges were made against him for the misuse of funds. Hopkins wired the Governor, "It is apparent these contributions were used for your political purposes. This practice is directly contrary to the policy of this administration and will not be tolerated nor permitted." Langer and some of his aides were found guilty of illegal practices and served prison terms. In Kansas, Hopkins kept a Republican in charge of relief during the time of FERA despite repeated efforts by Democrats to have him removed.[13]

Martin L. Davey, a lukewarm New Dealer, became governor of Ohio in January, 1935. A month earlier, Hopkins had received reports that Davey was interested in using the state relief organization to build a strong state political machine. After his election Governor Davey made it clear he wanted to replace Henderson, who was state FERA administrator, with a man named Walls. Hopkins felt Henderson, the administrator at that time, was suitable for the position, although he had made some mistakes. However, Hopkins agreed to the change in the interest of harmony.[14]

Hopkins had already received evidence concerning political activity by the newly elected governor, and this was supported shortly by a report from his field representative for the area, Charles C. Stillman, who had become convinced that "this State Administration is out to capture the State Relief Administration and make political pie of it all." Stillman gathered material to support his suspicions and by early March had some proof to support Hopkins in a move against Governor Davey.[15]

The clash between Hopkins and Davey began, however, before Hopkins had all the evidence. On March 4, Governor Davey wrote a letter to Hopkins in which he charged that the relief work of Ohio was inefficient and was not being properly handled. Too many of the home investigators were young social workers lacking maturity and tact. Some were young people just out of college with no previous experience. The governor felt people more mature and of local residence would be much better suited for the task. He maintained there was so much paper work that the social workers had to spend half of each day making reports. Furthermore, Governor Davey believed that since the state could do nothing in the way of relief without checking with the representatives from the FERA in Washington, that the federal office should have charge of relief and not the state. He charged, moreover, that the Democrats had been slighted in appointments. Too many Republicans had been appointed. He was certain that qualified Democrats could have been found.

Harry Hopkins, in his press conference of March 5, 1934, called this letter from Governor Davey an outrageous indictment against the hundreds and thousands of fine people in Ohio who had been administering relief. He did not believe the governor's opinion represented that of the majority of the people of Ohio. The people of Ohio did care about their 345,000 families who needed relief. The giving of relief, maintained Hopkins, was, under the acts of Congress and the direction of the President, to be a cooperative effort. He was certain the people of Ohio wanted to do their fair share. Many relief workers were Republicans and undoubtedly many were not Democrats, or at least not "Davey Democrats." The appointments, he said, "have been made on the basis of merit." Hopkins acknowledged over-all indirect control of FERA in Ohio, noting that "the act of Congress specifically required that I do it," and told Governor Davey that direct supervision and immediate responsibility "belong to you." [16]

This news made the front pages of the leading papers of Ohio. The Citizens League of Cleveland in its publication, *Greater Cleveland*, charged that Governor Davey had been "playing politics with human misery." He had, according to the paper, tried to introduce the spoils system into relief. The Cleveland *News* noted, "Probably no governor in the history of Ohio had taken such a spanking from the federal government. . . ." The spanking was "richly deserved" for Davey's attempt to unload the whole relief burden on the federal government. Such action, reported the Cleveland *News*, merited the contempt of Ohio's citizens. The *News* also pointed out that Davey, in his campaign speeches, had found the administration of relief generally sound in Ohio. Hopkins had the figures to prove this. The Cleveland *Plain Dealer* carried an article by Paul Hodges, who stressed the fact that before Governor Davey took office, the political affiliation of the social workers and relief personnel had not been asked.[17]

Harry Hopkins, on one of the few entries in his diary, noted on March 15, 1935, that "the Ohio politicians have been raising campaign funds thru our office, which pleases me not at all." A day later he wrote, "The evidence is complete in Ohio—the political boys went too far this trip and I shall take great delight in giving them the 'works'. Took the evidence to the President this morning—he wanted to get into the scrap and asked me to prepare a letter for him to sign to use—instructing me to take over the state. He later signed it and approved one of my own which was pretty hot." [18]

Both letters referred to were dated March 16, 1935. In his letter to Hopkins, Roosevelt said:

> I have examined the evidence concerning corrupt political interference with relief in the State of Ohio. Such interference can not be tolerated for a moment. I wish you to pursue these investigations diligently and let the chips fall where they may. This Administration will not permit the relief population of Ohio to become the innocent victims of either corruption of political chicanery.
>
> You are authorized and directed forthwith to assume entire control of the administration of Federal relief in the State of Ohio.[19]

Hopkins' letter to Governor Davey was much longer. It contains the basis for the action taken by the federal authorities.

> This is to inform you that pursuant to the order of The President the Federal Emergency Relief Administration will take ovcr the administration of Federal unemployment relief in Ohio effective at once.
>
> It has come to the attention of this administration by incontrovertible evidence that your campaign committee shortly after your election, proceeded to solicit money from the men and business firms who sold goods to the Ohio Relief Administration. The frank purpose of this shake-down, because it can be termed fairly by no other

name, was to help pay off the deficit of your campaign and the expenses of your inaugural. The further apparent purpose was to solicit these funds in order to retain their jobs.

The evidence of this corruption is, I repeat, incontrovertible. Investigators on behalf of this Administration have secured the signed and sworn confessions of the men who solicited the funds; and the names of the men who paid in to the fund which your committee raised. These affidavits show definitely the sources of an amount in excess of eight thousand dollars which was thus raised by this corrupt solicitation and paid in to your campaign committee.

This evidence, of course, not only establishes the utter unfitness of some of the men who are now in high positions in the Relief Administration; but it demonstrates the necessity of safeguarding the expenditure of Federal funds in Ohio.

Under the circumstances there is no alternative for this administration but to take over immediately the responsibility of directly administering the Federal funds available for Ohio relief. You may be sure that this will be done at once and that nothing will be permitted to cause delay in providing for Ohio's needy unemployed. You must understand, and understand clearly, that this action will not relieve the state of Ohio and its local subdivisions from continuing to contribute its share of the funds necessary to care for the needs of your citizens.[20]

Letters protesting the statements and actions of Administrator Hopkins came to the White House and the Washington FERA office by the dozen. J. E. Wyllie of Huntsville, Ohio, called for a "public apology" from Mr. Hopkins to Governor Davey. Another letter referred to Hopkins' comments at the March 5 press conference as an "unwarranted insult" to the governor of Ohio. George Anderson of Cincinnati, Ohio, requested the "discharge" of Hopkins and that he be replaced with an "American citizen with democratic principles." Many others stated that Hopkins was "decidedly wrong" about Ohio relief or that Hopkins "lacked the correct information" about the relief work in Ohio. Numerous county Democratic organizations passed resolutions calling for the removal of Hopkins or an apology to the governor. The Democratic members of the Ohio State Legislature passed a resolution to "deplore the gratuitous insult directed at our Chief Executive, Governor Martin L. Davey, by one Harry L. Hopkins." [21]

Despite the protests, Hopkins stood his ground. Most of the Ohio press and many responsible citizens supported his action. The threat of arrest Governor Davey had issued against Hopkins was not made good when Hopkins went to Cleveland in May. Hopkins' visit clinched his victory. The Cleveland *Plain Dealer* noted in its editorial of May 25 that Hopkins "gives the impression of being a straight hitter as well as a straight shooter." Most people who met him and heard him were "satisfied that so far as he controls the expenditures they will be made strictly on merit."

I believe the days of letting people live in misery, of being rock-bottom destitute, of children being hungry, of moralizing about rugged individualism in the light of modern facts—I believe those days are over in America. They have gone, and we are going forward in full belief that our economic system does not have to force people to live in miserable squalor in dirty houses, half fed, half clothed, and lacking decent medical care. —HARRY L. HOPKINS

V. A Variety of Interests

During the thirties the American people probed deeply into the problem of unmet needs and wants amid food surpluses and unused industrial plant facilities. Many believed the government should combine elimination of surpluses with the federal relief program. Hopkins supported this, believing it indefensible "to have food rotting on the ground or packed up in warehouses while people don't eat." In the fall of 1933, Roosevelt, Hopkins, and Secretary of Agriculture Henry A. Wallace agreed to launch the Federal Surplus Relief Corporation (FSRC), with Hopkins as president, to take surplus from the Agricultural Adjustment Administration (AAA) and distribute it to people on relief. The AAA supplied the funds during the initial stages.

In 1933, the FSRC bought and distributed primarily pork. The following year Hopkins extended FSRC activities. It purchased and distributed pork, beef, cotton, butter, veal, cheese, wheat, potatoes, rice, fresh vegetables, and occasionally additional farm products. In several instances the FSRC staff purchased these items directly from farmers. For example, beginning in the summer of 1934, beef and thousands of beef cattle were bought from farmers and packing houses. Drought throughout much of the Midwest made necessary the killing of large numbers of cattle normally not slaughtered. If not purchased and processed, the only alternative was to let them die of thirst or starvation.[1]

The purchase and distribution of beef cattle was one of the most difficult problems Hopkins faced as head of FSRC. The principal reason FSRC purchased beef and beef cattle from the packing companies was so they could buy more from farmers in drought areas. This did not help farmers to any great extent in the upper Mississippi valley areas, where cattle prices were so low that many farmers made less than one dollar of profit per head when they sold to private packing concerns. The governor of North Dakota requested that FSRC buy the cattle directly from the farmer and absorb the cost of marketing the animals. Ordinarily the FSRC did not do this; in general practice, Hopkins followed the principles of individual enterprise. Thus, private packers rather than the government processed the meat, despite occasional rumors that Uncle Sam would soon be in the packing business. The FSRC allowed the meat packers to make a profit on the meat processed and this arrangement gave aid to many packers. In addition, it benefited manufacturers of finished plate used in cans.[2]

Many persons had difficulty in understanding the work of the FSRC. Many complications made public understanding hard to achieve. In the case of several products there were surpluses in some geographic areas and shortages in other parts. Hence, people criticized FSRC for buying surpluses for relief needs when people not on relief desired them. Often, however, the product was of the perishable type and could not be shipped any great distance. Therefore, operating on the limited budget it had, FSRC staff often thought it better to give a product to individuals on relief rather than let it be wasted. Such actions gave plausibility to the claim that families on relief occasionally ate better than many not on relief. Obviously, this was not the usual situation.

Preventing spoilage was a difficult problem. In one case over 400,000 pounds of beef spoiled because it was not stored properly. In handling live cattle shipped from the drought-ridden western and midwestern states, mistakes were made in allotting cattle to grazers in southern states where the grass was less nutritious. Part of the difficulty in this venture was caused by lack of rain in the southern states. Many cattle, moved in the summer of 1934, later died.

By the end of 1935, it was becoming clear that the real value of the FSRC lay in its assistance to the farmers by removing surpluses rather than in providing food to people on relief. Plans were then altered so that relief became a very minor function of FSRC.[3]

FERA was the first relief agency to give real consideration to transients. Transients were seldom able to secure employment on local work relief projects, since most states had residence requirements which transients could not fulfill. Further, they were barred by law from participation in the CWA and PWA programs. Therefore, FERA established a special subdivision to care for this group.

FERA made the first transient relief grant in September, 1933, to the state of Alabama. By January, 1934, forty states and the District of Columbia had transient programs. FERA stipulated that the transients cease their migratory activities. Those desiring to return home or to go elsewhere could do so only after FERA checked with local authorities to see that they could be cared for. Local and state authorities had usually grouped transient families together at lodging houses or in abandoned buildings. Many of the homes for single transients were little better than flophouses, except where they built their own camps. The transient camp was the best method developed for housing single transients, but it had a basic defect in that it tended to isolate the transient from the private labor market. Experience showed the more enterprising men to be the ones who left camp first to seek jobs with private employers. In some localities, members of this group shifted back and forth from the camp repeatedly until they secured private employment providing a reasonable degree of security.[4]

The transient program presented problems other than the operation of camps and the relationship of these camps to the surrounding community. One of the most difficult was the separation of transients from local relief offices. FERA defined a transient as one who had resided less than the twelve preceding months in the state where he applied for relief. The next problem was the relief payment. Thus, with geographic separation and residence requirements as basic factors in the administrative operations, the relief payment to transients was difficult.

In addition to these problems, the FERA staff faced the problem of a suitable pay scale. Should FERA pay a uniform scale over the nation or vary it with each local community? Those in charge of the program for Hopkins felt that the local communities could not understand the problem of the one million transients and had mistreated them as a group. Permitting them to receive grants through local relief authorities would mean that in many cases the aid given would be so meager as to have little value. The FERA staff finally decided to pay transient workers a nearly uniform payment in cash or kind. It was difficult to explain to local relief recipients why they received, for example, only three dollars a week when the transients received perhaps ten dollars per week. Many persons believed that FERA was placing a premium on transiency. Hopkins maintained, as he did in trying to raise the relief standards of many states, that relief should not leave people overexposed to hazards to health and safety. Although laws limited Hopkins in directly raising relief benefits provided by the states, here was one place where he could impose a higher standard of relief.

The transient program was larger than many have realized. An average of 300,000 transient persons received assistance during the winter of 1934–35. Obligations amounting to $101,422,000 were incurred for all types of transient relief during the period from January, 1933, through December, 1935. During the last half of 1934 and the first six months of 1935, when transient relief operations were at their height, total obligations averaged almost $5,000,000 a month, including all types of transient relief in the form of cash payments, plus the cost of material and equipment used on work projects. When FERA came to a close, the transient work camps were often shifted to the WPA program. Those receiving direct cash payments were, for a time, aided by the FERA and then turned over to the state relief agencies.[5]

One of the most difficult aspects of relief during the years 1933–35 involved aid to the needy in rural areas. Conducting a relief program for urban people, who lived for the most part on a cash-and-carry basis, was direct and definite, since their pay envelopes were their only link to a cash income. For the farmers the problem of income and need was not related so closely. A farmer's income could stop, but need did not always follow immediately. Yet, when the need did appear, it was of greater magnitude for the farmer than for the city worker. Not only did the farmer need money for food and clothing, but also money to buy seeds and perhaps a new tool to plant and harvest another season of crops. The paradox of the rural situation was that as total farm income for the nation increased during 1934 and 1935, the actual number of farmers in need of relief also increased. In fact, the increase in those needing relief rose 75 per cent from October, 1933, to February, 1935.

The contrast in these two trends reflects the fact that most American farmers sought to get along on what they had as long as they could, thus completely depleting their resources by the time they sought relief. This meant that most of the farmers did not have the means by 1934 and 1935 to benefit from the AAA program. The severe drought in large areas of the country's agricultural strongholds in the summer of 1934 made the need for relief in rural areas greater; hence the situation became desperate for several hundred thousand farmers by the fall of 1934.

The preceding spring, Hopkins and his staff had initiated a rural rehabilitation program. This was an attempt to restore the farmer to his normal independent status. Therefore, it was rehabilitation as well as a relief program. Hopkins sought to aid the farmers in need of relief to the point where further relief would be unnecessary. In the long run, he believed rehabilitation the best type of relief for farmers. The FERA attempted to coordinate the giving of some cash relief with a program to provide tools, livestock, and better land or restoration of poor land, the point being that a farmer could serve his community, society, and himself better by improving his farm and increasing production than by working on a bridge or laying sewer pipe in a nearby town.

The Rural Rehabilitation Division of FERA attempted to fulfill three aims: to make the farmer self-supporting where he was, if that seemed practicable; to move the farmer to productive land if his land was of an unproductive type; and to establish stranded industrial groups on suitable land so they could become partially self-supporting. Most attention in time and money was given to the first two aims.

The Rural Rehabilitation Division, chartered in cooperation with FERA state corporations which could serve as legal entities, was responsible for selecting farmers needing rehabilitation assistance. Through it and the state rural rehabilitation corporations, farmers were given money and assisted by loans, and, in some instances, the corporations acquired mortgages on farm property so that foreclosures would not take place. Agricultural experts in the area gave technical assistance and advice to farmers attempting to help themselves. Farmers benefiting from the rural rehabilitation program were not eligible for other types of agricultural assistance. For the most part, therefore, rural rehabilitation dealt with the farmer who possessed only a few acres of land, or else with tenant farmers, mostly in the South. The administrative staff of the Rural Rehabilitation Division devised a system of repayment to utilize both the products of the farm and the cash income. Loans on cattle and similar stock or on equipment had to be paid, usually, by the end of three years. Repayment of loans on land could take from twenty to thirty-five years.

One of the basic reasons for establishing rural industrial communities of the self-sufficient type was that, as the FERA staff noticed, most rural villages with a high degree of self-sufficiency weathered the depression with little outside aid. On the other hand, in some areas the entire industrial activity collapsed when dominant companies moved their main activities to other communities. The most important of the planned self-sufficient communities were at Woodlake in Texas, Dyess in Arkansas, Cherry Lake in Florida, Pine Mountain Valley in Georgia, and Matanuska Valley in Alaska. The last of these was probably the most difficult to start and for a time the most controversial.

The Rural Rehabilitation Division and the FERA, as early as May, 1934, began to consider the establishment of a colony in Alaska to which several hundred persons could be sent. The final decision to develop an agricultural community about forty miles northeast of Anchorage was made early in March, 1935. This became known as the Matanuska Valley settlement project. Supplies and materials for construction of buildings and roads were sent from the United States. FERA selected families from lumbering and mining areas in Wisconsin, Michigan, and Minnesota. Transient workers from California assisted in the construction work. The few hundred selected were screened out of a possible

10,000. By mid-June, 1935, 1,336 persons were engaged on the Matanuska project, with transient workers numbering 425, colonists 897, and supervisory personnel 14.[6]

The project was almost immediately the cause for a series of fantastic rumors, stories, and ridicule. For instance, one newspaper account said that 2,000 persons were ill when the total number in the colony was less than 1,500 men, women, and children. Illnesses there were, but reports to Hopkins by the manager did not indicate any great amount of illness. Various newspapers sent reporters to investigate the charges and rumors. Several reporters found the situation not ideal, but discovered nothing sensational. Chase S. Osborn, representing the Detroit *Free Press* and the Sault Ste. Marie *Evening News*, said he was out of sympathy with the New Deal, but he reported no "critical" or "serious" or "sensational" condition. Don Bloch of the Washington *Star* indicated the project was basically sound. He noted that 4,000 family heads had applied to replace 32 families who had moved back to the states. Fulton Lewis Jr. concluded the "charges are exaggerated" and that the program was making suitable progress, although the quality of the products raised was not of sufficiently high quality for general market requirements. The record shows the Matanuska Valley Project was generally not guilty of the worst charges made against it.[7]

By the late fall of 1935 most of the homes for 170 families were completed. In addition, there were in operation a trading post, power plant, machine shop, garage, and a 40-bed hospital. Quarters for part of the staff were not completed until the following spring. The initial costs of the project came from federal funds. The major costs were eventually born by the colonists who paid off the government loans provided them for their land and homes. Crops, mostly vegetables and fruits, proved to be only moderately successful the first few years. Experimentation and experience taught valuable lessons. Matanuska Valley eventually became a very important agricultural area producing vegetable, fruit, and dairy products needed in Alaskan cities and towns.

Hopkins did not believe that the self-sufficient community, even though it served a useful purpose, should be developed on a large scale. The basic problems causing the need for such activity should have the most attention. Rural industrial communities could not provide a solution for rural unemployment as long as industry was highly centralized in urban areas, but Hopkins did think some of this activity necessary and he defended it when it was attacked. However, he never sought to push it as a means of combating the unemployment problem.[8]

Federal housing projects, social security, and unemployment insurance were activities related to relief and of great interest to Hopkins' staff. The inability to secure housing for relief recipients made the FERA staff more aware than ever of the acute need for low-cost but decent housing. The number of aged on FERA rolls crystallized the need for old age security programs operated on a sound, logical basis. Mass unemployment compelled an interest in plans to provide unemployment insurance. Hopkins, as head of FERA, was active in 1934 and later in numerous committees and groups studying these problems for the federal government. He carried influence with President Roosevelt and provided ideas for New Deal social legislation passed from 1935 on.

Hopkins believed the housing conditions to be one of the nation's acute problems, to be "evil," "unnecessary," and worse than any civilized nation need tolerate. Hopkins contended that "something has got to be done about housing and something is going to be done." President Roosevelt had planned to have Hopkins head the federal housing agency which Congress finally approved in 1934, but Hopkins had by then become involved in planning WPA. The housing bill passed by Congress did not stress low-cost public housing as Hopkins preferred. Consequently, Hopkins did not become more than a prodding bystander for more and better low-cost housing. He believed private construction companies had neither the financial means nor the motivation to build low-cost houses; nor should the government, except as a limited form of work relief, become engaged directly in housing construction. He stressed financing by the federal government on a long-term basis with low interest rates.[9]

Hopkins participated in the discussions which eventually led to the enactment of the Social Security Act of 1935. If the federal government could assist states in caring for unemployables—the aged, needy mothers and children, the blind and crippled—in the form of a permanent program, Hopkins could center his future relief program on various types of work relief activities. Further, if a system of unemployment insurance could be inaugurated in conjunction with the states, those persons only temporarily unemployed would be less likely to need relief. Therefore, as a member of the Committee on Economic Security, Hopkins took a keen interest in these programs which were eventually enacted into law. Much of what this committee recommended in its report in January, 1935, reflected Hopkins' views.

A trip to Europe in the summer of 1934 heightened Hopkins' interest in housing, social security, and unemployment insurance. This trip, taken at the direction of President Roosevelt, was primarily for the purpose of restoring Hopkins' health, or at least giving him a much-needed rest before the next large task. Roosevelt instructed Hopkins to "look over the housing and social insurance schemes in England, Germany, Austria, and Italy, because I think you might pick up some ideas useful to us in developing our own American plan for security." Then, as an afterthought, the President added that he believed the "sea trip will do you a lot of good." [10]

Hopkins did not bring back any ideas which influenced the American relief program to any extent. He stated upon his return that we needed to work out our problems in our own way. He liked one aspect of the British housing program—the low interest rates the banks were willing to make in order to encourage the construction program. Since Hopkins had already indicated interest in various types of insurance programs prior to his trip, it cannot be said that he brought back this idea from Europe. It can be presumed, however, that he did bring back certain impressions and facts which convinced him his ideas were sound or gave him ideas for revising.

By the fall of 1934 Hopkins had moved from the wings into the center arena of the New Deal show. President Roosevelt dominated the entire cast. Louis Howe, James Farley, Raymond Moley, Hugh Johnson, Henry Wallace, and Harold Ickes were well known and had made many headlines. But the very nature of Hopkins' task—and of his personality—soon made his name familiar throughout the country. Controversies with such men as Governor Davey of Ohio and Governor Talmadge of Georgia, and wisecracks at the expense of conservative business organizations, kept Hopkins in the limelight. Criticism of the work relief program and CWA served the same end.

Hopkins had clearly demonstrated by this time that his was a personality that instilled great loyalty in those who knew him and believed in what he was doing, but generated in those who opposed him a strong dislike and sometimes hate. The latter may have been because his critics sincerely opposed his views and his relief program, or it may have been because Hopkins conducted his program in a professional manner and with a great amount of personal purity and zeal. Hopkins continually beat his critics to the punch in denouncing cases of fraud and political interference. The more vociferous the critics, the harder Hopkins worked, and the better the program became. The critics were learning that Harry Hopkins did not believe in defending his relief program meekly. He defended it in dramatic and dynamic fashion by attacking the philosophy and the complaints of his critics. "Attack!" was the key word in Hopkins' actions in response to the assertions of the opposition. He "thrived in an atmosphere of protest." [11]

Hopkins proved time and time again that he could outwit his critics. He did in action what many people only dreamed could be done. He used ideas as steppingstones to an active, positive program to alleviate many of the wants and needs of millions of people. In Hopkins, America found a versatile man, one who played a chess game with his job, played poker with his friends, bet on horses with his administrative assistants, and played a ghostly game of chance with the destiny that hurled him to a pinnacle he never envisaged in his younger days. One Washington observer wrote at the time: "Give the Roosevelt Administration a dozen Hopkinses and a few more years and you will see them establish a new standard of efficiency in public service, a standard comparable to the prewar German public service or to the British Civil Service at its best in integrity and immunity to political influence." [12] But a few decades previous to this a famous British historian, Lord Acton, had observed that "Power corrupts. Absolute power corrupts absolutely." In the immediate years ahead Hopkins was to prove that both these observers of government and politics could be at least partially right. Hopkins continued his crusade to rid America of human misery, but he also became overly influenced by the power (although it was not absolute power) of his position. A conflict between the altruistic social worker and a shrewd politician in the making shaped much of the rest of Hopkins' career as relief administrator. This conflict had a direct bearing on the work relief activities from 1935 through 1938.

> Ickes came out at two—worried about who was going to run the new works program—he has heard all kinds of rumors and came to suggest that I be his deputy—said a new cabinet position should be created for me—that he would resign if President asked anyone else to administer the job. He thinks the Pres. has treated him badly on one or two things. . . . I told him that administration was up to the President, and I was making no suggestion. —HARRY L. HOPKINS

VI. Angling, Planning, and Wrangling

"Work Relief Corporation To Spend 8 to 9 Billions—Hopkins To End Dole." This headline, appearing over an article by Lewis Stark in *The New York Times* on Thanksgiving Day, 1934, surprised many liberals and Democrats, shocked in varying degrees conservatives and Republicans, and came with "bombshell suddenness" to Congress. As Delbert Clark wrote a few days later, "The fire-eating administrator of Federal Emergency Relief, Harry L. Hopkins, may safely be credited with spoiling the Thanksgiving Day dinners of many conservatives who had been led to believe that President Roosevelt's recent zig to the right would not be followed by a zag to the left." Clark called Hopkins' program the "End Poverty in America" plan.[1]

The recovery efforts of the Roosevelt administration were having only spasmodic success by the fall of 1934. There were still at least 10,250,000 unemployed workers. FERA listed 18,323,000 persons as receiving relief. It is little wonder Hopkins believed private industry could not provide jobs for the millions of unemployed employables. He believed these unemployed must have something approaching real work if psychologically, spiritually, and physically they were to be ready for re-employment in private industry when the opportunity for work did arrive.

During 1934 Hopkins and his staff considered several work relief programs which would cost the nation four to nine billion dollars. Several of the men involved believed a successful economic boost to the nation's economy would come only with large federal expenditures. In other words, mild stimulants to the economy were just that, and after each little push the economy would continue to sag. Lewis Stark, who wrote the Thanksgiving Day article, knew of these various plans and concepts. He implied that Hopkins desired to establish a Federal Work Relief Corporation as a permanent part of the American economy.

If Roosevelt supported the expenditure of eight or nine billion dollars for public works and work relief, it meant an important shift in his administration, for certainly he could expect no sympathy from industrial and financial circles, the National Association of Manufacturers, or the United States Chamber of Commerce. For a few days after the story broke no one knew for certain whether Roosevelt would actually support Hopkins. There were indications that Roosevelt was still trying to maintain harmonious relationships with various conservative groups.

During the summer of 1934, Roosevelt fought off attempts in Congress to change Section 7a of the National Industrial Recovery Act so it would be more favorable to labor. He used his powers under NIRA to prevent strikes in the automotive, textile, and steel industries. In September, he reorganized the National Recovery Administration in a way more favorable to business than to labor. Later in the fall, speaking to the American Bankers Association, he called for the cooperation of all groups on equal terms to form an "All-American team" to speed recovery. The President and the National Democratic Committee refused to support socialist-oriented Upton Sinclair in his campaign for governor of California. The Federal Housing Administration went into high gear with a friend of private business, James Moffett, at its head. He planned to stress private rather than government financing in developing the housing program. The President denied that he and Senator Robert Bulkley of Ohio had recently discussed further devaluation of the dollar. Donald Richberg, one of the high fixtures of the administration at that time, was assigned the task of coordinating the oftentimes conflicting agencies of the New Deal.[2]

President Roosevelt visited Warm Springs, Georgia, for two weeks in November, 1934. While there he talked to many senators, governors, and members of his official staff. Men from both the right and left advisory groups were present. Governor Talmadge, a severe critic of the New Deal, was one of the early visitors. Senators Robinson, Barkley, and Harrison also visited the President. Each attempted to condition the President to his particular concepts. The more conservative members of the official staff conferred with Roosevelt during the early part of this vacation period. These included Donald Richberg, James Moffett, Secretary of Commerce Daniel Roper, and James Farley. After Thanksgiving Day, with one or two exceptions, the more progressive members of the official staff appeared, including Rexford G. Tugwell, Harold Ickes, Henry Morgenthau, Frank Walker, and Hopkins. Ickes and Hopkins returned to Washington on the presidential train.[3]

Lewis Brown, president of Johns-Manville, Howard Heinz of the Heinz Pickle Company, and other business leaders had visited President Roosevelt during October and early November in an effort to bring the latter and the business world closer together. This led to other developments. It was understood the President, in order to achieve better understanding, would meet henceforth with the Business Advisory and Planning Council once a month. Henry I. Harriman, as head of the United States Chamber of Commerce, became the spokesman for business interests in this attempt to bring about cooperation between business and government leaders. Harriman stated, after holding a few conferences with government officials, "There is every indication that the administration desires cooperation of business and will in turn cooperate with business to revive trade and industry." Donald Richberg assured reporters and his audiences that the government would make no more inflationary moves. James A. Farley gave his word that Roosevelt intended to make no "swing to the left" as a result of the elections. There is no one, said Farley, "less apt to overturn the apple cart" than Franklin D. Roosevelt. He would follow a middle-of-the-road course. And Senator Joe Robinson, after a four-hour visit with President Roosevelt at Warm Springs, announced the administration aimed to balance the budget and to keep relief expenditures to a reasonably conservative figure.[4]

The record, now supported by evidence in part not known in 1935, points to another trend, only partly discernible in the fall of 1934. For example, on April 18, 1934, Hopkins held an interesting phone conversation with Colonel Henry M. Waite of the PWA staff. Enthusiastically he reported to the Colonel: "The big boss is getting ready to go places in a big way. We have been getting together with him. What he wants is this! He is giving us two weeks to prepare a brief on public works, housing—briefly, projects which someday we will get the dollars back on." Highspeed highways, grade eliminations, and rural electrification were acceptable projects. Roosevelt was willing, reported Hopkins, to spend five or six billion dollars. This was to be done in a three- to five-year period.[5]

Hopkins was heartily in favor of such plans. In August, 1934, he made clear to the press and the public his opposition to the dole system as used in England. He continued his drive for a large work program when he met with Roosevelt at Hyde Park, where both men talked over the relief and work relief situation with a group of city mayors. This group in turn asked for more public works, with responsibility for the unemployables returned to the states. This was precisely what Hopkins wanted, the goal to which he directed much of his energy during the next several months.

Shortly after the Democrats won their sweeping victory in the congressional elections of 1934, Hopkins exclaimed to Aubrey Williams and other staff members on their way to a race track near Washington, "Boys, this is our hour. We've got to get everything we want—a works program, social security, wages and hours, everything—now or never. Get your minds to work on developing a complete ticket to provide security for all the folks of this country up and down and across the board." These men took him at his word. They worked on plans in their FERA offices and weekends in the St. Regis Hotel in New York City where Hopkins often stayed while in "the city." Occasional conferences were held with members of the PWA staff, which was under the jurisdiction of Harold Ickes. Ickes had plans for public works which he also pushed.

A careful reader of the newspapers during the fall of 1934 knew that strong pressure from the liberal faction within the administration was being exerted on the President. Hopkins, in a speech to the National Conference on Economic Security, called for a bold stroke to unite all phases of economic security in a comprehensive program. Harold Ickes revealed a few days later that he and his staff were planning a five-year program of public works which involved the expenditure of several billion dollars. He believed a publicly financed housing program should be developed because the new federal housing program benefited the middle class rather than the lower income group. Mayor Fiorello LaGuardia, who held a considerable amount of influence on Hopkins, Roosevelt, and the national organization of city mayors, called for a large spending program by the federal government. And just before Thanksgiving, Roosevelt announced his support of a new low-cost housing program for income groups below the level served by the FHA. Members of the official family making such bold statements forced Roosevelt to think more along this line, or else take steps to reject openly the ideas of these men. The writings of Raymond Moley show a considerable amount of personal pressure being applied by the left-of-center group during the fall of 1934.[6]

Richard Hofstadter points out in his book *The American Political Tradition and the Men Who Made It* that critics of Roosevelt harped at him in rather abusive language just before and during the congressional election campaigns of 1934. The formation of the Liberty League and its role in opposition to him naturally irritated Roosevelt. The President increasingly despaired of working with the conservative Democrats, or indeed of working with the leading figures of the financial world in either of the major parties.

President Roosevelt, as political leader of the Democratic party, faced additional challenges by late 1934, despite the Democratic sweep of the 1934 congressional elections. Simultaneous with the increased boldness of the conservative forces, as centered in the Liberty League, was a challenge from political demagogues proposing programs more radical than the New Deal. Senator Huey P. Long of Louisiana was succeeding in building support for his "Share the Wealth" program. His following soon extended from the South into the Midwest. Long promised through confiscatory taxes on great fortunes to provide every family with an income of $2,500 per year and a homestead worth $5,000. This had much appeal to Americans living on a yearly income of a few hundred dollars in 1934 and 1935. Dr. Francis E. Townsend challenged the New Deal and Senator Long with his old age pension scheme, popularly called the Townsend Plan. Townsend proposed paying the aged $200 per month. Townsend at one time may have had as many as four million followers. Father Charles Coughlin in Detroit took a somewhat different approach, advocating silver inflation and the nationalization of banks, utilities, and natural resources. His helping to defeat the proposal for the United States to join the World Court was a demonstration of his power to mobilize public opinion.

Within his own party, dissension became more intense as liberal and conservative Democrats jockeyed for position with the President. Roosevelt had to choose. Should the New Deal continue its attempt to secure and to maintain support among industrial and business leaders, or should it launch reform, recovery, and relief programs which would steal parts of the programs from the "thunder on the left?" [7]

The climax to this particular struggle came in the annual presidential message to Congress delivered on January 4, 1935. President Roosevelt's remarks were hostile toward conservative business and industrial leaders. He issued a warning to those who might desire to oppose the new program and who would still support economic activities resulting mostly in speculative profits. "We find our population," he warned, "suffering from old inequalities, little changed by past sporadic remedies. In spite of our efforts and in spite of our talk, we have not weeded out the overprivileged and we have not effectively lifted up the underprivileged." He defined the profit motive, still to be sought and preserved, as "the right to work, to earn a decent livelihood for ourselves and for our families." Further, he asserted that "the ambition of the individual to obtain for him and his proper security, a reasonable leisure, a decent living throughout life, is an ambition to be preferred to the appetite for great wealth and great power."

President Roosevelt clearly supported a program which brought the federal government into a more prominent position as a leader in the recovery and reform efforts of the nation. The security of the men, women, and children of the nation became the central objective. Unemployment and old age insurance should be started; benefits for destitute children and mothers, and for sick and handicapped persons, should be increased and placed on a sounder basis. Relief, the President maintained, should be returned to the states and localities. Work should be found for destitute but able-bodied workers. Roosevelt was unwilling that the vitality of the people across the nation be further sapped by the giving of cash, by market basket relief, and by leaf-raking. The President made clear that he hoped to establish a program to aid the unemployed in keeping their self-respect, self-reliance, and determination.

Roosevelt believed that, with the exception of certain of the public building operations of the federal government, all emergency relief public works should be united in a single new and greatly enlarged plan. With the establishment of this new system, the Federal Emergency Relief Administration could be charged with the systematic liquidation of the direct relief activities and the substitution of this new work program could be made in an orderly manner. The new work program, said Roosevelt, should have these six guides: projects should be useful; projects should be structured to allow a high proportion of the money for wages; emphasis should be on projects which promised a financial return to the federal treasury; funds allotted for each project should be promptly spent; projects should be of a character to give employment to those on the relief rolls; and projects should be allocated to localities in relation to the number of workers on relief rolls.[8]

The administration's supporters quickly put the President's suggestions for public works into legislative form. A bill providing $880,000,000 for various forms of relief to be continued during most of 1935, and $4,000,000,000 for the new work program, passed the House of Representatives on January 24, 1935, by a vote of 329 to 78. After considerable argument and debate the Senate approved this bill with amendments on April 5, 1935. As can be seen from the dates of passage in each legislative body, the Senate held up final passage for seventy days, much longer than desired by the administration.[9]

Opposition in the Senate to the work relief bill was keen, persistent, and political in nature. The challenge to congressional power, states' rights in controlling relief and public works, and individual rights served as the first expressed points of opposition. Which of these was most important to congressmen is not clear. The *Congressional Record* records the fear that executive authority would be expanded to unreasonable limits. For example, Congressman Hess stated, "If this resolution becomes law, Congress will have granted to the President, and his appointees during the last two years, practically all its Constitutional powers, and may as well adjourn and go home."[10] Senator Steiwer of Oregon echoed this sentiment a few weeks later when he claimed the only thing the Senate knew about the proposed bill was that it:

> purports to clothe the President with authority to delegate in entirety the vast body of powers conferred upon him by this resolution, and we know that whatever the delegation may be the spending will be done at the discretion of the President and of those to whom the delegation is made, without substantial restraint and with but little control by Congress which is exercising its constitutional power to appropriate nearly $5,000,000,000 of the peoples' money.[11]

The vagueness in the draft of the bill presented to Congress was due basically to the failure of President Roosevelt to familiarize himself by January, 1935, with the details of the work and relief situation. It was not clear, therefore, to Hopkins, Ickes, or to anyone else vitally concerned with the program, whether Roosevelt really intended to stress self-liquidating public works or to stress work as a relief measure.

Certainly, a conflict on this point is clear in the six points listed in the presidential annual message. Thus, neither Hopkins nor Ickes could provide Congress with the details that members wanted. Daniel Bell, Acting Director of the Bureau of the Budget, told the Senate Committee on Appropriations that the bill, drafted by him, was worded so as to "meet every possible situation and give us authority to do things that would give relief and give it quickly. It may be we have not covered everything. We have tried." [12]

Related to this point of attack was the fact that the bill did not tell anyone in any specific manner for what the money would be used. Senator Arthur Vandenberg of Michigan, who was always a thorn in Hopkins' side, called the bill a "blank check" for the biggest sum of money ever appropriated in a single transaction, and the use of the money "so unbounded that it can warp the lives and livelihoods of every man, woman, and child in the land, and even the character of American institutions. . . . It is the most astounding contemplation, I venture to assert, in the history of Anglo-Saxon institutions." Senator Vandenberg said he agreed with what a columnist had written two weeks before —that Congress should strike out all the text and substitute two brief sections, viz:

> SECTION 1 Congress hereby appropriates $4,880,000,000 to the President of the United States to use as he pleases.
>
> SECTION 2 Anybody who does not like it is fined $1,000.

"This measure," the senator from Michigan added, "requires Congress to abdicate; it requires the country to lean on a dubious dream; it requires posterity to pay the bills: it creates more problems than it solves. This is not recovery's road." [13]

Another question: Were there enough sound projects on which this large amount could be properly spent? Senator Steiwer pointed out that PWA had 63 per cent of its projects in progress and 23 per cent to start as yet. In the case of non-federal projects sponsored by public agencies, approximately 55 per cent were not started yet. All of the remaining money to be allotted PWA would aid the economic activity of the nation. Certainly for a time, he argued, a smaller amount than the $4,880,000,000 would be sufficient. He called attention to the comments President Roosevelt had made at one CWA conference: "We might as well be perfectly frank. It has been exceedingly difficult, honestly, to allot the entire sum of $3,300,000,000 given for PWA to worth-while projects." The senator believed the task would be even more difficult in 1935 than in 1933 and 1934.[14]

Opposition to the work relief bill existed in part as a result of either poor or shrewd drafting. Combining the amounts for work relief and continued direct relief in one bill made the decision to vote pro or con difficult for some senators. Several were in favor of relief but not the proposed $4,000,000,000 for work relief. If they voted against it, additional time would be required to draft a new relief measure. Some congressmen thought this an important factor when the House considered the measure. Louis Ludlow, a long-time Democratic member of the House, said: "I am for relief for those in distress, and I am against great outlays for public works. I shall vote for the bill because if I were to vote against it I would be voting to cut off relief from the hungry, cold, and naked, thousands upon thousands of whom would be subjected to untold suffering in the dead of winter if this bill should fail." [15] A good many senators were unable conscientiously to use such an excuse. In any event, by the time the Senate finally voted, winter had passed and spring had come.

There was serious disagreement on the wage scale for the new work program. The administration, including both the President and Hopkins, backed the security wage scale. Senator Pat McCarran, supported by several anti-administration

Democrats, several Republican senators, and senators closely aligned with labor interests, supported the prevailing wage scale concept. If this latter method were used, the cost of projects would increase and fewer workers could be employed. The employment of a total of three and a half million men and women was one of the primary objectives of the work program.

The Senate adopted the McCarran amendment on February 22, but this was done to a large extent for reasons other than pure opposition to the security wage scale. Roosevelt had just pressed the Senate in its consideration of the entrance of the United States into the World Court, and many Democrats in the Senate had questioned his doing so at this time. Resentment by both Democrats and Republicans, including some who voted for entrance into the World Court, showed itself in the vote on the prevailing wage scale. The Senate later rejected the McCarran amendment, but only after the administration had assured organized labor that the government would not let the security wage have an undue influence on the regular wage scale for labor. Hopkins and Roosevelt secured only a partial victory, however, for in several subsequent appropriations Congress included the prevailing wage scale.[16]

Patronage was of great importance to the senators. Senator Vandenberg and his colleagues were opposed to this work relief bill for reasons mentioned earlier, and also because neither the administrator nor provisions for approval of appointments were known. Steve Early wrote Marvin McIntyre on March 29 that Senator Glass had told him that Senators Bennet Clark, Pat McCarran, and others threatened to filibuster against the bill unless confirmation of certain appointees by the Senate was written into the bill. Hopkins, Admiral Peoples, President Roosevelt, and other key members of the official family wanted the new agency to have a free hand in picking personnel. Hopkins himself was moved to oppose Senate approval of appointments mainly because he objected to political interference, although some of his critics have contended that he already envisaged a future for himself as President and wished to build his own political machine. McCarran, at any rate, succeeded in getting the Senate to require its approval of appointments to positions paying $5,000 or more per year.[17]

Who was to head this vast undertaking? Not knowing who would manage the spending of over $4,000,000,000 of the taxpayers' money disturbed many senators as much as any other single factor. For weeks the President gave no indication of his choice. Probably he did not know. He received suggestions from many different sources. The administrative arrangements proposed varied greatly. Several congressional leaders like Representative Culkin feared "Honest Harold" Ickes might head the new organization. He did not want that. In fact, he agreed with Representative Cox of Georgia who went so far as to say that Ickes was the most hated and despised man connected with the government. Ickes had shown, said Cox, that he lacked even "the necessary training and experience to erect a sizable gasoline filling station." Senators Vandenberg and Steiwer also showed concern on this point. Senator Byrnes indicated to Hopkins that several senators did not want Ickes to head the program, although the senators steering the bill through the committee and onto the floor of the Senate for the final vote seemed to favor him.[18]

Ickes soon conferred with Hopkins about the new organization and the person to head it. Ickes told Hopkins that he preferred to see the establishment of a new department with Hopkins heading it as secretary. Ickes would have brought into this new department the social service activities of the government. Included would be federal relief and social security activities. If this were not feasible or possible, then Ickes was willing to make Hopkins deputy administrator of public works with a definite assignment of duties. Ickes thought Hopkins took to the first suggestion and "I think he would not be averse to the second one." [19] Harry Hopkins' view of this conference was markedly different. He recorded: "Ickes came out at two—worried about who was going to run the new works program—he has heard all kinds of rumors and came to suggest that I be his deputy—said a new cabinet position should be created for me—that he would resign if President asked anyone else to administer the job. He thinks the Pres. has treated him badly on one or two things. . . . I told him that administration was up to the President, and I was making no suggestion." [20] Meanwhile Hopkins was being informed by Morgenthau and Senator James Byrnes that he would receive the appointment as head of the new program.

Ickes approached Louis Howe in late January concerning the President's plans for head of the program. Ickes told Howe he would not mind being eliminated as PWA administrator provided he was informed ahead of time and was given, as he had requested before, full control of all conservation departments in the government. Howe revealed that Hopkins had been to see him, trying to find his place in the new scheme, something Howe did not know.

During February and March, uncertainty concerning the administrator for the new work program continued. Ickes reveals in his diary that he believed efforts were made to "torpedo" him. On several occasions he went to see a member of the White House staff to ascertain the President's thoughts or to register a complaint. Ickes was in favor of a substantial work program, but he obviously thought Hopkins could not administer it so as to contribute to the continued success of the New Deal, of which Ickes was a fervent supporter.

In early April Ickes and Hopkins compared drafts of their proposals. Ickes observed that Hopkins' draft made the President head of the program. He also noted that his name was immediately after that of the President. The proposal also provided an outline for a committee which would receive and channel applications. A third committee, on which Hopkins would serve as chairman, had, according to Ickes, been "given the real power." Ickes concluded that within a short time Hopkins would emerge as the "cock of the walk" as the executive order was drafted.[21] Ickes believed this draft was the proof that McIntyre had given out the story that Hopkins was to be the "big man" in the new work relief organization. Hopkins suggested to Ickes that he send a copy of the proposals developed by Ickes and the PWA staff to Roosevelt. Steve Early, later the same day, also told Ickes to send his proposal to the President. Ickes decided to do so and to thrash the situation out, for he believed he was in the "strongest position I have ever been so far as both the Congress and the public are concerned." [22]

What underlay this feud between Hopkins and Ickes? Why was it so bitter? Obviously, both wanted to be close to Roosevelt; they wanted the power the position would give. "The Battle of Relief," as Arthur Schlesinger, Jr., has aptly called it, was certainly in large measure a power struggle. With control of billions of dollars for relief and public works came influence in local, state, and national politics. Certainly, however, a study of Ickes and Hopkins reveals that both were sincere believers in their approach to work relief and public works. Ickes did not believe in Hopkins' more flexible approach and light public works projects. Hopkins thought PWA valuable, but inadequate to meet the needs of several million unskilled and semiskilled workers. The net result was that these two men maneuvered for the coveted position as head of the new works program until the very last when Roosevelt finally announced his choice.

Ickes and Hopkins each completed a plan and submitted it to FDR. When Hopkins submitted his own proposed draft to President Roosevelt, he attached a note to it in which he pointed out that Admiral Peoples, Rexford G. Tugwell, and Daniel Bell had approved the draft, but on showing the draft to Ickes he noted it was "quite apparent that he has a number of reservations regarding the administrative set up." Hopkins said he had given Ickes a copy of his executive order and that Ickes would probably express his reservations.[23]

In his proposal Hopkins made the President chairman of a National Works Program Allotment Board. Several top government officials would be members. The task of this particular board would be to assist the President in the final determination of funds for various types of projects. A publicity agency, the Application and Information Bureau, would have the role of receiving applications for projects, following the progress of each proposed project, and announcing its approval by the National Works Program Allotment Board. A third agency, the National Works Council, would implement the action taken when approval was given, coordinating the projects in the states. It would make certain that labor, supplies, equipment, and local funds were all available before the project actually got under way. All factual information about the projects, accounting, and purchasing would be handled by the National Works Council. The fourth agency designated by Hopkins in his proposal carried the title Administration of Civil Works. Its task would be to initiate and carry on work projects similar to the better projects under FERA and CWA. Hopkins' draft also called for participation by various other government agencies, including the Rural Electrification Administration which would soon be engaged in building thousands of miles of electric power lines in rural areas.[24]

Ickes' major objections to Hopkins' proposal were four. First, the National Works Program Allotment Board had too many members (seventeen). It would be unwieldy.

Second, the relationship of the administrator of the National Works Authority to the other agencies was not clear. Ickes noted that applications for PWA projects must be initiated through the National Works Authority and that PWA field representatives would apparently be selected by, and subject to the direction of, its administrator. Third, Hopkins' proposal authorized the National Works Authority to issue all administrative orders dealing with the administration of the act without consultation with the National Works Program Allotment Board and the agencies concerned. And fourth, all requests for opinions and decisions with respect to the administration of the act would have to be originated, or be approved, by the National Works Authority. According to Ickes, the order provided for a central disbursing unit which presented grave administrative difficulties, brushed aside existing planning boards, concentrated all powers and functions under the act in the National Works Authority, made subordinate to the National Works Authority all other agencies administering the act, and rendered virtually superfluous the National Works Program Board.[25]

The Ickes draft of the executive order made each of the agencies, including the new ones, self-sufficient with power to select their own personnel. They could issue their own rules. Ickes gave emphasis to a central planning board which would work with state planning boards. His plan, as Ickes himself stated, withdrew most of the power Hopkins had given himself. As he records in his notes: "I cut him [Hopkins] down very sharply in my draft."

The time for President Roosevelt to make his choice came in late April. Roosevelt thought Ickes to be "a good administrator" but "too slow." Hopkins got things done. Since Roosevelt wanted "speed, flexibility, quick re-employment, and a sharp stimulus to consumer purchasing power," Hopkins was to him the better choice. Yet, Roosevelt's respect for Ickes' honesty and ability to produce durable public works was so strong that he wanted Ickes involved. He therefore came forth with a plan of organization which attempted to provide various checks and balances on both Hopkins and Ickes, leaving them both active in the work program and competing against each other.

Frank Walker, the in-between man of the various factions of New Dealers and Democrats, Roosevelt announced as a key figure in the new work organization. He would be head of the Division of Application and Information. This division was to receive all suggested plans for the useful expenditure of public funds. The source made no difference. Whether local, state, or federal in origin, proposed plans went to the DAI. Here they were to be sorted, checked, tabulated, then passed on to the Advisory Committee on Allotments, of which Harold Ickes was to be chairman. This committee recommended the projects which would be considered by the President for final approval. Its membership consisted of the secretaries of Interior, Agriculture, and Labor; directors of the National Emergency Council, the Progress Division (of the new works organization), Procurement, the Bureau of the Budget, Soil Erosion, Emergency Conservation Works, Rural Resettlement, Relief and Rural Electrification; the Chief of Engineers, United States Army; the Commissioner of Reclamation; the chiefs of the Forest Service, Bureau of Public Roads, Division of Grade Crossing Elimination, and the Urban Housing Division; together with representatives of the Business Advisory Council, organized labor, farm organizations, the National Resources Planning Board, American Bankers Association, and the United States Conference of Mayors.

The third division was the Works Progress Division (soon changed to the Works Progress Administration). Hopkins, as head of this organization, found himself assigned the apparently minor role of investigating, regulating, and reporting functions of the program, checking man-hour costs and the availabilities of men in any particular area. Hopkins had the right to recommend and carry on small useful projects designed to assure *maximum employment* in all localities.

Stated briefly, this arrangement meant that Walker and his group received projects and kept track of them until they were finally approved or rejected. Ickes and his group surveyed the caliber of proposed projects and recommended or disapproved them. The President himself gave the final approval or disapproval. Hopkins and his staff were to make sure that men on relief or otherwise in need of work were available for each proposed project, that man-year costs were right, and that the project fitted in with other activities of the government in a given area, i.e., CCC, PWA, federal road work, and other federal activities. Hopkins could, if he wished, conduct projects through his own division. This last provision later allowed Roosevelt and Hopkins to make WPA the most important part of the program.[26]

Hopkins had his doubts concerning aspects of the organization and procedures as finally set forth by the President. He opposed the high degree of centralization in getting projects approved. What he had wanted was federal control with the work program under one set of officials organized from the localities throughout the nation to the top administrator in Washington, each level of officials having certain duties and authority. He had written the President in connection with his executive order draft, "It seems to me that the crux of the whole matter, is going to rest with the centralization of the work in 'Kokomo, Indiana' and a thousand places like it; there must be no division in authority." Hopkins thought there should be a clear-cut administrative unit under federal management controlling only the ultimate selection of projects. State level administrators could check proposed projects, forward the better ones to Washington, and when informed they had been approved, charged with administration of them until completed, being responsible for their actions to the administrator in Washington. He was convinced also that if three and a half million persons were to be put to work it would be "only through the instrumentality of an outfit like the Civil Works Administration." Such an organization could be controlled as to number of projects and personnel, for its projects would not last over a year and could be quickly started and completed. Lastly, Hopkins made the point that the $4,000,000,000 would not allow many projects involving "heavy construction" which required large sums for materials "else three and one-half million persons will never get on direct employment." [27]

What Hopkins was seeking was a means to get suitable projects going quickly, once they had been adequately screened. He looked upon the work program as one gigantic operation which should be under one head. His experiences with the Bureau of the Budget and other federal agencies had further convinced him that so much red tape would occur under Ickes' and Roosevelt's approach that the work program would not get started before the summer was over. He worked, therefore, to devise a system whereby applications would never have to come to Washington to run through the mill of inspection and receive formal approval from several agencies.[28]

For his part, Ickes was reasonably well pleased with the announced organizational plans, although he thought the arrangement could have been made more streamlined so that its operation would be more efficient. He believed Frank Walker to be the "best possible choice" for the position as coordinator, for Walker was not one to "try to aggrandize power to himself at the expense of others." Ickes believed he would really outrank all the other men in the work relief organization. This would, he thought, surprise many.

On the evening of April 26 the key group to be concerned with the work program met with the President to formulate further plans. The President noted that the work program would have an important bearing on the election in 1936 and he therefore expected the program "to run smoothly" and "to go like clockwork and that he would accept no excuses." Ickes thought Hopkins was "playing up" to Walker during the evening. Later, when Hopkins suggested that all publicity should go through Walker's office, Ickes disagreed and stated that PWA definitely planned also to screen its own personnel rather than to have Walker or some other agency do it. Thus, friction between the men, inherent in the beginning of the work program, quickly became an important factor with which Roosevelt had to deal not once but numerous times within the next few years.

Hopkins made this notation in his diary on May 12: "All day planning the work program—which would be a great deal easier if Ickes would play ball—but he is stubborn and righteous which is a hard combination—he is also the 'great resigner'—anything doesn't go his way, threatens to quit. He bores me." [29] In a talk Hopkins made to PWA personnel on May 7, Hopkins or one of his staff had written this opening paragraph:

> Now you are a long way from Washington, and you see these stories in the newspapers about rows. I know if you thought there was a fight here, that your sympathies would all be with me. You know Harold Ickes is always in the newspapers, always in a fight; while I am a mild sort of person and wouldn't think of getting in a fight. But I want to tell you the low-down on this thing because you really should know it. The real low-down is that the fellow who is making all the trouble around here is Walker. He is the one that really stirs up all the trouble; if you want to blame anyone, blame Walker. That is one of the things he is here for, to be blamed for everything

> that goes around. I certainly intend to do my share of it. I want to have a fine summer here.[30]

Someone had crossed out this paragraph in one copy and marked it "not used." Whether he actually used it is not known. It was a chance to add some humor to a tense situation, but perhaps Hopkins concluded developments on this subject were too tense for humor.

Ickes in the meantime was becoming more critical of Hopkins. Neither Hopkins' ideas nor his role in the new work program suited Ickes. At approximately the same time that Hopkins was recording that Ickes "bores me," Ickes told Frank Walker in the presence of Hopkins that he "did not believe the program would work out." He made the statement with particular reference to the process whereby only persons on relief rolls could be accepted on the work projects as laborers. Hopkins had supported, but apparently not originated, this idea of the President's. Ickes thought such a policy "bad psychology and bad politics." Self-respecting and independent persons who had been able to keep going would resent "the need" to "go on relief" to get work under the work program. Therefore, maintained Ickes, the least independent and least provident would be aided the most.

During the early weeks of organization there was much confusion. Hopkins recorded on May 14 that he thought Walker was "bewildered" by the complexity of the new setup. Ickes concluded the organization was "just as unwieldy" as he thought it would be. He found no snap or efficiency. Ickes still believed one man should be head, but not he. On May 21, after a conference at the White House, Ickes noted he continued "to live in a maze so far as general work relief is concerned." What was now needed, apparently, was some individual to step forward and push the program and dominate it, even though the charts and program did not call for that. Seemingly this was what Hopkins attempted to do in the next several months, either because he saw the need for it, or wanted the power, or a combination of both of these fundamental driving forces.

At the May 21 meeting Ickes and Hopkins disagreed on the tempo of the program. Hopkins began to talk about hitting the peak November 1, after indicating earlier a desire for a July 1 deadline. Ickes and Walker thought that November would be too late because of weather. Ickes believed the program was being worked out by charts and not on the basis of experience. Further discouragement came to Ickes at this meeting when the President talked of projects where no financial return would be expected. The President also told Ickes to make each PWA loan on an individual basis. Ickes did not believe this would work because cities would all want the same percentage arrangements for the loans. By June 1 Hopkins seemed to loom larger in the program. Ickes was told by his staff that Harry Hopkins had "Public Works pretty well stymied." Ickes feared his men might be right.

The meeting of the Allotment Board on June 17 seemed to indicate to Hopkins additional gain for the WPA. The President and others were giving careful consideration to his type of project. Ickes thought it was "becoming ever clearer that Hopkins is dominating this program and this domination will mean thousands of inconsequential make-believe projects in all parts of the country." Ickes believed Roosevelt's administration would "suffer" if it proceeded with the Hopkins program.[31]

Newspaper reporters quizzed the two gentlemen concerning their differences at their press conferences on June 20, 1935. Ickes said: "There may be occasional differences of opinion as to details of approach and methods of achieving our mutual goal [but] . . . we have the common object in trying to give work to the unemployed. Harry Hopkins and

I are good friends. We have worked happily together for two years and will continue so to work together." [32] Hopkins was perhaps less candid in his answer when asked about this statement by Ickes. At his press conference this colloquy occurred:

Query: Can you comment on those stories?

Mr. Hopkins: What stories?

Query: Of a row between you and Ickes.

Mr. Hopkins: There is nothing to that. I haven't got time to row.

Query: All along we have been going on the idea that Mr. Ickes was of the belief that projects would be approved on the basis of their economic utility, counting on indirect employment to spread throughout the nation. We had the idea that you preferred projects which would be distributed to meet the local unemployment needs in each particular area, and also would have low cost projects because you did not count indirect employment.

Mr. Hopkins: No, I am sure that both of us want to do the job the President has told the American people he is going to do, and that is to take three and one-half million people from the relief rolls and put them to work. That is the objective and there is no disagreement about that.[33]

Harold Ickes presented his viewpoint on the relative merits of PWA and WPA by means of a conference and letter to Roosevelt in late June. WPA, said Ickes, could contribute up to 100 per cent of the funds for a given project. In contrast to this, PWA was limited by law to a 45 per cent grant. This established unfair competition between the two agencies. Local governments would not submit projects to PWA if they could build them with WPA money. There was no reason why they should pay roughly half the total cost when they could get by with paying less, or even nothing. Ickes stated that a clear demarcation line must be drawn between what PWA could do and what WPA could do. He believed if the municipality was willing to make any contribution, and the proposed structure was of a permanent nature, PWA should do it. PWA had the experience and it already had personnel, while Hopkins' organization would have to create more staff and gain experience to do the same thing. Ickes believed the original intention to have approximately one-half of the fund spent for self-liquidating projects could be carried out best by emphasizing the role of PWA.[34]

President Roosevelt talked to Ickes about his letter and called a conference of Hopkins, Ickes, and Walker on June 27 to discuss several matters. The President pointed out that WPA could not compete against PWA and that they should not compete for projects. Walker said he believed there was too much confusion for local and state officials seeking approval of their projects. Hopkins, according to Ickes, "scoffed at this suggestion," but Ickes thought Walker's point well taken. The President told the men to get together and draft a document which would clear up the situation.

At this conference Ickes thought Hopkins was discouraged to begin with and even more so by the time the conference was over. In talking with Walker and Ickes before seeing the President, Hopkins supposedly complained to the other two men about the organization of the work program. Hopkins thought there should be only one administrator. Ickes agreed. Walker and Ickes told Hopkins in turn that he had so many projects to check they did not have time to check them individually at the Allotment Board meetings and, therefore, they did not want to vote on them. They would prefer to vote for a lump sum and let Hopkins be responsible for his own program, which was in essence more what Hopkins actually wanted. Ickes has also stated that on this occasion Hopkins told them that he (Hopkins) should go back to New York and find a job and let Ickes run the show. Neither Ickes nor Walker made any comment on what Ickes called "this petulant statement." [35]

Between June 27 and July 2 Walker, Hopkins, and Ickes held several conferences. Finally, they submitted an agreement. The agreement stated that applications for construction projects (other than repair and maintenance projects and certain others assigned to WPA) with estimated cost over $25,000 should be submitted to PWA. Slum clearance and low-cost housing projects were also assigned to PWA. The agreement defined the areas of activity for WPA. These included non-construction projects (white collar projects), small works projects costing under $25,000 upon completion, and various other propects such as parks, playgrounds, and street repairs. If PWA rejected a project, the applicant could then apply to WPA.

The agreement did not prevent competition between WPA and PWA. True, a $25,000 limit was set for WPA, but at the same time new areas of operation were offered for WPA. If PWA rejected a proposed project, it was now sent to WPA which might approve it. All types of light construction projects were now possible for an imaginative WPA administrator. All Hopkins had to do was to have any proposed project of a few million dollars broken into small projects and WPA could do them. In fact, certain areas of activity were not limited by the $25,000 figure, and one section of the agreement listed nineteen areas in which projects were acceptable regardless of cost. Hence, if Hopkins wished, he might build an airport costing as much as $3,000,000. In reality the agreement meant little.

During August, Hopkins continued to present to the Advisory Committee on Allotments hundreds of projects. Ickes argued this was bad practice because proper evaluation could not be given them and this consideration consumed too much of the agenda. Ickes became further incensed when he learned that a project from Atlanta, Georgia, originally being considered by his agency was also being evaluated by WPA officials. If Atlanta's officials could get WPA to approve their sewerage project, there would be a very large financial saving to the city. PWA could give financial terms of a 45–55 ratio only. Ickes promptly raised the question as to what other cities would do if Atlanta received more favorable terms from WPA. Ickes also claimed that Hopkins' office was holding up hundreds of suitable PWA projects because there was a lack of unemployed labor in the area. Ickes asked for the right to look over the WPA lists of projects submitted to see if any PWA projects were on them. He also sought to bring pressure on the President to have Hopkins' check of PWA projects speeded up.

Thus, by the fall of 1935, Hopkins had built WPA into a dominant position. Factors working for this growth and for the limitations on PWA were the loan requirements for PWA grants, the ability of Hopkins' staff to subdivide larger projects so WPA could do them, control of judgment on labor supply, and the plain fact that hundreds of local sponsors could secure a quicker response from WPA; therefore, they continued to work with WPA.

Ickes was certainly convinced now that there had to be a showdown between himself on the one hand and Hopkins and Morgenthau on the other. He was certain that the letter from the President which caused this last difficulty had originated in the office of the Secretary of the Treasury. He was "tired" of voting Hopkins "money by the carload" which he could spend "at his own sweet pleasure," when every PWA project had to be closely scrutinized. The President, he concluded, must surely have a "blind side" as far as Morgenthau was concerned and "Hopkins seems to sing a siren song for him." To Ickes, Hopkins had now become a "lawless individual bent on building up a reputation for himself as a great builder, even at the expense of the President and the country. I think," continued Ickes, "he is the greatest threat today to the President's re-election." [36]

On the same day that Ickes recorded the above comment, Hopkins told Mayor Kelley of Chicago that Ickes was "taking a flyer" at him. Hopkins was going to see the President about it. The New York *Daily News* reported that Hopkins had been boarding with the Roosevelts too much and had interfered with some of the public works setup devised by Ickes. Hence, Ickes was going to see the President and get him "to countermand the orders of this Hopkins upstart, or else." A clash of principles, followed by a clash of personalities, had to be reconciled. President Roosevelt had this task before him as he met with these two men and others at a major conference in Hyde Park in mid-September.[37]

As part of the background for this important meeting, additional information, which the President had and some of the others did not, must be considered. First, Harold Ickes had written a lengthy and important letter to the President. In the letter Ickes argued that PWA, which might have been slow in starting its original program in 1933 and 1934, now possessed an efficient decentralized system of administration. The government should give it more money to work with rather than create new agencies in another organization. WPA was even given "veto power," said Ickes, over much of the proposed program of PWA. The WPA program, which was slow in starting, would be inefficient and would suffer from "graft and corruption" if conducted as outlined at that time. Believing that the public works and relief programs would be the key issues in the campaign of 1936, Ickes feared that not only relief, but the entire works program, including PWA, would become unpopular. This he thought "would be a great pity," for he anticipated the need for a good public works program for several years.[38]

Frank Walker, head of the Division of Application and Information, expressed his opinion as to the course to pursue in a memorandum to Roosevelt dated September 10, 1935. Presumably the President read this before the meeting on September 12. Walker stated that three million jobs could not be allotted by November 1 as promised. Therefore, the administration could not abandon relief in any substantial amount by that time, nor probably within the current fiscal year. He believed the works relief program as contemplated was "impractical" and could not be "expeditiously and effectively carried out." In view of these facts and beliefs, Walker suggested that "all WPA projects not at this stage initiated, be abandoned." He suggested also that $1,000,000,000 of the money appropriated by Congress in the Emergency Relief Appropriation Act of 1935 "be not allotted for any purpose." Walker believed the entire relief situation as it existed in the fall of 1935 should be studied before further steps were taken to aid those in need. He did not suggest, however, that relief efforts be suspended.[39]

The conference at Hyde Park told the several officials in charge of the various agencies what they could count on. On September 12, Hopkins, Walker, Ickes, Bell, Tugwell, and several others conferred with the President for over ten hours in the large living room in the south end of the Roosevelt home. The President trimmed and transferred funds from agency to agency. Finally, he came to the necessity of allotting money to PWA and WPA. From what he had thus far saved he gave to Hopkins the minimum amount he needed and then gave the rest to PWA, an amount of only $200,000,000. Ickes argued strenuously that such an amount was not nearly enough. He pointed out that his office had received applications for projects totaling over $2,000,000,000. The President, however, stayed by his decision and closed the issue.

The crux of the situation by September 12, 1935, was this.

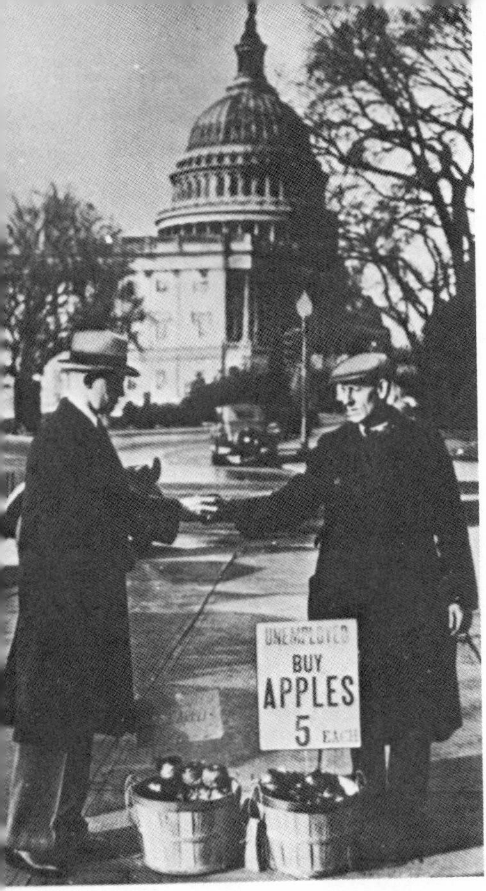

Congressman buys an apple from a jobless man, 1930. (UPI)

Despite a heavy rain, jobless wait in bread line at Grand and Christie streets in New York, 1930. (UPI)

Al Capone, Chicago's "Public Enemy No. 1," feeds 3,000 men daily at a rented store on South State street. Soup, bread, coffee, and doughnuts are served at a cost of $300 a day. These unemployed are waiting for the dinner bell. (UPI)

HARRY L. HOPKINS
(Franklin D. Roosevelt Library,
Hyde Park, N. Y.)

ABOVE: "And Everywhere that Harry Went The Ram Was Sure to Go"
(Columbus [Ohio] *Dispatch*, Sept. 6, 1936)

CENTER: "When Three's a Crowd"
(Philadelphia [Pa.] *Record*, April 29, 1935)

RIGHT: "Anyway—The Little Fellow's in Line"
(Philadelphia [Pa.] *Inquirer*, April 8, 1935)

CWA project in Minnesota, 1934
(Franklin D. Roosevelt Library, Hyde Park, N. Y.)

HOPKINS
WORK RELIEF PROGRAM

WORK RELIEF PROJECTS
DOODLESACKPFEIFFER
RHYTHMATIGGERS
PAY WINDOW
WORTH-WHILE PUBLIC IMPROVEMENTS
THINGUMBOB DESIGNER
BOON-DOGGLER
DINGBAT MAKER

CWA

"The Sower"
(Washington [D.C.] *Star*, July 18, 1938)

Construction work on bridge across Elkhart River in Indiana, 1935.
(Franklin D. Roosevelt Library, Hyde Park, N. Y.)

"The Big-Check Suit That Was Hung On Harry" (Kansas City [Mo.] *Star*, Nov. 28, 1938)

"A Great Record!" *(Parkway Transcript*, Roslindale, Mass., Jan., 1939)

"Christmas, 1938" (Washington [D.C.] *Star)*

Hopkins, whose agency had the task of checking availability of men, materials, and costs, had rejected by this time approximately 2,000 PWA projects on the basis of costs of materials in relation to direct wages to labor, and, in some instances, a shortage of relief labor. Ickes did not like this, for otherwise they were acceptable projects. This led directly back to the original point of disagreement and to the issue which President Roosevelt himself had to settle. Was the primary goal of this new works program the expenditure of money on projects with no regard to the number employed? Or was the primary goal the placing of the three and one-half million workers at jobs on acceptable projects which had lower material costs? On September 10 the balance from the $4,880,000,000 appropriated in the spring of 1935 was $1,232,322,301. This meant that if the main purpose of the works program was to put the unemployed employables to work, the projects remaining to be selected must have low man-year costs and low material costs. PWA man-year cost per project usually averaged $1,200 to $1,500. Occasionally it was higher. The projects selected until September 10 would put approximately two million to work. Therefore, the President had available $1,200,000,000 to put the remaining one and a half million people to work for a period of one year. This meant selecting projects with a man-year cost of $900 or even less, if possible. PWA's projects for the most part could not meet this requirement. WPA's projects could meet it. In deciding that WPA should have the opportunity to select and conduct projects with most of the remainder of the money, President Roosevelt was being reasonably consistent. He had always indicated that putting the unemployed employables to work was the key thing, although he operated under the illusion for too long that PWA type projects would accomplish this. The President's questions and statements at the first meetings of the Advisory Committee on Allotments indicated clearly his interest in the projects with low man-year costs. To Harry Hopkins then fell the task, and it was a hard one even though he sought it, of juggling money, manpower, and projects in an effort to get one and a half million persons to work for twelve months with $1,200,000,000.

Hopkins, having won this skirmish with Ickes, felt quite pleased with the results. Ickes foresaw failure and a possible rejection of the whole New Deal by the people at the next Presidential election. His reactions to the Hyde Park Conference were in part similar to other utterances, some by Republicans, critical of the WPA program. Ickes recorded his impression on September 13.

> I didn't leave Hyde Park in a very pleasant state of mind. We caught a late train out, although the President had asked us to stay all night. While I was there he also asked me to take the trip to Boulder Dam and San Diego the latter part of the month and said he would be glad to have me take the sea voyage with him through the Panama Canal also.
>
> I have no confidence myself in Hopkins' program. I think it is the greatest present threat to the President's re-election. It looks to me as if the WPA will be perhaps the major issue in the campaign next year. Its absurdities, its inefficiencies, its insufficiencies, its bunglings and its graftings will be aired in the press and from the platform and I don't see how we can defend it. The whole program seems to me to be based upon an economic and social fallacy. The more I think of it, the more convinced am I that the only sound procedure is a program of worth-while public works. I happen to believe that secondary employment is more important than employment at the site, because secondary employment means employment in the factories, in the mills, and on the railroads, fabricating and transporting the materials to be used at the site to build

the projects. However, no one has been able to mention indirect employment to the President for a long time. He simply has no patience with the thought. Hopkins has finally convinced him that the goal ought to be to put men to work, regardless of what they were being put to work at, and if there is no legitimate work, to put them to work notwithstanding.[40]

In early October, President Roosevelt gathered his two hard-working feuding lieutenants under his wing and took them on a trip across the continent and on a long cruise in the Pacific to the Cocos Islands and back through the Panama Canal. Two excerpts from the U.S.S. *Houston*'s paper, *The Blue Bonnet*, tell the tone and purpose of the cruise other than rest.

Buried at Sea

The feud between Hopkins and Ickes was given a decent burial today. With flags at half-mast—the band's trumpets muted—Pa freshly shaved—the officers half dressed—the President officiated at the solemn ceremony which we trust will take these two babies off the front page for all time. Hopkins, as usual, was dressed in his immaculate blues, browns and whites, his fine figure making a pretty sight with the moon-drifted sea in the foreground. Ickes wore his conventional faded grays, Mona Lisa smile and carried his stamp collection.

The ceremony, tho brief, was impressive. Hopkins expressed regret at the unkind things Ickes had said about him—and Ickes on his part promised to make it stronger—only more so—as soon as he could get a stenographer who could take it hot. As the sun burst thru the fading moonlight bathing all (Wilson needed it—Pa bathes twice as often and covers more territory but never reaches his plaster belt—it's disgusting Mr. President)—well as soon as the moon flattened out, the two feudists turned facing the sea to pledge their fealty. It was soon over. The President gave them a hearty slap on the back—pushing them both into the sea. "Full steam ahead," ordered the President.

Welcome Gladiators

The Blue Bonnet is anxious to pay its respects to the President's two civilian Aids [*sic*] aboard ship, Secretary Ickes and Hopkins. This paper remains neutral during the recent unpleasantness between these apostles of the New Deal. However, we would be faithless to our readers if we failed to make a few pointed observations about the irrelative movements. We haven't seen much of Harold because the sea has been a little too much for him and just as he is about to heave into full view, his stomach gets in the way. He was born with the well-known silver spoon in his mouth (Hopkins is said to have remarked that it should have choked him then and there) and never worked a day in his life until Roosevelt put his name in a hat along with other contributors to the campaign and pulled his out.

The truth of the matter is that he hasn't worked much since—he has changed the names of a couple of dams—written a couple of books—corresponded with Senator Tydings—appointed Bob Moses—got some of Farley's stamps—given Steve Early headaches—Henry Morgenthau the ague—Wallace, writer's cramps, and Roper the pip.

Hopkins' fine figure and open mouth have been real inspiration to the ship. He has a retiring, aesthetic quality about him that belies his advance publicity. One has but to see him playing "upstairs" in his rompers to realize that an angry word has never crossed his lips or an evil thought galloped thru his mighty brain. One can well understand how Hopkins gets the short end of the stick when the money is passed around in Washington. His case rests on justice and truth—not upon intrigue.

As we have watched this famous pair, we are sure they will both go far and we are quite confident of the place—the ash can! [41]

The cruise and chance to relax did clear the air to a degree. Ickes and Hopkins did become better acquainted with each other. However, the "two babies" were on the front page the following spring when once again Ickes and Hopkins found there was not enough money for both of them to do the programs they both believed in.

Reflecting on the series of events during the spring and summer of 1935, Secretary of the Treasury Henry Morgenthau, Jr., observed, "It seems almost tragic to think that the fate of the unemployed in America could be held up so long by these men both seeking power. . . ." For the efficient employment of a few hundred thousand Americans the September decision and the cruise came too late.[42]

The foundation upon which this nation stands is the dignity of man as an individual . . . his right to free expression in politics and religion, and in the labor by which he builds his way of life. Work is America's answer to the need of idle millions. . . . Work, not charity . . . peaceful work, not regimentation to build machines of war . . . useful public work, to benefit us all.

—INSCRIPTION ON THE WPA BUILDING:
NEW YORK WORLD'S FAIR, 1939

VII. The Works Progress Administration

Eager and intense activity, plus confusion, marked the beginning of the WPA. Men with sleeves rolled up worked over desks piled high with papers. Messengers ran from one to the other of the nine buildings occupied entirely or partially by WPA and from office to office within these buildings. Desks and files were placed wherever there was available space. The staff knew no set office hours. Even the lesser personnel would grab a sandwich and a cup of coffee for lunch and rush back to work. Lights burned to early hours in the morning. Elevators ran all night and telephones were frequently busy until midnight. Housed in nine different buildings, trying to establish work projects more extensive and complex than those of CWA, WPA, nevertheless became a working organization within a short time. Hopkins' ability to get the utmost from his staff was the primary reason for this success.

WPA lived mostly in the present. Past records were seldom consulted, or needed, during the first year of WPA's existence. Much of the business was done by telephone, no record of it being kept. One official later remarked that after a year on the job he still did not know what was in the files about the work of his predecessor. He had, he said, often wondered if it might not be useful to find out what was in the files, but he had never had the time to explore their contents.[1] That these men and women were rushed, that they worked as hard as any human beings could or should, cannot be denied. As General Hugh S. Johnson, a critic of much of WPA's activity, once observed, WPA "undertook more than human flesh" could do but "if devoted and unselfish effort to the point of physical destruction was ever put forth, these men have done it. It is a wonder they are still alive."[2]

In June, 1935, as WPA was being launched, reporters asked Hopkins who his top administrators would be. Hopkins quickly replied, "I made up my mind that I am going to use our (FERA) people. This crowd here—four or five fellows—have been with me since the beginning, and they suit me. I cannot hire any better and if they cannot do it, I cannot get any better to do it." Hopkins knew the skills of these men and women. He was used to working with them. He knew they were loyal to him and to the principle of work relief.

Corrington Gill, possessor of a live-wire intellect, who sometimes "got mad" at Hopkins for always being "ahead of me," continued in charge of research, statistics, and finance. He spent much of his time working on the procedural changes in forming the WPA program. Aubrey Williams, a capable administrator despite his lack of tact at times, continued as first assistant administrator. Later he became head of the youth program (National Youth Administration) and other educational programs. It can be said in reference to these two men that Hopkins could trust the brain of Gill and the heart of Williams. Jacob Baker, who supervised the work program of the FERA and the CWA, headed the white-collar work and self-help activities of WPA until assigned to work for the government in another capacity. Mrs. Ellen S. Woodward, at one time a member of the Mississippi state legislature, was in charge of the

Women's Division of WPA. Lawrence Westbrook, not formally listed as an assistant administrator, nonetheless performed this role, advising Hopkins on various problems. Dallas Dort continued his work as the key investigator and soon became head of WPA's own investigation department. Pierce Williams, Howard O. Hunter, Alan Johnstone, and other field representatives for FERA became field representatives for the WPA program. Hunter eventually became head of the Federal Works Agency in the early 1940's. David K. Niles soon became director of the Information Service of WPA. He proved to be of great value and later served on the secretarial staffs of presidents Roosevelt and Truman. Naturally, one of Hopkins' main tasks was to help each of these persons to develop his own ideas and phases of the total program, at the same time keeping a harmonious relationship which would allow him to concentrate on the major problems.

To assist his staff in coordinating its activities, Hopkins established a Committee on Procedures. Donald C. Stone, executive director of Public Administration Service, a private nonprofit administrative consulting service, became chairman of this committee. The committee consisted of men from the Public Administration Service, the FERA, and the WPA. This group studied the entire WPA program—local, state, and the operations of the Washington office. Disagreements occurred between the committee and some of the top administrators. To minimize the conflict and duplication of orders, it worked closely with the Division of Information and Publications which issued all orders and regulations for WPA. In this way it could stop attempts to bypass its suggested procedures. The difficulty was that the committee served as a negative rather than a positive force. Nonetheless, as long as Hopkins was head of WPA it continued its work, primarily for two reasons. First, as Donald Stone pointed out when he resigned in October, 1935, the committee had been able to assist in the efficiency of the program. Second, as time passed the personnel of the committee consisted largely of experienced representatives from all phases of the program. They could view WPA activities in the light of practical experience. Therefore, they could and did make suggestions of real value.[3]

Hopkins believed strongly that personal contact was one of the most effective means of putting information across to a group of administrators; whenever possible and logical he called state administrators to Washington where his staff could work with them directly for at least a few days. Operating under this philosophy, he called the first major WPA conference in June, 1935. Hopkins and his staff attempted to answer the many questions of the state administrators. Perhaps the real value lay, however, as Hopkins believed it might, in having the state administrators meet his staff and hear from him directly his thoughts on the intents and purposes of WPA.

At a press conference, May 2, 1935, Hopkins told reporters, in two very brief sentences, what WPA was supposed to be. "The purpose of this whole program," he said, "is this three and one-half million men. That is the motivation of this whole thing." In the first session with the state administrators Hopkins drove home this point.

> Our job . . . is to put 3,500,000 people to work, and the President has asked the Works Progress Administration, in attaining that objective, to take two distinct responsibilities. The first, and I believe the most important, is that the Works Progress Administrator is to place at work on projects which are to be directly administered and controlled by the Works Progress Administration a very large number of men and women. [The second job is] . . . correlating and planning a whole program to put 3,500,000 to work.

Hopkins' various experiences in dealing with personnel problems resulted in a very strong warning to the state administrators to select a competent staff. A reading of the minutes for this conference in June, 1935, shows that Hopkins built up steam as he came to this part of his remarks. In the back of his mind were probably remembrances of several tough situations. To those who have had administrative responsibilities, his words ring true.

> Ninety per cent of this depends on the people we have to run it. Seventy-five per cent of my job is over and finished when I have a good State Administrator in a particular state, and if the State Administrator isn't any good, then my troubles are doubled. Why, in the whole relief administration, when I think of it now over the past year, I believe I have given three-fourths of my time to half a dozen states, and if I have [*sic*] been a little smarter I would have fired some people long before I did in those half a dozen states. I was fiddling around, compromising with people that you know are incompetent, just because I am a good-hearted son-of-a-gun. That shouldn't be done. You have no business doing that in the public's business when you are spending the public's money. We are not going to do it this time.
>
> Just as my job is easier or anyone's job around this national office is easier if we have a good State Administrator, so a State Administrator's job is easy if he in turn has a fellow that knows his business. Therefore, obviously, the thing to consider is, do these people know their business and can they do a good job and deliver the goods. I don't care what their religion is, and I don't care much what their background is, as a matter of fact, if they have got executive ability, if they have got integrity, if they know how to move, if they are willing to take some chances, if they are not afraid to sign their name on the dotted line. We are going to assume all these fellows we have appointed are

> honest. Great guns! you should take that for granted. None of us should be proud of the fact that we are honest. My Lord! the thing we are proud of is really doing this job.

And later on Hopkins revealed his deep personal belief in what he was doing. To him, this effort to put people to work was extremely important.

> And some of us have the only chance we will ever again in our life have to do this job for all the people. Every one of us in this room is being paid for by the nation, they pay us, we work for all the people. This isn't our money. We are just agents of America, doing a job, and in a crisis like this—because when we have ten or eleven million people out of work don't let anybody tell you this isn't still a crisis—we have been given the greatest opportunity to serve not only the people but the nation, that we will ever have again in our lives. I tell you, I have to pinch myself sometimes when I think how some of us have been catapulted into these positions and I will tell you now of the faith and confidence that I have in you, the devotion which you have given to this thing for the past two years and I know I do not have to appeal to this crowd for support. What I need to do is to be sure that I can keep up with you in the kind of service you have been giving to this nation in the past two years. I am proud to do this job with you and I want you to be proud to do it with me.

With these thoughts and words Hopkins attempted to build strength into the WPA administrators. Several caught the spirit, or had it and were encouraged to renew it, while others never rose to the occasion or, pressed hard by local politics, soon let expedience win over principle.[4]

The major operating unit of the WPA was the state, which provided a centralized agency to serve as intermediary between the local district offices of WPA and the Washington office. This organization was feasible because the state had been the intermediary agency under FERA. If work relief were at some future date to be returned to state and local control, the state could more easily become the head of the combined direct relief and work relief activities. The major weakness of organization by state was the uneven distribution of the work relief load. In March, 1938, Alabama had only 34,560 workers on WPA projects and Nevada only 2,648; Illinois, typical of the populous states, employed 181,938.

Below the state level the main organization was the district. In using the district rather than the county for local operations, WPA could shift the load more evenly. In other words, a heavily populated urban county might have one or more districts while two or three lightly populated counties might form a single district. Districts were in theory to be as nearly as possible comparable in work load, measured by potential relief employees. Secondary factors included compactness and accessibility in reference to district headquarters and transportation costs for the workers. The boundaries of the districts were originally determined in WPA headquarters in Washington even before the state administrators were appointed. Hopkins and his staff did this to avoid tugs and pulls by local groups on the new administrators and to avoid political squabbles at the very beginning. Also, it was logical and wise to outline district boundaries before submitting projects sponsored by the local agencies. It should be noted that WPA made an effort to avoid fixing WPA district boundaries according to congressional districts. On occasion they purposely established boundaries in such a manner as to weaken local or state political machines, thereby lessening the pressure on WPA staffs. In only a few states, and here only because the newly appointed state administrator requested it, did the WPA districts and congressional districts coincide. The efficiency gained by the district method was illustrated in Kentucky, for example, where the number of district offices decreased from 126 in 1933 to 39 in 1935, and finally to 6 district offices under the state WPA.

Hopkins and his staff originally established five divisions within each state office. These corresponded roughly to the divisions in the Washington office—divisions of personnel, finance and reports, field relations, projects, and labor. Experience proved these divisions to be unsuitable from the administrative standpoint. After a comprehensive study by army engineers, Hopkins and his assistants reorganized the state offices so that there were four divisions known as operations, women's and professional propects, employment, and finance and statistics. Thus, by early 1936, Hopkins had WPA in the form it was to keep until absorbed as part of the Federal Works Agency in 1939.

The several regional offices served as important links between Washington and the state offices. Washington determined the area of each regional office and assisted in securing quarters and staff. The heads of the regional divisions and their staffs were to advise, instruct, report, and recommend policies in use, and those which might be put in use, to both state and Washington offices. The field representatives of these regions served, therefore, as liaison officers to a large extent. Although confusion existed at first in getting the proper relationship among the state, regional, and Washington headquarters of WPA, the state administrators soon learned that the field representative of the regional office was a personal representative of the top administrator, Hopkins. The field representative could interpret the various orders and circulars of instruction to the state officers, for he was in almost daily, at least weekly, communication with Hopkins by phone or personal visit to Washington headquarters. With a constant stream of reports, surveys, and observations on projects and personnel,

Hopkins was able to obtain a fairly complete picture of the vast activities of WPA.[5]

Experience with people who attempted to use FERA and CWA funds improperly led to the formation of WPA's own investigative organization early in the development of WPA. Dallas Dort, another of Hopkins' men who worked for WPA by choice even though he had better opportunities outside that agency, was Hopkins' first chief investigator. The purpose of the W-Men, as some people called them, was to check for fraud, corruption, and questionable activities. This division of WPA was responsible directly to Hopkins and to no one else. The offices established throughout the nation were not secret and could be located by any inquiring citizen who wanted to do so. Actually, anyone with a complaint or an irregularity to report could have it checked by writing to Hopkins himself or to President Roosevelt, who sent numerous memos to Hopkins to have this or that matter checked which someone claimed to be a misuse of WPA. The investigation division was to assist WPA wherever and whenever possible. If this meant exposing unsavory facts, that was to be done. The FBI trained approximately half of the original investigative force.

In 1940 the investigative force dealt with a monthly average of two hundred cases. During the year 1938, while Hopkins was still administrator, it must have been more than that, for the political campaigns were particularly bitter that year. The relationship of cases of fraud, corruption, and politics to political influence was made clear on one occasion by the joint efforts of the chief investigator and the deputy administrator. The chief investigator prepared a list of the geographical incidence of complaints received by his division. The deputy administrator independently listed the states administratively most troublesome as he had observed them or heard about them. The two lists coincided entirely.

Political interference proved to be a problem which the WPA staff by itself could not eliminate.[6]

For the most part Hopkins was able to keep the number of WPA personnel in a reasonable proportion to the number of persons at work. The highest number employed aside from the workers themselves was in December, 1935, when the program was being expanded and developed. The ratio of WPA personnel to employed relief workers was, as one would expect, highest in the late summer and early fall of 1935 when WPA was still in the basic organizational stage, and when projects were being submitted on a vast scale never to be equaled again. In mid-February, 1936, when approximately 38,000 were on the staff, only 2,225 were attached to the Washington office. The salaries paid were not large when considered as a whole over the nation, nor was the proportion of higher-salaried individuals to the lower-salaried personnel excessive. In March, 1937, when 30,347 persons were on the entire administrative payroll, over 24,000 of these received under $2,000 per year. The average annual salary in the Washington office was $2,251; in the state offices it was $1,633; and in the district offices, the average was $1,401.

The highest administrative costs for WPA came with the beginning of the program. During the period from the summer of 1935 to December 31, 1936, WPA spent a total of $2,325,285,492, of which $99,994,132 or 4.3 per cent was for costs of administration. For the calendar year of 1936, the administrative costs were 3.6 per cent of the total money spent. For the fiscal year of 1936, the administrative expense was 5.1 per cent of the total expenditures. Three years later administrative costs were running between 3.4 and 3.7 per cent. During Hopkins' last year as head of the WPA, each dollar appropriated for WPA was spent in the following manner: eighty-six cents in project wages, ten to eleven cents for materials and equipment, and between three and four cents for costs of administration.

Congress eventually provided a set amount for WPA for administrative expenses. Five per cent seemed to Congress a fair proportion for administrative expenses. WPA usually kept below this. Within each state, administrative costs varied considerably depending on the efficiency of the personnel, type of projects in operation, quality of workers, geographic factors, and political interference.[7]

Administrator Hopkins predicted in early August, 1935, that the new work program would be in full swing by November, 1935. He believed the WPA staff could have over three million workers on the job before Thanksgiving. This prediction, an expression of hope, proved to be false. The report for early November, 1935, shows 1,737,610 employed on the work program. The failure to begin the projects on the scale anticipated was partially due to the red tape within the various work agencies, including WPA; also, the system for approval of projects was a rather cumbersome and confusing one. In practice the WPA and the PWA staffs soon circumvented the Division of Applications and Information, in an attempt to eliminate some of the steps necessary for approval. The DAI was supposed to classify and number the applications and then forward them to the proper agency. Thus, WPA and PWA found they received a project application, sent it to DAI, which kept it a day or two, and all that happened was its return with a number stamped on it. Therefore, the staffs of these two agencies began to phone the DAI to get the appropriate project numbers, which were thereupon written on the application forms. By midsummer of 1935, once the WPA staff approved a project application it went directly to the Advisory Committee on Allotments. Roosevelt officially eliminated DAI in mid-September. One reason, other than desire to speed approval of applications for projects, was the fact that the work program conference at Hyde Park in mid-September, 1935, resulted in the decision to have more projects with lower man-year cost. Therefore, WPA could handle these projects by itself, as it was already doing in practice. The correctness of this decision is seen in the fact that by September 1, 1935, the WPA staff had approved far more projects than any other work agency; under the acts of 1935 WPA processed 102,686 projects of the total of 110,239 approved for the work program.

Hopkins and his top staff had other complications with Washington red tape before the WPA program really got rolling. Once WPA approved a project it was submitted for approval to the Advisory Committee on Allotments, the Treasury Department, and the Office of the Comptroller-General. These agencies checked the projects to make certain all was in proper financial order and that no illegal projects, as defined by the act passed by Congress, had been approved. The comptroller-general maintained for quite some time that each project had to be approved by his own staff, the Treasury Department, and the President.

Hopkins disliked this arrangement because these offices lacked the necessary staff to expedite the huge work program. Thus it was that by September, 1935, millions of dollars of projects had been approved by all necessary offices except the treasury and comptroller-general. Particularly in the case of this latter office it would seem that Hopkins' criticism of the red tape seemed justified. The comptroller-general's office would return a WPA project application because it was not, in its opinion, satisfactory. No statement, however, would be attached telling what was incorrect or deficient. Hopkins asked the comptroller-general to make a list of projects, by type, which he would approve. This request was refused. Hence, by trial and error, the WPA personnel learned what was acceptable and what was not. The net result was a considerable amount of extra paperwork and much confusion. By October, 1935, of $2,700,000,000 in projects approved by the President, the comptroller-general's office had issued warrants, necessary for the commencement of a project, for only $900,000,000. Hopkins finally obtained an agreement with the comptroller-general's office, whereby he learned immediately when a project was rejected and upon what basis the rejection was made. WPA's staff could then make the necessary corrections so that the project could be approved in a few days.[8] Harry Hopkins' attitude toward this is reflected in a letter written to his brother, Lewis, on September 10, 1935: "It has been a tough job loaded down with government red tape and of an almost unbelievable variety. They have tied pink ribbons on everything but the telephone poles and may have to do that yet." [9]

While Hopkins busied himself trying to eliminate red tape outside his own agency, the red tape plague grew within the Washington WPA office. Soon state and local WPA administrators complained of the vast number of forms required. The state administrator of Michigan claimed, for example, that if the payroll reports and forms were not so demanding, he could drop 500 of the 1,400 persons working on payroll alone. The director of the district office in Grand Rapids, Michigan, reported he could dismiss at least twenty employees if "it weren't for all the reports and statistics" demanded by the Washington offices of WPA. In some instances district supervisors hid clerical help on the work payrolls because they could not get away with listing them as clerical help, but could not keep the administrative work going without this extra assistance. Lorena Hickok, Hopkins' personal observer in the field, wrote Hopkins: "I tell you we've just gone statistics crazy, that's all. Reports, duplicate copies, triple copies, quintuple copies—demands from everyone who rates a private office and a secretary in Washington! Whew! People constantly bobbing into your office in the field from Washington demanding this, that, and the other thing. Huge regional staffs cluttering up the scenery. This is pretty frank, but that's what I get all the time from state, district, and local directors." [10]

Hopkins knew his office required a large number of reports, but he probably did not know the nature of all of them. Many of the reports and related material could have been eliminated. On the other hand, WPA was not responsible, by any means, for all the reports and statistics which were demanded. As Donald Stone of the Public Administration Service noted, WPA was criticized by many for a lot of material going in and out of its offices, but the law required this information, or by the very nature of the over-all setup, it was necessary. In paying the workers, for example, the security wage system required local and district offices to maintain more records than a regular set pay scale. Stone did not believe WPA's paperwork and orders were out of keeping with the program it conducted.[11]

The WPA staff selected projects for the work program assigned to WPA on the basis of several criteria. These can be briefly summarized:

Projects should be useful.

Projects should require a large proportion of money needed for wages and a low proportion for materials.

Projects to be preferred were those to which the local sponsor contributed a fair share of the cost.

Projects were to be encouraged which would give a financial return to the federal treasury.

Projects should be such as to be capable of immediate prosecution with most of the personnel coming from the relief rolls.

Projects should have a low man-year cost.

Projects must be reasonably well located in relation to the source of labor and supplies.

Projects must be of a nature to fit in with other federally sponsored projects in progress in the surrounding area.

In actual practice, a few of these factors proved dominant. Hopkins wanted people to work on reasonably sound projects as quickly as possible. Therefore, projects which would fit the type of workers immediately available and which fitted the engineering criteria, could be placed in operation quickly. Utility to the community and local preference often took second place. Nonetheless, once WPA started and had enough projects approved, other considerations carried more weight in approval than immediacy of operation. Factors such as manpower available, type of project submitted by the sponsoring agencies, activities of PWA and other work agencies in the area, and funds available were always influences which could not be ignored. To encourage selection of the best projects, WPA headquarters always approved more projects than could be implemented. Thus, state administrators and local authorities had more leeway and could provide more continuity than they could have done otherwise. Hopkins told state administrators that "within limits of human ability you *must* provide employment for all eligible workers; you *must* complete projects, or project units, once begun; you *must* so plan your material purchases that no project need be delayed for lack of it and yet you *must not* accumulate surpluses of unneeded materials." [12]

The selection of projects placed in operation proved to be a product of choices made by WPA and the local sponsoring agencies.

Before analyzing the official criteria for selecting projects, mention should be made of the criteria of politics. Politics in WPA is to be described in later chapters, but at this point it is pertinent that the WPA staff, particularly from 1936 on, had to give attention to the desires of New Deal congressmen. There had to be coordination between WPA headquarters and James Farley and FDR as key leaders of the Democratic Party organization.

Legally the initiation of projects was with local sponsors

(except for federally sponsored projects), but the certification of workers eligible for work relief was the responsibility of local relief offices. The approval and operation of the projects, assignment of workers to them, and the determination of the conditions of work and wages were the combined responsibilities of the district, state, and federal offices of WPA. At the end of the first year of WPA's operation about 98.5 per cent of the projects were initiated by local and state agencies. These sponsoring agencies spent $95 of each $100 spent on WPA projects. Thus, federally sponsored projects provided only a small proportion of total projects placed in operation. Many projects, particularly in recreation and the arts, were encouraged by WPA headquarters, where it was believed that the local sponsor should assume full responsibility for adequacy of design, conformance with local laws and regulations, and recommendations of appropriate planning agencies. Expenses incurred in doing these things could be counted as part of the sponsor's contribution.

During the first two years of WPA's operation, the municipalities sponsored more projects than any other one sponsoring group—39.3 per cent of the total. Other sponsoring agencies and their percentages were: townships, 14.5; counties, 26.7; states, 15.6; federal, 3.7; other, 0.2. Types of projects emphasized were those for roads and streets, public buildings, sewer systems, recreation, and conservation.[13]

Man-year cost, based on material and equipment costs and wages, largely determined the type of project WPA could conduct with funds available. Harold Ickes stated it cost PWA $330 per month to keep a man on the job. WPA could not expend at this rate and still put to work the expected millions of people in Roosevelt's promise to the nation. By 1938 WPA's cost for keeping a worker on the job was approximately $82 per month. By and large, WPA always had to keep its man-year costs below $1,000. While a number of projects could be constructed on which the man-year cost could be as high as $1,500, this also meant many projects with a low man-year cost of $500 would have to be completed to maintain a suitable average. The low man-year cost was largely responsible for the type of construction projects in operation under WPA. It made necessary large numbers of projects with very little material costs which in turn limited rather severely the type of projects completed.

Another basic factor that helped to determine the nature of WPA projects was the quantity and quality of available manpower. The major groups of unemployed in 1937 arranged by skills were: semiskilled, 23.3 per cent; skilled and foremen, 11.7 per cent; clerks and similar workers, 12.9 per cent; new workers, 12.7 per cent; and other laborers, 15.7 per cent. An important function of WPA was placing in operation projects fitting as many of these characteristics of unemployed workers by occupation as it could and at the same time, if possible, fulfill the other criteria for selection of projects. Hopkins and his staff worked hard to provide flexibility. Projects varied from mosquito control to serving school lunches; from the beautification of cemeteries to giving beauty treatments to patients in hospitals for the mentally ill; from repairing library books to making Braille books for the blind; from improving airplane facilities to building over a million privies in rural and semirural areas; from repair and construction of bridges to painting murals in public buildings; from training housekeepers to performances of symphonic orchestras; and from cleaning children's teeth to teaching adults to read and write. Needs of the communities, material and equipment, amount of funds sponsoring agencies had, and the occupation of workers in a given area combined to give WPA a larger conglomeration of projects conducted by a single government agency than ever before in the history of this nation.

Hopkins and his staff had to face another knotty problem

because Congress usually stipulated, in providing WPA funds, that 90 to 95 per cent of the workers be from relief rolls. This is one reason for the importance of occupational background of WPA workers in determining the projects to be completed. It is true that within the area of a state careful maneuvering could bring about conditions whereby the number of non-relief workers on a particular project could be reasonably high, thus allowing WPA to handle construction projects which it could not have handled otherwise. Nonetheless, it meant, from an over-all point of view, that WPA projects must be of a limited nature since most of the workers were semiskilled and unskilled men and women.

Roosevelt and Hopkins were convinced from their earlier experiences with CWA that the 90 to 95 per cent requirement was justified. Only 50 per cent of the CWA workers came from relief rolls and they thought too many not in need had benefited at the expense of others whose needs were desperate. Further, WPA was in large measure strictly work relief, whereas CWA had been a measure to bolster immediately the economic life of the nation. Others, however, criticized the 90 per cent provision. Hugh S. Johnson referred to the 90 per cent provision as "silly." To him it had "neither human sympathy nor common sense." He and others maintained there were families not on relief rolls as badly in need of work relief as those on relief. Such stipulations tended to destroy the pride and will power of the heads of many families. Many of the critics of WPA thought it wrong to force a man to go on relief in order to qualify for a WPA job.

That WPA employees came primarily from relief rolls created certain conditions which were detrimental to the WPA program. Hopkins and his staff faced the unpleasant fact that WPA became a haven of refuge for many persons who never made a really serious attempt to find private employment. These people, unwilling or unable to get and hold regular jobs in private industry, found WPA wages and hours and the security of the position the best in several years. They were reluctant to leave WPA even for a brief period of time. Added to this group were those who had earned a livelihood for themselves but had received compensation in the form of food and shelter. They found the direct cash payment of WPA much more to their liking. The presence of these workers on WPA work projects naturally decreased WPA's efficiency. But despite the desire of many to keep their WPA jobs, after two years only 16 per cent of WPA's employees had been with WPA continuously. That is, there had been no break in their employment from the time they started on WPA until November, 1937. Many of these had not been with WPA from the very beginning. In the first eighteen months of WPA's existence one and a half million different persons left WPA. When Harry Hopkins resigned as administrator of WPA in December, 1938, well over five million different workers had been employed on WPA projects.

One of the most common charges made against WPA was the refusal of private jobs by persons on WPA rolls. Complaints brought out the fact that at times private contractors or private employers could not get WPA workers to quit the WPA for a job with them. Hopkins acknowledged that occasionally such cases occurred, but stressed the fact that often such situations were greatly exaggerated. Hopkins and the rest of the WPA staff tried to encourage WPA workers to take private jobs, provided the standards of employment were fair and just. WPA, either rightly or wrongly, did not ask or expect WPA workers to accept private employment with an income which would necessitate supplementary aid from relief agencies, nor did it expect them to accept jobs for which they were not suited. Hopkins clearly stated his policy to state WPA officials on January 11, 1936:

It is expected that WPA workers will accept available jobs in private employment, whether of a permanent or temporary nature, provided:

(1) That the temporary or permanent work shall be a full-time job;

(2) That such work shall be at a standard or going rate of wages;

(3) That such work shall not be in conflict with established union relationships; and

(4) That workers shall be offered an opportunity to return to the Works Progress Administration upon completion of temporary jobs. . . .

It seems to me extremely important that all workers be given every reasonable opportunity to accept temporary employment because this often results in a permanent opportunity, and obviously workers are going to be loath to accept temporary jobs unless they can be given definite assurance that the WPA work will be open to them upon completion of the job.[14]

If a worker refused suitable private employment he was supposed to be dismissed from his WPA job. Every effort was to be made to accept former WPA workers who lost the private job they had taken if the fault was not their own, and if they were again in need. There is little doubt, however, that project supervisors, anxious to complete their projects, sometimes discouraged their better qualified help from taking private employment. These situations when known were investigated by WPA field representatives.

The portion of the public critical of the WPA accused WPA workers of losing their sense of values and the ability to think and act independently. Most of the WPA workers who hung on to their WPA jobs probably disagreed, the difference here being that they reached a different conclusion. In their own way they surveyed the situation and decided they could best fulfill their family responsibilities by staying on WPA. Few men who had a wife and two or three children would leave WPA for another job which guaranteed nothing better.

The accusations against WPA workers and refusals to take private employment were extremely irritating to Hopkins, who perhaps had too much faith in the WPA worker. He was probably irked further by the number of false and ridiculous charges. WPA investigated the charges of refusal of work for private employers whenever and wherever they occurred. On one occasion a produce company charged they could not get workers to handle fruit ready to be canned because workers would not leave the local WPA projects. Investigators found that in twenty-nine canneries in the general area only one needed additional help, and there only a few women were needed to clean strawberries. Over half of the twenty-nine were not operating. In another instance a contractors' association asked that WPA stop construction in a state because they could not hire enough electricians. WPA immediately supplied a list of over three hundred unemployed electricians in that particular state. The construction association apologized to WPA but hired no electricians.

There was a serious difference of opinion as to what grounds would justify a WPA worker's refusing private employment. The private employer who wanted cheap, unskilled labor seemed to hold that any private job should be accepted by a WPA worker. This was particularly true of employers engaged in seasonal economic activity. They would immediately raise a yell when the cheap labor they had enjoyed for years was no longer waiting at their employment office door. Bakke reported in the study of the unemployed worker in New Haven, Connecticut, that "in the cases of the few job refusals we have encountered, the jobs offered were not comparable in wages, working conditions and permanence to relief work." [15]

What actually was a legitimate shortage of labor? Hopkins pointed out on one occasion that WPA had a large number of carpenters on its rolls. A reasonably large proportion of these men had been carpenters all their lives and were members of unions. Most of the men, however, were 50 to 55 years old, and private contractors usually specified they wanted men only 45 or younger. They could not always get them and accused WPA of causing a shortage of carpenters. There was, noted Hopkins, a shortage only according to their specifications, for which WPA could not be held responsible. Many shortages, true shortages, were only temporary. For example, in Memphis, Tennessee, on one occasion a shortage of bricklayers existed because several large private construction projects were going up at the same time. On the other hand, at Atlanta, Georgia, bricklayers were unemployed because there was not enough construction work.

It is interesting also that one of the major criticisms of WPA workers was they showed too much initiative at times. The Committee to Investigate Unemployment and Relief reported that in one community 63 per cent of skilled WPA workers in the building trades did some work on the outside to supplement their income. The average they seemed to be earning per year (1938) through such activity was $102. The committee felt concern about this trend and its effect on privately employed workers and others in need of jobs. Hopkins argued WPA should not discourage this type of activity as long as it clearly did not prevent another from securing employment. He believed opportunities for part-time employment must exist, for occasionally contacts made resulted in full-time employment. He believed WPA should not make a sweeping ruling cutting out such work, but should let local WPA offices judge each individual case. Punitive action should be taken only when a WPA worker had worked at substandard rates or at rates incompatible with continued WPA employment.[16]

WPA began its program with a wage and hour policy known as the security wage system, intended to provide work of a reasonable number of hours per week which would maintain an emergency standard of living. Wages received, on the national average, would be $40 to $50 per month for unskilled and semiskilled workers—about $20 per month more than under direct relief of FERA work relief. Hopkins' belief that hours and wages should approximate conditions of private employment was partly responsible for this decision to use a higher level security wage system. The prevailing wage system was not used at first, since it would raise the wage scale and fewer persons could be placed on jobs by WPA. Gill estimated the prevailing wage would cut by one-third the total number put to work by WPA. Since the number placed on the job by WPA was to be one of the basic factors guiding its operations, the security wage schedule seemed necessary.

The American Federation of Labor and other labor groups opposed the security wage from the very beginning. Lorena Hickok reported to Hopkins that organized labor did not like this provision and would oppose it. Hopkins had warning from the beginning, then, that this part of the program would be subjected to heavy criticism and attacks by organized groups. To help offset this criticism the wage schedule set up by WPA allowed for certain variations in regard to geographic location, general level of wages, type of work performed, and skill of the worker. WPA also created a payroll system whereby allowances could be made for time lost each month through no fault of the worker. Examples of these are weather conditions or forced changeover to another project. Thus there was, under provisions of the 1935 relief act, to be no real correlation many times, particularly in the northern communities, between actual number of hours worked and the hours credited a worker for a monthly period.

The principle of an hourly scale security wage system began to disintegrate with the very beginning of the operation of projects in the WPA program. By mid-September of 1935, Hopkins had stipulated that state administrators could determine the minimum hours per day, with an eight-hour day as the maximum. And by mid-November, 1935, Hopkins allowed state administrators to pay 10 per cent of all WPA workers in the state a wage scale determined on the basis of prevailing wages. Whether because of experience, as Hopkins claimed, or due to pressure from labor unions, Hopkins recommended to Congress in the spring of 1936 that the prevailing hourly wages be paid, still allowing only so much per month. This was in essence still a security wage concept except for the hourly rate. Naturally, many of the congressmen and senators who had preferred the prevailing wage were pleased to help write this provision into the new WPA regulations. Henceforth, until 1939, WPA wage roles were based on prevailing rates of pay of each community where a WPA project existed.

The change to the prevailing hourly wage schedule proved to have two basic defects. First, it led to great variance in pay for equal work and caused much unnecessary confusion. While it eliminated some of the difficulties incurred in payroll forms under the security wage system, it also added confusion and detailed information of only a slightly different nature. For example, by 1938, in New York alone there were 125 different working schedules, and for the nation as a whole, over 4,000 different schedules. Most of these varied because of the necessity of adjusting hours and rates to fit the total amount to be earned for any one monthly period. This meant that many projects where skilled workers were involved had workers who only worked half a month to earn their quota for the month. In the District of Columbia it was found that a carpenter on a WPA project earned his monthly security wage with only 42 hours' work at the prevailing wage of $1.75 per hour. It was learned that in five cities (Atlanta, New York, Baltimore, Omaha, and Pittsburgh) 5,049 skilled workers checked on WPA projects took their monthly WPA paychecks and still had time to work for private employers.

The second major weakness of the prevailing hourly wage system was its failure to provide the unskilled and semiskilled WPA worker with sufficient income for the basic needs of life. As noted previously, this group was the dominant portion of those on WPA rolls. For the average unskilled and semiskilled worker the total time he could work each month was more important than either the kind of work or the location. This type of worker found the WPA wage and hour system defective in that he lost too much time because of bad weather, changeover to new projects, and rotation of workers. Despite the fact that workers were able to make up time lost through no fault of their own, the income earned by them was, on the average, never as high as had been expected. In a study completed in 1940 a sample of workers who had been on WPA an average of 39 months (but not continuously) showed they had in fact worked only 57 per cent of the time. Similar studies indicate a majority of WPA workers did not receive in pay the equivalent of an emergency standard living wage. For all practical purposes, then, the wage-hour schedule of WPA, while Hopkins was head of it, gave more financial aid than direct relief, but did not actually provide the security wage which he and President Roosevelt had hoped would be given.[17]

Perhaps the most popular WPA relief agency was the National Youth Administration. Aubrey Williams served as executive director of the NYA division as one of his functions as deputy administrator of WPA. The major objectives of NYA were these: to provide funds for part-time employment of school and college students; to employ young persons, chiefly from families on relief, on projects which would develop useful skills; to support job training efforts through apprenticeship training arrangements; and to encourage the development of worthwhile leisure-time activities.

A national advisory committee assisted Williams and his aides, and there were also state and local advisory committees. Men and women with practical experience in industry and business made suggestions which kept the training more realistic.

Student aid became the most important function of NYA. During the last five years of the 1930's hundreds of thousands of young people secured diplomas and degrees who otherwise would have been unable to complete high school or college. The NYA staff set forth three main stipulations to school and college officials: student aid recipients must be selected on the basis of need; they must carry at least three-quarters of a normal course of study; and the work performed must be useful to the college or school. It was also accepted practice that use of these students would not displace personnel already employed in the colleges and schools.

Work projects for youth were started in 1936. NYA selected projects on the basis of work experience they might provide for the particular type of young people available for assignment. Thus, in one city playground work might prove best, while in another community, perhaps only a hundred miles away, a light construction project might be the best type of project. About 50 per cent of the young people selected for these projects had no previous work experience. The NYA student aid program and work projects were warmly supported by many youth and educational groups. Programs such as NYA and the Civilian Conservation Corps, dealing with youth, seemed to consistently have a popularity not always enjoyed by FERA, WPA, RRA, and PWA.

Apprenticeship training eventually became a very important phase of the NYA. A federal committee on apprenticeship training was instrumental in securing support of labor and industry, although unfortunately several labor and industrial groups opposed this program. Several thousand young men eventually received training through this arrangement. It was the only technical training many of them ever received.

Of minor importance in NYA activities were the camps for unemployed young women. These were somewhat like the camps for young men in the Civilian Conservation Corps program. These young women, many from urban slum areas and underprivileged families, needed training in skills, employment, and a lift in morale. Leadership and work experience provided at these camps were expected to make some improvement in their outlook on life.[18]

As mentioned earlier, Hopkins believed in appointing administrators sympathetic to work relief. He made one important exception to this guide—a very important exception. This was the appointment of General Hugh S. Johnson, former head of the National Recovery Administration, as WPA administrator for New York City. General Johnson was known to have strong reservations concerning WPA. He had referred to it as "boondoggling." Johnson held it was not public works, which it really was not in the same sense as work done by PWA. He thought it "a new if more ambitious kind of leaf-raking."

It may be that Hopkins actually wanted General Johnson for the job as WPA administrator in New York City. There is evidence to indicate this. Johnson was an experienced administrator. Obviously the post would be hard to fill, for in size it was larger than several state organizations and there were many difficult and diverse groups with which the administrator would have to work. There is some possibility too that Roosevelt thought he could do Johnson a favor by giving him another post. He had removed Johnson as head of the NRA program in the fall of 1934. Evidence is clear that Johnson did not want the WPA job. Before he finally accepted it, he stipulated that certain things must be recognized. These were: no compensation except expenses ($25 per day); he could resign as of October 1, 1935; he need spend only four days a week on the job; Hopkins, and not the mayor of New York City, was his boss; he could select his own assistants and he could hire and fire, having to ask only Hopkins' permission; he could have five army and navy men detailed to work with him; and he could have a personal part-time assistant. Apparently a secret part of the agreement stated that after a study of the situation he could do the following: take a census of unemployment in New York City; set up an employment agency; give men not on relief rolls a job if they had as great a need for the job as one on relief; let people stay on relief jobs even if they got some work on the outside; depart from the $1,100 yardstick for man-year cost if necessary to do a worthwhile job.

Johnson had many headaches as head of the WPA organization in New York City. The transfer of individual projects or the decision not to transfer them from the New York State ERA work program was time-consuming. Matters were made worse by a series of strikes by WPA skilled workers, backed by other workers, who claimed the pay scale was not high enough. They wanted prevailing wages. Johnson believed communists were behind the strike. Hopkins told Johnson that if that were the case he should "just close down that project." Johnson finally appointed a committee to study complaints of the skilled workers and it recommended the prevailing wage be paid. Opposition had barely subsided when Johnson resigned in October of 1935.

By this time Johnson had stated his criticism of WPA. In mid-September of 1935 he wrote President Roosevelt that most of the projects in New York City were "not good," and they had lots of planning compared to most in the country. More emphasis should be given, thought Johnson, to the engineering phase of the planning. Otherwise Roosevelt would be embarrassed, in 1936, with "monuments to a blunder." Hopkins' organization was "utterly unfitted" to know what the engineering job "was about." He had no form of organization, only four assistants to whom he tossed jobs at random. "It is pitiful. The field representatives are second raters and the system cannot control this approaching avalanche of trouble." Therefore, Johnson recommended that Roosevelt "gently pipe the whole effort down. Let no new projects be *started*." And then in a few weeks or months, as those started were being finished, he should announce that in light of "approaching normal re-employment" it seemed "unwise to commit too much money to enterprises of unknown final cost." Direct relief at federal expense, if need be, should be restored except for really sound public work activities. Along any other course "there would be vast and inevitable disaster."

When Johnson resigned he sent Hopkins a long memo of his views concerning the WPA program in which he made the following points. First, the security wage was harmful to skilled workers and to unions and should be dropped and replaced by a prevailing wage system. Second, generally speaking, WPA projects were not worth the money spent, except those construction projects involving some degree of engineering and planning. Third, the payroll schedule in New York City should have been left on a weekly basis even though the national policy was bi-weekly payments. Fourth, there was too much red tape, particularly in materials and equipment where each project was responsible for these items. Some projects had surpluses of items while others were temporarily in need of those same items. There was no quick process to transfer from one project to another. Fifth, workers should be allowed some time off for sick leave to avoid undue hardships. WPA did not allow this. Sixth, the necessity of having to go on relief before being eligible for

WPA destroyed WPA as a morale builder. And seventh, he recommended direct relief be used rather than an extensive work program. Johnson concluded that if, as he had heard, new plans of the federal government were to be all work and no dole, then "imagination must become more fanciful still, disregard of expenditures more prodigal, and practical result more parsimonious. I earnestly hope that such will not be the case." With this blast Johnson left WPA and relegated his criticisms to sharp, caustic thrusts in his newspaper columns and radio broadcasts.[19]

The feeling between Hopkins and Johnson, or at least between WPA headquarters and Johnson, had become rather hostile by this time. When Johnson charged later that WPA had not answered many of his telegrams and letters, members of the staff made a thorough check of all communications between the Washington and New York offices and found that headquarters in Washington had failed to answer four communications, and Johnson's office had failed to answer eight. Actually, although Johnson disagreed with much of WPA's activity, he did have a great respect for Hopkins and thought "under the circumstances" WPA in New York City had given, by 1936, a "remarkable performance." Hopkins claimed when Johnson resigned that he was not sorry he had appointed him. He did not agree with Johnson's remark that WPA had been "a flop." [20]

This chapter has been devoted to a description of the more significant aspects of Hopkins' role in organizing the WPA and to some of the criticism directed against the agency. Since a large volume can be written on the WPA itself, it is obviously necessary to leave out several details of lesser import. Of the important phases of the administration of the WPA program for which Hopkins was directly responsible there are three which need additional consideration: first, the interesting relationship between the procurement of funds from Congress and the number of WPA workers on the job at a given time; second, the story of politics in the WPA; and third, the events in Hopkins' personal affairs that influenced his administration of WPA and other agencies. These are discussed in the remaining chapters.

If the total of sponsors' contributions under this year's appropriation is to be raised, as I have requested, it is about time to start raising them now.

More contributions please! —F. D. R.

VIII. Fluctuating WPA Rolls

Neither Hopkins nor the Congress of the United States ever implemented a system of appropriations and distribution of funds on a planned basis. This was not entirely the fault of Congress, or Hopkins, or Hopkins' staff. Suggestions for a long-term work program were never popular; therefore, Congress was unwilling to appropriate money for a period of several years. WPA was not strictly a work agency since relief was part of its responsibility; therefore, its activities fluctuated with seasonal variations in employment and with the general upward and downward trends in employment. These conditions made it impossible to implement in a satisfactory manner any well-conceived, systematic plans for a work program.

There were certain unseen and unforeseeable factors which Congress and WPA could have properly planned for only after they occurred: the drought and floods of 1936, the floods of early 1937, and the recession of 1937–38. In each instance Congress found it advisable to appropriate additional amounts of money. If the work relief programs were the right thing to do, it is clear that the plans Hopkins drafted along with those of Ickes in the fall of 1934 for a long-range work program of four or five years, expending eight to nine billion dollars, were much better than those put into operation. Congressional and public opposition prevented such programs as Hopkins and Ickes envisioned. Some New Deal leaders were not anxious to advertise in 1935, prior to the 1936 election, that unemployment was probably to stay for several years.[1]

When Congress appropriated funds during the years 1935 through 1938 for the work program, it stipulated how much should be spent for various types of projects. The actual allocation of funds was left to the President. Congress gave him the responsibility for shifting portions of the funds from one type of activity to another, but mostly within the general areas prescribed in the acts passed. Thus, WPA had only a varying and indirect influence on categories of activity in expending its money. For example, by October 31, 1936, after Congress passed the second major appropriation bill for the work program, combining its stipulations and adjusted allocations by President Roosevelt, amounts to be spent for various types of projects were as follows:

Highways, roads, and streets	$413,250,000
Public buildings	143,925,000
Parks and other recreational facilities, including buildings therein	156,750,000
Public utilities, including sewer systems, water supply and purification, airports, and other transportation facilities	158,175,000
Flood control and other conservation	128,250,000
Assistance for educational, professional, and clerical persons	98,325,000
Women's projects	98,325,000
Miscellaneous work projects	71,250,000
National Youth Administration	71,250,000
Rural rehabilitation, loans, and relief to farmers and livestock growers	85,500,000

Within each of these areas the WPA staff had some degree of flexibility in allotting work projects. It was in these areas, as we have noted, that sponsors' contributions in materials, type of workers available, weather conditions, and other federal projects in a given state had their influence.

Hopkins did not like the earmarking by Congress of all

the funds. He and President Roosevelt sought two changes in appropriations for the work program. One was to appropriate the money directly to the agency spending the funds or portions thereof. The second was to list categories of acceptable projects, or types of projects themselves, and allow the work agency itself to decide how much of the total amount available would be spent for various types of projects. Beginning in 1938, Congress did as President Roosevelt preferred and appropriated money directly to the agencies. Congress began in 1939 to list acceptable projects, leaving it up to the WPA staff to allot money for each type as it wished.[2]

In the spring of 1937, Hopkins had his toughest battle with Congress over appropriations for WPA. By this time Congress was divided into three distinct groups concerning the scope of the work program. One group, headed by Congressman Maury Maverick, wished to create a welfare department, give it $2,500,000,000 to spend, direct it to study the needs of the unemployed, and stipulate that it recommend various types of work projects. Congress would then approve the proposed projects individually as the welfare department presented them. A special tax of some sort would be levied to make it a pay-as-you-go proposition. The second group, consisting of a large number in the House of Representatives, plus a few senators, who wanted WPA's activity expanded, wanted a permanent WPA with an annual $2,000,000,000 appropriation for its various programs. This group believed that the work relief activities were not extensive enough to have the greatest possible positive effect on the nation's economic recovery. It wanted expansion rather than contraction of work program activities. The third group, alarmed by the huge amounts named by the first two, wanted drastic cuts made. Democratic senators James Byrnes and Isaiah Bailey and several Republican senators were members of this congressional bloc.

It is interesting to note that Hopkins did not support with vigor, at this time, the energetic plans of either of the first two groups; however, he did feel that Senator Byrnes and others sought to curtain the work program too extensively.[3]

In the spring of 1937, after Congress appropriated special amounts to relief and work agencies to help the flood victims of the previous January and February, the regular work appropriation hearings and discussions began. Senator Byrnes and Senator Bailey demanded that the $1,500,000,000 Hopkins asked for be cut drastically. Senator Byrnes asked Hopkins if he thought he could get along on $1,000,000,000 for twelve months. Hopkins replied curtly: "I can but the unemployed couldn't." Hopkins received support for his request of $1,500,000,000 from several liberal senators, mayors of medium and large cities, local relief groups fearful of having to bear more of the relief costs, several governors, and WPA unions such as the Workers' Alliance. Hopkins was also against Senator Byrnes' proposal to make sponsoring agencies contribute 25 per cent of the cost of each project. Hopkins argued that many localities could not provide this percentage, would get no projects, and then local relief authorities would cut relief standards, which in his opinion were too low already.[4]

Hopkins devoted considerable attention to his relations with Congress, particularly from 1935 on. While he continually ignored several congressmen because of their obnoxious ways of opposing the New Deal or because their habit of asking unreasonable favors irritated him, he gave special attention to senators and congressmen who supported the work relief program. At the same time, he had a keen awareness of Roosevelt's delicate maneuverings relative to other legislation and issues—entrance of the United States into the World Court, agricultural legislation, social security legislation, and bills affecting labor and labor unions. At times, therefore, Hopkins and his staff found it necessary to handle some congressmen carefully, even though they were not supporting work relief.

Roosevelt also wanted to keep the support of progressive Republican senators Robert LaFollette of Wisconsin and George Norris of Nebraska. Senator Pat Harrison of Mississippi, chairman of the Senate Finance Committee (1933–41), Senator Carl Hayden, a strong supporter of public works, Senator Alben W. Barkley, the majority leader in the Senate (1937–48), and Senator Joseph Robinson, the Senate majority leader (1933–37) were key Democratic senators to whom special attention was given. Sam Rayburn, majority leader in the House of Representatives during the 75th and 76th sessions of Congress, was contacted frequently by Hopkins. Hopkins and WPA were a part of the New Deal team and program; therefore, they had to operate within this context, not independently.

Hopkins disagreed openly with several key senators and representatives despite the need to keep congressional support. Senators Byrnes, Bailey, McAdoo, and Bilbo, all Democrats, on more than one occasion found Hopkins unwilling to agree to their approach to relief or to comply with their wishes in regard to projects or appointments within their states.

These men and congressional leaders in the House of Representatives sometimes complained to FDR. Representative Moser on one occasion told Roosevelt that Hopkins appeared on the hill, summoned certain Congressional leaders together and simply told them what they had to do. Congressman Moser said the President could do that and nobody would resent it, but not Hopkins. Some congressmen said to him, "Why, Hopkins won't even see some of us when we come up to his office. . . . This fellow is demanding blank checks and autocratic authority to do things, and he has the worst setup in the whole U.S. I don't want a darn thing to do with it." Representative

Starnes of Alabama stated that he resented Hopkins' coming into the halls of Congress and holding meetings in the office of the majority whip. Hopkins, exclaimed Starnes, "entered the sanctum sanctorum or the office of the majority leader, or the holy of holies." [5]

Hopkins had done just what Congressman Moser and Starnes accused him of doing. In May, 1937, Hopkins complained to Daniel Bell, Acting Director of the Budget, that the House had earmarked most of the funds for this, that, or the other thing. Hopkins suggested that, since they needed a fire escape on his building, maybe he could get them to earmark some of it for that. He told Bell, "They are great boys up there!—It is damned discouraging. . . . I hope they *earmark* all of it. I think I will call up Sam Rayburn and tell him to earmark the whole damn works." Within twenty-four hours following this conversation Hopkins made a visit to Capitol Hill. He told Governor Earle of Pennsylvania on the phone that he had talked with "some of the fellows up there" (Capitol Hill) and some of them realized they had "pulled a boner," but they were "out on a limb." Governor Earle agreed to get some strong editorials out in favor of WPA getting the full amount of $1,500,000,000 and to put pressure on the congressmen of his state.[6]

Hopkins' main hope for cooperation lay in the Senate. While some senators opposed the sum of $1,500,000,000 they believed WPA should receive more than the House seemed willing to grant. Hence, when the bill was before the Senate, Hopkins began to put pressure on men who usually supported WPA but who needed prodding. On June 15 and 16, Hopkins made a series of phone calls to several governors, field representatives, and Mayor La Guardia of New York. The latter agreed to contact Senator Copeland of New York, Senator Hiram Johnson of California, and Senator Lundeen of Minnesota. Governor Leche of Louisiana agreed to talk with Senator Overton. Governor White of Mississippi was willing to talk to the senators from his state, but he and Hopkins both agreed, finally, that Senator Bilbo would vote the opposite way Senator Harrison would, so the total vote picked up would be none, and it would be better to leave them alone. Field Representative Howard Hunter reported that in his area, the Midwest, senators Herring, Donahey, Gillette, and Bulkley were doubtful.[7] Hopkins won his battle with Congress on June 29, when it appropriated $1,500,000,000. The amount to be spent was divided as follows:

Highways, Roads and Streets	$415,000,000
Public buildings, parks, and other recreational facilities including buildings therein; public utilities, electric transmission and distribution lines, or systems to serve persons in rural areas, sewer systems, water supply and purification, airports and other transportation facilities; flood control, conservation, eradication of insect pests, and minor miscellaneous work projects	630,000,000
Assistance for educational, professional, and self help, and clerical persons and women's projects	380,000,000
National Youth Administration	75,000,000
Total of	$1,500,000,000

This particular skirmish with Congress over the amount of appropriations was a crucial one for Hopkins. As Arthur Krock noted in June, during the early spring it looked as if Hopkins' "star had paled," as President Roosevelt appeared willing to approve further cuts in the work program. For Hopkins this was then a twofold test: first, a test of his personal influence and relationship with President Roosevelt; and, second, a test of his ability to convince enough people that the work program should continue. Hopkins was at this time the most aggressive "social-economic reformer" among the New Deal leaders. Hopkins, convinced that the work program was essential, went all out on this particular occasion and won his battle, although he had to use a considerable amount of pressure as has been indicated. Hopkins' belief that purchasing power in the hands of the "submerged third" would do more good than a balanced budget in 1937–38 had won the approval of the President.[8]

An important aspect of administration of WPA funds with which Hopkins dealt was the percentage and total amounts of contributions by sponsors of projects. It is a credit to Hopkins, as well as an indication of the improving economic situation of state and local governments, that the percentage of local contributions rose from 1935 through 1938. At the same time, it must be recalled that by early 1936 state and local governments were caring for most of the unemployed not hired by WPA or any other federal work agency. President Roosevelt kept harping on the fact that sponsors should contribute 30 per cent of project costs. In late August, 1937, not being satisfied with the percentage provided by sponsors, Roosevelt sent a memo to Hopkins stating: "If the total of sponsors' contributions under this year's appropriation is to be raised, as I have requested, it is about time to start raising them now. More contributions please!" Roosevelt's directions were carried out in part. The WPA staff succeeded in raising the percentage of state and local contributions from 9.8 in 1936 to 20.8 in 1938.

When the dates of appropriations of money and dates of emergencies such as floods and droughts are examined, there is a reasonably sound correlation between the time money was made available to WPA and the increase or decrease of the WPA rolls. Yet the number on relief and the number unemployed did not correspond as closely as some would have preferred. Thomas E. Dewey of New York, for example, pointed out that in 1938, during the four months prior to the elections, some 327,000 persons were added to WPA rolls. During this same period nearly 1,000,000 persons were rehired in business and industry. In 1936, and again in 1938, opponents of the Democratic party printed stories and graphs which indicated the only reason for expansion of WPA in the fall seasons of 1936 and 1938 was politics. It is true officials were most anxious to get relief cases transferred to WPA rolls just before election in the hope of winning additional votes. It is also true that Hopkins was willing to have WPA help the Democratic party. Local Republican leaders were as active as Democrats in trying to put their supporters on WPA rolls. Defenders of the WPA pointed out at that time, and have since, many reasons for the rise and fall of WPA rolls, all much more important and influential than politics. For example, WPA rolls for 1936 appear to have expanded unduly in the fall of 1936. But when farmers placed on WPA work relief projects during the months of July through December, 1936, are subtracted from the total number on the rolls, the regularly employed number of WPA employees followed the usual seasonal increases. In fact, from March, 1936, to November, 1936, the number of employees involved in the regular activities dropped approximately 400,000. This does not explain the great expansion of 1938, except that if WPA is to be criticized for having expanded its rolls during 1938, then the alternative would have been less rapid expansion, which would have subjected WPA to the criticism that it was slow in putting people to work with the amounts provided by Congress to combat the 1937–38 recession. If WPA's primary function was to help rid the nation of the recession, then its expansion during 1938, with the peak in November, was logical. WPA could only put people to work once it received adequate amounts of money. These amounts came in March and June of 1938 and not 1937, which in retrospect would have been more logical if a work program backed by federal expenditures was to be used to combat the recession.

Broadly speaking, project employment lagged during periods of rising unemployment. In the winter of 1937–38 the ratio of WPA employment to total unemployment reached the lowest level it was ever to have prior to 1940. The curtailment of WPA rolls usually exceeded the decline in unemployment. Indeed, in view of the time funds for WPA were approved, and the victims of various unforeseen disasters which struck the nation had been aided by the WPA, if WPA rolls had expanded or decreased in any other manner, then the opponents of WPA would have had a more legitimate basis for attack. Of five basic influences on WPA rolls in the fall of 1938, it seems that these four were much more important than politics: additional aid to tenant farmers, aid to victims of the New England hurricane, regular seasonal increase (whenever funds were available), and the recession. That politics and WPA were closely allied in 1938 will be shown in a later chapter. It does not necessarily follow, however, that WPA increased the number of employees solely for political reasons.[9]

Congress, as well as much of the public, believed that WPA rolls should rise and fall as unemployment rose and fell. This was a wrong assumption, for WPA did not provide employment for all of the unemployables, and those losing their jobs did not always need aid immediately.

The census of 1940 shows there were 3,042,000 on emergency relief work projects in the nation when the questions were asked, and that 4,919,000 persons were at that time looking for work, feeling they were employable. This was, incidentally, 14.9 per cent of the labor force. This meant that unemployment could fluctuate at least to the extent of affecting 1,000,000 workers without necessarily affecting

WPA rolls which usually totaled less than 3,000,000. At all times local agencies had from 500,000 to 900,000 unemployed employables certified for WPA work which WPA could not use because of lack of funds. Further, relief agencies did not certify all of those unemployed who considered themselves employable; therefore, there could be no exact correlation between the rise and fall of employment and WPA rolls.

A study made in 1939 and 1940 of 138,000 WPA workers dismissed in the late summer of 1939 shows that only 13 per cent were able to secure jobs after several months. Of this 13 per cent, one-half were earning less in February, 1940, than they had while on WPA. Fifty-four per cent of the 138,000 were back on WPA rolls by February, 1940, and 12 per cent more on relief. The WPA staff observed that "the discharged WPA workers have not benefited to any great extent from the industrial recovery this fall (1939); they are not the first to be rehired when business improves." Of the 3,300,000 nonagricultural workers who lost their jobs in the period from September, 1937, to June 1, 1938, only an undeterminable portion needed relief, and not all at the same time.[10]

Other important elements influenced WPA rolls' erratic reaction to unemployment trends. Congress did not provide funds for WPA and other agencies consistently, and in the case of the recession, not until after it had begun were extra appropriations made. The working population increased about 500,000 each year. From 1929 through 1936 this meant a net increase of at least 3,500,000 possible workers. Hopkins pointed out in 1937 that what WPA had on its rolls was approximately this net increase. Increased productivity of industry due to better machinery caused temporary unemployment. Hopkins also observed that from September, 1934, to November, 1936, the average number of hours per week for a worker engaged in manufacturing establishments had increased by seven. Thus, employers had stepped up production by two means—better techniques of production and working those already employed a longer period of time. Thus, production could increase several per cent over the period of a few years, 1933–36, without necessarily influencing the number unemployed. Nearly 75 per cent of WPA employees were unskilled or semiskilled. Of those who were skilled laborers, many were not wanted by private employers because of age or race. Others could not always find in a given community work corresponding to their skill. In June, 1936, one analysis showed that 50 per cent of WPA workers were 40 years or older and that 70 per cent of those in the age group 45 to 64 years were manual workers in nonagricultural occupations. Thirty per cent of all experienced workmen on WPA rolls were between 45 and 65. Hopkins said that of these people the majority were physically employable but not economically employable. In other words, they really could not compete equally with others for jobs because even if capable they were not wanted; young men were preferred rather than older men, white rather than colored, and so on. Seasonal influences were of fundamental importance in determining the number on WPA rolls. In fact, the seasonal cyclical factor was of more importance than the over-all trend of employment *prior to* the recession of 1938.[11] The following excerpt from Hopkins' testimony before a congressional committee in January, 1937, will illustrate the influences of these factors.

With a deficiency appropriation of $790,000,000, it is contemplated that $655,000,000 would be made available for the Works Progress Administration, including the National Youth Administration. With this amount it would be possible to employ 2,200,000 on Works Progress

Administration projects in February; 2,150,000 in March; 2,000,000 in April; 1,800,000 in May; and 1,600,000 in June. In terms of dollars, the monthly obligations are estimated as follows: February, $151,700,000; March, $146,000,000; April, $134,500,000; May, $120,000,000; and June, $103,000,000.

The employment schedule, involving a reduction of 600,000 workers between February and June, anticipates a large and widespread increase in private employment over the period. Normally, there is a seasonal increase of about 800,000 private jobs during these 5 months; but an increase of from 1,200,000 to 1,500,000 private jobs will probably be necessary to remove 600,000 persons from the W.P.A.

Viewing the situation from another angle, our studies of the seasonal variation in relief show that the number usually declines about 15 per cent from February to June. This would mean that starting with 2,200,000 Works Progress Administration workers in February, we should ordinarily expect a decline of about 340,000 workers, leaving 1,860,000 on Works Progress Administration projects during June. To reduce Works Progress Administration employment to 1,600,000 workers, therefore, it will be necessary for 260,000 Works Progress Administration workers to find jobs over and above seasonal expectations.

These estimates are based on studies of our past experience during periods of reemployment, which indicate that the creation of two and one-half new jobs in private industry results in the removal of one family head from relief or from the W.P.A. On this basis, private employment will have to increase to the extent of 500,000 to 650,000 more than seasonal expectations if Works Progress Administration employment is to be reduced to 1,600,000 in June.[12]

The various influences just mentioned caused WPA rolls to fluctuate in a manner inconsistent with unemployment and the rise and fall of the industrial index. These influences also indicate in part why WPA rolls did not correlate closely with the general relief rolls. Relief rolls were no criteria for judging expansion or curtailment of WPA rolls. The Temporary Emergency Relief Administration in New York State reported in 1937 that "the peak of relief need lagged as far as two years behind the low point in payrolls." It learned also, as Hopkins learned, that rehiring on a sizable scale occurred only several months after industrial revival began.[13]

It is impossible to evaluate the damage done by the inconsistent expansion and curtailment of the number receiving aid from the WPA. Of course, this condition was typical of the entire economic system whereby the worker was expendable. That is, if industry did not need him, it dismissed him. If our economy had maintained the expansion necessary to hire all those desiring work, WPA quite obviously would not have existed. Therefore, WPA was after all no more than a reflection of our own economic system with its seasonal unemployment, its unemployment (temporary if not permanent) due to technological changes, and its mass layoffs of the late twenties and early thirties. When WPA had the most money, it soon had its rolls at their highest level. When Roosevelt and Hopkins hoped, as they did in late 1936 and in 1937, that recovery was well under way, they naturally curtailed WPA as a means of saving money. Further, they hoped to encourage a psychological reaction whereby industry and business could believe that the government would curtail WPA as soon as industry began to take up the slack. This was, in essence, the usual American approach. Had it actually been more akin to the so-called planned society approach as charged by many New Deal opponents, WPA would not have been as flexible and responsive to economic trends.

The alternative to flexible WPA employment would have been the creation and maintenance of an agency which would have had prescribed for it a set number of workers to be used. A happy medium might have been chosen, but it is just as likely that Congress and the administration might have selected a figure so low as to have been of little value or one so high that more people might have been kept employed on WPA rolls than necessary, particularly in 1936 and the first three quarters of 1937 when our economy did seem to be expanding rapidly. Certainly Hopkins would have been equally criticized had he maintained that WPA should always have had 2,000,000 on WPA rolls whether our industrial index was 110 or 85 or whether there were 6,000,000 workers or 11,000,000 workers unemployed. In the last analysis, the conclusion must be that most WPA workers were employed or dismissed in response to two key factors: first, money appropriated by Congress for each fiscal year; and second, the expansion or contraction of American industrial activity. Of less importance were floods and droughts. A rather minor influence was politics.

This thing is too damn serious in terms of all these people, to think of this in terms of petty partisan politics. This is a great national endeavor . . . , and we certainly would be a pretty low form of life if we used this opportunity to try to take advantage, politically, of anybody.

—Harry L. Hopkins

The whole rotten mess [WPA] stinks to high heaven and, like a dead mackerel in the moonlight, it stinks and shines and shines and stinks! —Congressman Hamilton Fish

IX. Politics Galore!

When Hopkins first went to Washington he did not engage in political maneuvering in the same manner ward heelers, city political bosses, or many seasoned congressional leaders did. As Stanley High observed, in 1933–34 Hopkins "was not only indifferent to politics and politicians, he was generally impatient with them." [1] Certainly his skirmishes with men such as Governor Talmadge of Georgia and Governor Davey of Ohio and politicians of lesser stature support this statement. Then, as High noted, and as indicated in the preceding chapter, Hopkins found it necessary to cooperate with the leading politicians on Capitol Hill to secure funds to put into operation and maintain a program he believed to be essential at that time. Thus, he began to cultivate some of the more important leaders, such as Congressman Pat Boland, Senator Robert Wagner, Senator Robert LaFollette, Jr., and others. On the basis of Hopkins' appointment book, records of his phone calls, and the list of appointments and engagements kept by Mrs. Hopkins at their home, he did not contact extensively those on Capitol Hill who were considered to be the less influential political leaders. That Hopkins learned how to put personal pressure on congressmen was clearly shown in the efforts he made to secure passage of the full amount he thought necessary for work relief in 1937.[2]

Many people considered WPA a political asset for Roosevelt, but in many ways WPA was a political liability. It affected only a few million workers, many of whom never bothered to vote in elections and who probably did not vote in the elections of 1936, 1938, and 1940. On the other hand, there were several million voters within the Democratic party who approved of a work program of a non-political nature but not a politically manipulated program. In addition to this, President Roosevelt and other Democratic leaders desired to gain and keep the support of liberal Republicans and independents. A poorly administered work relief program would lose the vote of many of the latter two groups whose support Roosevelt had secured in the elections of 1932 and 1934. Roosevelt needed to keep the support of the liberal Republicans and conservative Democrats. In other words, with a free press and a free radio, with the records of WPA open to public inspection and always subject to call in court proceedings, an exposure of gross maladministration could lose more votes than WPA could gain. Hopkins expressed his ideas on this point when he stated, "Whoever says this four-billion dollar program is a political asset is crazy." And it was with this in mind that he told his newly appointed state administrators in June, 1935:

> I have been in this game [giving relief] now for two years, and if there is one way not to do it [buy an election], it is by giving relief, because none of the clients like you. They all think you're terrible, and you are not going to buy any elections that way.[3]

Since early in the history of our federal system senatorial confirmation has been an important factor in the appointive power of the President and high-level federal government administrators. The President is expected to confer with congressmen, particularly senators, before appointing men to federal positions in their state or congressional districts. The Senate insisted in 1935 that senatorial courtesy be honored in the operation of the new work program. Therefore, the Emergency Relief Appropriation Act of 1935 provided that "any administrator or other officer . . . named to have general supervision . . . over the program . . . and receiving a salary of $5,000 or more per annum from such appropriation, and any State or regional administrator receiving a salary of $5,000 or more per annum from such appropriation (except persons now serving as such under other law), shall be appointed by the President, by and with the advice and consent of the Senate." Inclusion of this statement in the act establishing the work program meant one thing above all else to Hopkins and his staff—political patronage. It could not be held off to the extent it had been in the FERA program.

The terrific pressures and influences which United States senators can bring to bear on a public official became increasingly a part of Hopkins' activity as head of WPA. If a senator was too disgruntled with WPA, he might launch a campaign against Hopkins and WPA. Appointment of state WPA administrators would now have to be made with the utmost caution and political analysis. The figure of James Farley loomed larger in the shadowy background of Washington politics. It was at this time that Hopkins nearly resigned as relief administrator.

Hopkins personally handled the appointment of state administrators, for he was anxious to obtain men sympathetic to the WPA program and who would meet the approval of the particular set of United States senators involved. In May and June of 1935, he had lists made of young businessmen throughout the nation who were in sympathy with the general aims of the administration. He did not stipulate that they be active Democrats.

The problem of finding capable men in sympathy with the work relief program and at the same time approved by the senators of the particular states brings out the fact that executive appointive power, wherever senatorial confirmation is involved, reflects the different factional claims of the predominating political power. Therefore, the officials finally selected represent dual forces, the singleness of responsibility is undermined, and the cohesion necessary for a successful program is endangered. The success and failures of the WPA program can be judged in better perspective if this basic fact is considered.[4]

In several instances Hopkins attempted to avoid senatorial confirmation of state WPA administrators. One way he did this was to appoint state FERA administrators as state WPA administrators. In each case these persons proved they had the ability to run a sound program. In Indiana, for example, Wayne Coy had, and later added to, such a fine record that he became one of Hopkins' most reliable men, being promoted to a field representative for WPA. In some instances state FERA administrators were appointed because it would prevent Hopkins from having to engage in a long-drawn-out factional dispute between state Democratic party leaders. Louisiana, where Senator Huey Long threatened to filibuster if any appointment was made that he did not like, is an example of this. Thus, in fourteen states, either because they were able men or because of political pressure, Hopkins appointed state FERA administrators as head of WPA state organizations, thereby avoiding senatorial confirmation.[5]

Hopkins also used the device of paying state WPA administrators under $5,000 a year as a means of avoiding Senate confirmation. In a few cases where political appointments had to be made, Hopkins, who knew the state FERA administrator to be a capable man, made the political appointment of a WPA administrator to satisfy the senators, then named the state FERA administrator as deputy WPA administrator. The latter would actually administer the WPA program in that state.[6]

In thirty-two states Hopkins made appointments requiring Senate approval. These and the sixteen he made in which he avoided Senate approval fall into three general categories: first, political appointees without any previous qualifying experience; second, businessmen with a suitable local reputation; and third, individuals with qualifying experience and varying degrees of political sponsorship. It did happen, of course, that occasionally political sponsorship and suitable qualifications for the position coincided. In general, WPA headquarters found little cause to be enthusiastic about the quality of the state administrators. One WPA official estimated that, of the original appointments, the suitable and successful state administrators numbered only 50 per cent. In half the states WPA had better administrators than FERA had had administering its program. Before the first year was over, it was necessary to dismiss one state administrator outright and in one way or another to get rid of several others. Hopkins' desire to get 75 per cent of his problems solved and work done by good appointments never materialized on the state level under the WPA program.

A study of the quality of a group of these state administrators was made in 1936. While subjective, it does indicate something of the detrimental influence of the Senate confirmation authority on the WPA program. Twenty-two state administtrators were investigated and evaluated. Of these, twelve were political appointments. Only four of these twelve proved to be capable administrators. Of ten nonpolitical appointments, three were unsuccessful and seven successful. Evidence and events between the spring of 1935 and the end of 1938 indicate Hopkins might have done considerably better in appointing state administrators if he had not had to consult the senators. He was highly successful in selecting his Washington staff, for example, where political influences were at a minimum.[7]

The official policy of WPA in regard to politics was to keep it out of the program. One of the main functions of the Division of Investigation, headed by Dallas Dort, was to check reports of political use of WPA funds or interference with the hiring or firing of WPA workers by politicians. Beyond this, Hopkins and his staff kept an eye on politicians whom they felt sure would try to use WPA for political purposes. Mrs. Roosevelt would occasionally complain to Hopkins about incidents of political interference which she had noticed or which had been called to her attention. She told this writer that Hopkins had his staff investigate all of these incidents and he was always most willing to see what could be done. But it was, he told her, often beyond the control of WPA. In answering a particular complaint, Hopkins wrote her in part:

> I realize that the local political organizations have no hesitancy in writing letters to try to convince their several clients that they have an inside track in the W.P.A. This goes on all over the country and I, of course, cannot control their activities. To say the least, many of the things they do are very embarrassing to us, and very stupid. But, a great many politicians are unbelievebly [*sic*] stupid.[8]

Miss Lorena Hickok, Hopkins' personal observer in the field, reported carefully on the political developments on the state and local levels.[9]

Beginning early in 1936, WPA started to issue what became a whole series of regulations and rules governing political action and political interference with WPA workers and officials. One of the first of these, which set the general tone for the rest, reads as follows:

> No employee of the Works Progress Administration, either administrative or engaged on a project, is required to make any contribution to any political party.
>
> No Works Progress Administration employee's job will be in jeopardy because of the failure of said employee to make such contribution.
>
> No employee of the Works Progress Administration shall at any time solicit contributions for any political party and evidence of such solicitation will be cause for immediate discharge. The question of whether or not to contribute to any political party is a matter entirely for the voluntary decision of said employee.
>
> No person shall be employed or discharged by the Works Progress Administration on the ground of his support or nonsupport of any candidate of any political organization.[10]

In September, 1936, WPA workers were told they were to be free to vote in "the same manner as other citizens." WPA made it a point to see that workers had time off to exercise their franchise privileges.[11]

WPA also set a definite policy in regard to WPA workers and officials running for public office on a political ticket. On February 21, 1936, Hopkins sent out a directive which stated that "persons who are candidates for, or hold elective offices shall not be employed on administrative staffs of the Works Progress Administration." This ruling was later interpreted to mean all supervisory personnel and the WPA workers themselves. In some instances Hopkins had to send a specific order or to instruct directly a state administrator to remove certain officials from the state or local WPA staff.[12]

Hopkins and his staff continued to send to local and state WPA administrators numerous statements about interference with WPA workers by local Democratic or Republican party bosses. Certainly political use of WPA cannot be laid to improperly drafted orders on this point. Hopkins frequently restated WPA's position in his radio addresses. He also invited the public to send to his office directly any evidence of violation of policy.

To carry out such a policy perfectly was impossible. Even the most honest and sincere man in the United States, unless he created a vast spy system for that purpose, could not have controlled the thousands and thousands of local and state politicians who desired to make what, in their eyes, was the most of WPA. In reference to these men Hopkins commented, "I cannot control a politician who does not work for me." [13] Hopkins had no control of political activity by ward leaders and others who mailed forms to WPA workers and approached them immediately after they left work. There was no law against passing handbills to WPA workers as they left WPA jobs in the evening or as they came to work in the morning. Only when political interference occurred on the project site within hours of employment could WPA act to punish the violators. Hopkins did hope to keep WPA workers from being fired, but in placing workers on WPA rolls, he and his organization in Washington had only limited powers due to the vastness of the program. Local relief agencies usually determined who was eligible for WPA employment. This was a powerful political weapon in itself which, under the law, WPA could not control.

"A Congressman wants an airport—another wants a river dredged." So wrote Hopkins in his diary on July 15, 1935, just as WPA projects were first being approved. This reveals another phase of the political picture. Congressional interference in the program coupled with Hopkins' own political desires resulted in a series of incidents that led to serious charges of politics against WPA and Hopkins. WPA had three political leverages which it could hold over

Congress. The first of these was the location of projects in the districts of loyal congressmen; the second, selection of lesser personnel and employees to suit the congressmen; and the third involved direct pressure to get the local WPA organization to give or withhold support of a given candidate for office. The last of these three became illegal but was used to some extent. The other two were used whenever necessary or advisable, in election years or in nonelection years. They were used primarily to secure support in Congress for New Deal measures.[14]

At the same time congressmen had certain leverages over WPA. As previously noted it was at times difficult to secure all the funds for the work program Hopkins and Roosevelt thought necessary. A favor for a congressman might mean an important vote on a bill pending in Congress. Some congressmen were in a position to ask that favor after several years of loyalty before assuring continued support of the New Deal legislative program. A second leverage of congressmen was that of approval of top WPA personnel. Ramifications of this have already been noted.

In dealing with appointments in California, Hopkins consulted with his field representative in the area. In a phone conversation with Robert Hinckley, Hopkins said that patronage was now "in the cards" and that was what Congress wanted. A man by the name of Thompson was ruled out for consideration for a position because he was not "friendly" with the senior senator on the other "side of the political fence." In the case of Illinois, Senator Hamilton J. Lewis opposed the appointment of Robert Dunham as WPA administrator because neither he nor Senator Dieterich had been consulted. The Washington *Times* reported on July 16, 1935, that besides Dunham six other suggested appointments by Hopkins were opposed by prominent senators. Senator Murray opposed the appointment of Roy Hart in Montana; Senator Adams of Colorado opposed the appointment of Paul Shrivers; and senators Trammell of Florida, Gore of Oklahoma, Schall of Minnesota, and King of Utah opposed the proposed WPA administrators for their states. The appointments in Maine and Massachusetts were made without the full agreement of Democratic party leaders. Several of Hopkins' choices were eventually appointed to take office despite announced senatorial opposition and pressure from Democratic headquarters in Washington. Sometimes conflicts were successfully resolved, but not in all cases.[15]

In several states the senators and other leading Democratic figures kept up a running battle with the WPA offices in the appointment of state WPA administrators and other top state personnel. Senator Theodore Bilbo of Mississippi was one of these. He did not like the original appointment. Once it was made and approved, he tried to bring about removal. He appealed to President Roosevelt directly and put pressure on Hopkins. In March, 1937, he even asked the President to stop WPA in Mississippi and called it a "farce." Shortly afterwards Roosevelt told Hopkins that "Bilbo says the present setup is unfairly one-sided against him." He suggested that Hopkins look into the situation. In 1938 a change was made in the state administrator, and again the headquarters of WPA and the senator from Mississippi could not agree on the appointment. In June of 1938, Aubrey Williams, in the absence of Hopkins, appointed Roland Wall as state administrator. James Roosevelt informed his father that "this is the man Senator Bilbo is so opposed to." The President asked that it be held. Wall was apparently selected for a short term, and later Hopkins and Bilbo differed on his successor. The latter continued his claim that the WPA organization in Mississippi was not favorable to the New Deal.[16]

In Nevada, senators Pittman and McCarran disagreed concerning the WPA administrator of their state, and Hopkins had to try to keep both of them happy. In this instance he stood by his man, who was in the good graces of Senator Pittman. In Washington, the WPA organization was for a time unfavorable to Senator Schwellenbach. There the WPA administrator became involved in politics so deeply that he allowed WPA workers on the job to be assessed for contributions to local Democratic organizations. This gave Hopkins a chance to remove him and replace him with a man who, regardless of political affiliations, was a more qualified administrator. In Indiana, Governor Paul McNutt, shortly after being elected to the governorship, became involved in a factional fight between Senator Van Nuys and Congresswoman Virginia E. Jenckes, both Democrats, in the course of which they made accusations about WPA in Indiana which brought joy to the hearts of Republicans. Despite the furor, Hopkins stood by his state appointees. In Montana, Senator James E. Murray, who opposed the appointment of Roy Hart as administrator, complained to Hopkins that Hart had appointed too many Republicans to office, thereby injuring the chances of the Democrats in the election. In California and Michigan, Hopkins faced very strong opposition from state and local Democrats in his appointments. The most clear-cut cases, with the most complete records available, occurred in Minnesota and Massachusetts.[17]

In Massachusetts, Hopkins appointed Arthur Rotch as WPA administrator. Rotch had served Hopkins in the FERA organization and Hopkins apparently thought that he would make a capable WPA administrator. Further, the appointment would eliminate having to receive the blessings of the leading political figures of the state. Hopkins made the appointment even though he knew that Rotch was not popular with the Democrats who were active supporters of Governor Curley. In July, 1935, Hopkins told President Roosevelt that "Arthur Rotch and Governor Curley had a long talk the other day and apparently things are going much better. For how long nobody knows!" James Roosevelt, particularly interested in the Massachusetts organization, attempted to secure appointments for a few of his friends, but Rotch seemed most reluctant to cooperate although in a few months he did find a position for one of the six recommended by the younger Roosevelt. James Farley informed Hopkins in November that he was getting complaints about Rotch and he wanted to talk to Hopkins about it. In a letter to Joseph McGrath, chairman of the Massachusetts Democratic State Committee, Representative John McCormack declared, "The best thing for the Democratic Party is to have a complete cleanup from Rotch down." Rotch stated in later years that President Roosevelt and Hopkins instructed him to administer the program in Massachusetts on an absolutely nonpolitical basis, and that the only politician who gave him trouble was Governor Curley. Interestingly enough, McCormack gave Rotch the impression that he was supporting him. Rotch claims that early in 1936 a field representative of WPA told him to "play ball" or resign. He resigned.[18] Hopkins agreed to the resignation and asked President Roosevelt to invite Rotch down for a short chat, for he had done a reasonably good job and had taken "a terrible beating." How bad that beating must have been is partially revealed in Hopkins' conversation with the man whom he appointed to replace Rotch temporarily. Hopkins told his successor that "you can take some bullet-proof vests along." To which Paul Edwards, the new appointee, replied, "I'll need them." Hopkins was sure that there were plenty of "cemetery lots we can put you in." [19]

Hopkins did not like the Massachusetts situation and complained on one occasion that all Governor Curley was seeking was publicity. Hopkins left the impression that he thought Curley was trying, at times, to put the President "on the spot." The elimination of Rotch from the scene did not improve the situation. During the remainder of 1936, Hopkins continued to receive complaints from Farley and local Democratic leaders in Massachusetts. It was alleged that the Republicans were getting all the good jobs in the state relief and WPA organizations.[20]

With Victor Christgau, state administrator for Minnesota, Hopkins eventually gave in to political pressures. In this instance, the pressure, as it did sometimes on other occasions, came from the highest political source, the President of the United States. Governor Floyd Olson of Minnesota opposed the appointment of Christgau but apparently caused him little trouble. The main difficulties leading to Christgau's removal did not arise until there was a change in governors. Lorena Hickok reported to Hopkins in mid-1936 that Christgau had given Minnesota a "good WPA show." She noted that if Governor Olson died, a new "crowd" of Democrats would try to dominate the picture and ask that Christgau be removed. Governor Elmer A. Benson had been in office only a short time before he demanded that Christgau be removed from office. Benson apparently disliked Christgau so much that he even suggested that Hopkins promote him if need be to get him out of Minnesota. Senator Lundeen was in the group which opposed Christgau, and finally, as the situation became more heated, the President entered the picture. He told Hopkins Christgau must be removed. Hopkins had no plausible charge to make against Christgau except that he had spent too much time with his personal affairs. Hopkins did offer him a position in Washington which Christgau refused. Hopkins made it plain in a press conference shortly afterwards that it was the Benson-Farley groups who were responsible. Christgau, in answering the letter from the President demanding his resignation, called attention to the fact that no charges had been made against him, even by his opponents, and neither the honesty nor the integrity of his administration had been questioned. He quoted the field representative for the area as stating that Christgau had a "splendid organization." In closing he told the President of

Hopkins' offer of a position on the Washington staff of WPA. The evidence in this case seems to indicate that removal of Victor Christgau was on the grounds of politics and no other.[21]

A correspondent for *The New Republic* observed in May, 1935, that members of Congress were more concerned about the personnel of the work relief setup and the distribution of the big fund than they were in the rest of the President's program. Certainly the brief accounts just preceding, which have been taken from only a portion of the available material of a similar nature, are indicative of the truthfulness of the statement. Some states remained relatively free from WPA politics; others became sources of constant political bickering. Part of this difficulty obviously lay with the efforts of senators to keep their state political machines in order. Part of it came from Democratic party leaders such as James Farley and Franklin D. Roosevelt. Much of it came from the squabbles of political factions within the same party in a locality. Really serious charges of politics in WPA on a large scale occurred in only a few states. These were in West Virginia, Pennsylvania, Kentucky, Missouri, and to a lesser extent in Mississippi, Illinois, and Tennessee. In the remainder of the states no serious charges on a large scale were ever made.

In a letter dated November 3, 1935, Lorena Hickok reported to Hopkins that the relief situation in West Virginia was "just one awful political mess." She called attention to the fact the relief program was controlled by Governor Kump and the work program by senators Neely and Holt. She did not know "who is worse, C. L. Allen, the relief administrator, or Wicher McCullough, the works progress man. Certainly McCullough hasn't had a chance." McCullough was being ridden hard by the politicians, particularly United States Senator Rush Holt.[22] Shortly after WPA began Senator Holt was entirely dissatisfied with the WPA organization in his state. As a result of charges of politics in the program, directed against McCullough, the state administrator, Hopkins sent Alan Johnstone to West Virginia to investigate. Early in March, Johnstone reported to Hopkins that WPA in West Virginia was in good shape, and Hopkins should stop worrying about it. He had found instances where Senator Holt and his brother, a WPA official, had collected some money from WPA personnel. The difficulty here was that Holt felt WPA was favorable to Senator Neely and not himself.[23]

The charges made at various times by Senator Holt and the result of the investigation show that both the charges and the conclusions of the investigation tended to overlook certain basic factors. When stripped of all the verbiage, Senator Holt charged that WPA had increased the salary of top personnel far beyond reason and that several state WPA personnel had put pressure on the workers to get full political cooperation. In some instances he claimed WPA had closed down projects as a form of political punishment. He also said his brother had been discharged after Senator Holt had attacked WPA on the Senate floor. He asked that he be reinstated and the wrong corrected. The brother involved had been discharged, reported Johnstone, three days before the senator's attack on WPA. The discharge was recommended by Wayne Coy, a field representative, after he found the offices Holt headed to be overloaded with supervisory personnel. Cases of processing of unapproved projects had also been uncovered. Coy had recommended his discharge as early as February 14, 1936, before charges had been made.[24]

Records of the United States Employment Service and of WPA indicated that 60 per cent of the administrative staff for the state had been appointed without political recommendations of any type. Of those having them, many were recommended by both Senator Holt and Senator Neely.

Neely had been in the Orient during the formative days of the WPA, and therefore Holt's charge that McCullough had told an assistant that Neely was dictating the WPA program in West Virginia had to be questioned. Of the 55,000 on WPA, 40,000 had been originally placed there by the United States Employment Service; the remainder by WPA after December 10, 1935, when it became clear that the USES in the area did not have sufficient personnel to place names before WPA officials rapidly enough. WPA had then obtained lists of eligible workers from the local relief officials as in several other states. McCullough claimed that he had never told Senator Holt that West Virginia's 50,000 WPA men would make him governor of the state. He himself had announced early in the fall of 1935 that he was not a candidate for the governorship of the state. Johnstone called attention to the fact that the records show that Senator Holt had attempted to interfere in some appointments. There were clear-cut cases where he threatened supervisors by telling them to appoint a certain person or he would take the matter directly to the Washington office.[25]

It appeared that Senator Holt had some reasonably good questions as to the operation of the WPA program in his state. Yet he mixed figures of WPA and of the state relief organization with statements that were so obviously biased that his account of the situation was not an accurate one. On one occasion Senator Holt described the WPA supervisory system in this fashion.

> They have a man here in charge of the W.P.A. and under him they have a State W.P.A., and under the State W.P.A. they have a district W.P.A., and under the district W.P.A. they have an area W.P.A., and under the area W.P.A. they have a county W.P.A., and under the county W.P.A. they have a project W.P.A. How on earth can we

> expect the man down at the bottom to get anything after they get through with that, I should like to know, after knowing the men that handle it? [26]

Senator Holt did not think much of Johnstone's investigation. He thought it was like sending " 'Baby Face' Nelson down to investigate John Dillinger." In the report there were "more lies per square inch . . . than in any other report in the history of the United States." [27] He referred to Hopkins as "Cockey Harry, the wisecracker of the administration." And he informed the Senate that he kept going back and forth checking on WPA and would do so until "the people know that Harry Hopkins should go down on record as the greatest teller of untruths, the greatest spender of money that this nation has ever known." He thought Hopkins was perhaps "too damned dumb" to know what was going on down in West Virginia. In Holt's opinion, better names for WPA might have been "Witcher's Political Army" or "Whitewashing Political Activity." [28]

In Missouri, Hopkins appointed as state WPA administrator Matt Murray, an employee of the Pendergast Democratic machine in Kansas City. The appointment was criticized shortly after WPA started, but Hopkins defended it on the grounds that Murray was a capable engineer. He had been approved by an engineering society as having the necessary qualifications for the position. In May, 1936, Arthur M. Curtis, assistant to the chairman of the Republican National Committee, charged Hopkins and WPA with political activity in Missouri. He cited specific cases where politicians had been allowed to affect the status of workers. Hopkins ordered an investigation and called the charges "all political and publicity stuff." He wanted to turn it to WPA's advantage by stating publicly the facts in an answer to the chairman of the Republican National Committee. Hopkins stated that "in each and every instance" the charges were "untrue." Hopkins then summarized the results of the investigation, contending that no one had lost work or been refused a job because of political pressure. Of Chairman Fletcher's action Hopkins said publicly:

> With the smug complacency which apparently goes with the Chairmanship of the Republican National Committee, Mr. Fletcher has seen fit to accuse me of playing politics because I am feeding the hungry, clothing the naked, and sheltering the destitute regardless of their sex, age, creed, color, race or place of residence. If that be politics, I plead guilty, but decline to enter into argument with Mr. Fletcher. Hunger is not debatable.[29]

Little more was said in reference to Missouri during the 1936 campaign, but further charges, rather serious ones, were made during 1938.

By 1938 WPA had become involved in a political skirmish in Missouri between Governor Lloyd C. Stark and the Pendergast machine. In June, Governor Stark sent a long telegram to President Roosevelt charging that Matt Murray was using the WPA in Missouri to strengthen the hold of Pendergast over the state. Pendergast was now about to gain control of the state supreme court also, particularly if Judge James M. Douglas, who had proved himself capable, was defeated by the Pendergast man in the primary. Stark called attention to the fact that Douglas would vote to uphold some of the more progressive legislation which had been passed by the state legislature, and that Pendergast and his outfit were against these acts. Stark told Hopkins directly a few weeks later that one of the WPA men in the state had said that he "did not have a thing to do for the next six weeks except to work on that primary." Stark sent some material to Hopkins in an attempt to prove his charge and Hopkins had the charges investigated, but he never did change his mind about Murray. He told reporters that Murray might be receiving $8,000 from Kansas City as an engineer on the Public Service Commission, but he had worked full-time for him and if they wanted to pay him for services not rendered, that was their business and not his. Murray had done a fine job in view of the circumstances and he would not fire him. The material sent to Hopkins by Stark and the persistence of Stark's charges past 1938 indicate that in some areas politics and WPA in Missouri were combined. But it is interesting that Colonel Harrington, who succeeded Hopkins as WPA administrator and who was not nearly so involved in politics, told Hopkins in 1939 that he preferred Murray and thought he "had done a good job as WPA administrator in Missouri." [30]

According to Aubrey Williams, Senator Guffey of Pennsylvania was one of the most difficult senators with whom Hopkins had to cooperate. In the appointment of the state administrator in Pennsylvania, Hopkins created one of his most difficult problems. Edward Jones, the man selected for state administrator, was a Guffey man serving in Governor Earle's state cabinet. He was probably more under the influence of the senator than the governor and worked in behalf of the Guffey Democratic political organization in the state. Miss Hickok reported to Hopkins in July, 1935, that she had heard that Guffey and Jones intended to run the Democratic party in Pennsylvania and make Earle take the back seat. Earle said he was going to be governor of the state in action as well as title. She thought that Jones would do a reasonably good job, but she had her doubts about him.[31]

In March, 1936, Senator Arthur H. Vandenberg of Michigan wrote Hopkins calling his attention to charges of political pressure on WPA workers in Indiana County, Pennsylvania. Ex-governor Pinchot also charged that "persons on relief are required to contribute part of their compensation to the Democratic campaign coffers." [32] Hopkins had these and other reports of politics checked. A portion of the damaging criticisms charged local Democratic officials with demanding funds from WPA workers. One of the letters given extensive newspaper publicity was to Mary C. Shearer, a worker on a WPA project, from Harry W. Fee, chairman of the Democratic County Committee of Indiana County. She was told she must contribute twenty-seven dollars to the campaign chest, or "it will be necessary to place your name on the list of those who will not be given consideration for any other appointment after the termination of the emergency relief work." The results of the investigation showed that only one dollar and twenty-five cents had been contributed and that the WPA administrator in the area had told the Democratic chairman that this was illegal and must be stopped. He told the workers that they need not contribute and that their jobs would be safe whether they did or did not contribute. He had done this verbally. He had also posted the notice on the bulletin board. Hopkins wrote Senator Vandenberg in part:

> I am sure you know that I cannot be held responsible for the acts of the dumb politicians who take it upon themselves to write letters to our employees. I am responsible for protecting our staff from any "raiding" on the part of any political party or their representatives. This I have done, and in this particular case our policy was carried out to the letter. The politician who asked for the contributions was told in words of one syllable that our staff was under no obligation to contribute and that their jobs would be fully protected in case they did not contribute, and not one single person on this staff was removed from office because of his failure to contribute, nor will he be.[33]

In April, 1936, Lorena Hickok reported that she thought Jones had tried to keep politics out and do a good job, but he lacked the personality to go with his job and had therefore had trouble with various groups. She thought many of the men he had appointed were able, but "down the line politics" had crept in because Senator Guffey had put pressure on the boys. She said that Jones and Johnson (head of the state relief program) had attempted to get some of the politics out of the program. Jones had been irked by Wayne Coy's visit in which the latter was stressing efficiency so much. She thought the program could be better; it was not as good as Coy's in Indiana, but it was much better than the program in New Jersey. In a press conference, August 20, 1936, Hopkins told the newsmen that he still thought Jones was a "good man." [34]

Political tension mounted as the campaign entered the final weeks, however, and William Hard, an up-and-coming journalist now turned to writing about politics in WPA, accused the Democrats in Pennsylvania of using WPA as a source of votes and funds. In some instances the Republican committee chairmen throughout the state asked the WPA workers for money and support. On the other hand, the Democratic forces did take over some of the offices of WPA by the time the November election took place. Lorena Hickok wrote Hopkins in mid-October that in the Pittsburgh area and a few other places WPA was really political. She knew that generally speaking the projects were good. "But, my Lord, it's political!" She revealed that right on the projects people would talk of how they were working for the Democrats. One woman boasted how she had raised $3,000 on her project. They were excusing their actions on the ground that if the Republicans were in power, they would do the same thing. In Philadelphia she noted that many Democratic committeemen were holding WPA jobs. She had hoped that they might be at least a little discreet, but they openly informed her that they would be right in there "working like Hell at the polls. . . ." She commented in closing that William Hard had good reason to pick Pennsylvania as a place to get evidence to use in the campaign.[35]

On August 31, 1935, President Roosevelt sent Hopkins a confidential and personal memo which noted that "relief in Ky—too much in Repub. hands—See Fred Vinson & talk with him about it." Hopkins' datebook does not reveal that he conferred with Vinson in his office, nor is there any recorded telephone call related to this topic. Charges of political activity in WPA were not prominent in the election of 1936. But in 1938, when Governor Happy Chandler decided to run against Senator Barkley for the Senate, politics and WPA became a controversial topic in the state of Kentucky, in the WPA offices, and in the leading newspapers of the country, particularly the Republican press.[36]

The honeymoon period of smooth and quick response from Congress to President Roosevelt's requests ceased by the time of Roosevelt's annual message to Congress in January, 1935. And even though Roosevelt won a sweeping victory in 1936, many conservative Democrats spoke out against the Roosevelt programs of 1935–36 and 1937. We have seen a phase of this as it related to the passage of acts appropriating money for the work program. Similar skirmishes and divisions in voting occurred within the Democratic ranks involving the Social Security Act of 1935, legislation for aid to agriculture, and the attempt to enlarge the Supreme Court. Hence, Roosevelt's note reveals his increasing concern for supporting senators who had been loyal to him in most of these legislative battles. Having additional objectives in mind, he needed support in the future. Happy Chandler would not be a New Deal supporter. New Dealers wanted Senator Barkley returned to Washington. Each man had his own state political machine. This senatorial campaign in 1938 proved to be a rough one, a vigorous campaign. WPA, therefore, became one of several organizations accused of political manipulation in Kentucky.

During the summer of 1938 Thomas L. Stokes, writing a series of articles about political pressures on WPA workers in Kentucky, accused district supervisors in Kentucky of drumming up business for Senator Barkley. One supervisor was charged with asking his men to support Senator Barkley by contributing 2 per cent of their annual income. In another instance Stokes reported workers had been shifted to poorer jobs. Supposedly, several had been dismissed because they favored Chandler rather than Barkley. They had been asked to register as Democrats so they could vote for Barkley even though they might vote Republican in the fall elections. George H. Goodman, state WPA administrator, denied workers had been dismissed because of failing to cooperate politically. One worker had been dismissed because he made speeches of a political nature on the project site. Another had not been denied a job but had refused to accept one because the pay was less than $1.50 per hour. On July 1, Hopkins issued his first denial of charges made by Stokes, saying the charges were substantiated in only two cases. In one of the situations a timekeeper handed out registration cards. One foreman on another project solicited funds for Barkley. The timekeeper had already been reprimanded for his action and Goodman had been instructed to take action against the foreman. Stokes responded that "the whole atmosphere and tone of WPA in Kentucky is political and has been at least since early March." He disagreed with Hopkins' statement, feeling Goodman had made it clear in March of 1938 that the WPA in Kentucky was to back Barkley or else. Stokes confirmed the fact that in both instances WPA had taken steps to correct the violation, but he was not convinced that his other twenty charges were all mistakes.[37]

The charges made by Thomas L. Stokes and others were presented in the fall to the Senate committee investigating campaign expenditures. The Sheppard Committee, as it was known, was not friendly toward the New Deal. It asked Hopkins to defend his position and that of WPA. Hopkins agreed that in some instances violations of WPA regulations did occur, but not always with the intent in mind that critics of the New Deal and WPA thought. In Russell and Pulaski counties, for example, an area engineer had asked the workers for their political affiliation. This was done to secure information to answer a charge made by a Colonel Woodson that only 10 per cent of the WPA workers in the county of Pulaski were Democrats. He prepared a sheet which asked the workers to state whether they were Democrats or Republicans and not to state a preference for any candidate. The engineer reported no funds were solicited and no one was fired. In two instances papers in behalf of Senator Barkley and Governor Chandler had been circulated on projects, but the area engineer had not known of it until later. The circulators were not affiliated with the WPA in Kentucky. He reported that higher-ups in WPA in Kentucky had told him to "stay out" of politics. Hopkins himself concluded the proven cases were small, since there were over 70,000 persons employed in Kentucky on projects and some 1,800 different projects were in operation.[38]

After the election in November, the attacks on WPA in Kentucky subsided somewhat. The Sheppard Committee kept holding hearings from time to time and, in the spring of 1939, an Ernest Rowe, after being dismissed by Goodman, made available a letter from Goodman in which he outlined the procedures to be followed in obtaining political contributions from WPA project workers. After suggesting contributions of 2 per cent and indicating the type of persons to be collectors, Goodman stated that there was to be "no discrimination against any employee who, because of home expenses or other reasons, does not feel able to assist financially in the campaign." He instructed that a record be kept of all contributions. Goodman had prepared this letter on May 23, 1938. He did not deny that he had written it. On May 27, 1938, Goodman wrote Rowe telling him to destroy all correspondence of a political nature which "carries a meaning which would subject us to criticism by the wrong interpretation." Here was a case, as Stokes claimed, where a state administrator was certainly not following or enforcing the regulations issued by the WPA headquarters. Hopkins did not dismiss him, however. Actually, the Sheppard Committee found that, of the two men, Governor Chandler had had more success than Barkley in obtaining funds from state highway workers and other officials using state and federal funds. Barkley got only $24,000 from employees of governmental agencies, while Chandler had secured $70,000. Hopkins later admitted that he should have taken more drastic action in Kentucky in the summer of 1938.[39]

Not all complaints concerning the political activity of WPA came from Republican or independent sources. Hopkins claimed in a news conference, April 16, 1936, that WPA offices received more complaints from Democrats than from Republicans. There is certainly a large amount of truth in Hopkins' statement. Many of the charges of political activity had to do with squabbles between factions within the Democratic organizations in a state. In Michigan the chief complaints Hopkins received, except for one area, were that the Republicans controlled WPA and other federal agencies in that state. And even after some changes had been made, several Democrats were dissatisfied because the wrong people headed the work relief organization. Harry Glass, Jr., a member of the Michigan House of Representatives, wrote Louis Howe in the summer of 1935 that "Mr. Hopkins' hysterical efforts to keep public works jobs beyond the range of political preferment, his quixotic belief in the existence of 'nonpartisanship' in this country has resulted, in Michigan at least, in a most dreadful scourge of Republican appointments." He said that WPA was the last hope of the Democrats in Michigan, but "with this great organization in the hands of Republicans aided and abetted by Mr. Hopkins, who in his statement refers to politicians as though they were the actual enemies of the president, we are facing a complete breakdown in the morale of the Democratic organization." Here Mr. Glass was referring to a reported statement of Hopkins to H. L. Pierson, head of WPA in Michigan: "You are better off to appoint a good independent Republican in sympathy with the program than a Democrat who is not." [40]

Lorena Hickok and others reported to Hopkins from time to time that the state administrator for Michigan favored the Republicans. One of the complaints about lack of proper political sensitivity on the part of H. L. Pierson and his successor, William Haber, was sent along to Hopkins by James Farley.

> The W.P.A. is still impossible to local Democrats. For months they have been going over the heads of local committee men making appointments of Republicans. I understand this situation is general in this part of Michigan, but worse in this county and district. All efforts to influence Mr. Haber and staff have failed.[41]

Hopkins and his staff checked this and the other charges made from time to time but found little to criticize. In the upper peninsular area, Lorena Hickok reported that the Democrats were in strong control but, except for interference from local politicians, the state WPA of Michigan was a reasonably clean show. On one occasion Hopkins wrote Farley that he was sure that Haber was not a Republican, although he had "voted the Republican ticket some time ago." He believed him to be loyal to the President and did not believe for a minute that he was "using his office for political purposes." [42]

Congressman Jerry Voorhis of California wrote that in his experience with WPA and politics, he had found that the degree and type of politics varied from state to state. He had become convinced that the influence of local and state political leaders on the WPA program was more damaging than influence from federal authorities. In his state, he claimed, WPA workers had never told him of having to obtain political backing to get WPA jobs. He had never had to provide any. He knew that in one state the Republicans did dominate WPA and attempt to use it for their own political ends. In other states the Democrats who were most skillful in using WPA for political purposes were not the supporters of the administration in Washington but the Democrats within the party who opposed the New Deal program.[43]

Much of the political maneuvering which went on in the WPA program cannot be attributed to the influence of the Washington staff of WPA, but occurred in spite of the efforts of that group to stop it. There was ample room for politics in the certifying of people on relief, making them eligible to receive consideration for employment by local WPA supervisors. Many people did not realize this and attributed manipulations of local relief boards and administrators to WPA. Some people seemed to think this distinction needed to be stressed more by WPA headquarters. Raymond Clapper, an honest critic of much of the work program of the New Deal, pointed out in the spring of 1938 that "the most insidious attempts to gain political advantage out of WPA are beyond his [Hopkins'] reach, and can be broken up most effectively by local exposure." Clapper knew that at that time a governor in a certain state was building his state machine largely by putting pressure on local relief officials to put people on relief rolls and certify them as eligible for WPA employment. Hopkins realized that such activity, beyond the control of WPA itself, required more stringent laws. He recommended to Congress that laws be passed making such activity less likely. Hopkins believed administrative personnel should be placed on civil service. Indeed, as one authority on the federal relief and work program concluded, the administration, despite its desire to have men friendly to it in the key positions, took a stronger attitude against politics in WPA than did Congress and locally entrenched Democratic leaders.[44]

Hugh Johnson, always critical of the over-all work program and of WPA, came to the defense of Hopkins in the midst of charges of politics made by Senator Rush Holt in February and March, 1936. Johnson claimed that "the charges of graft and politics are cruelly false and unfair." He knew that in an organization as big as WPA there were bound to be some "peculation and political heeling." But as to the character of the administration itself and of the bulk of its "colossal" organization, there could be no doubt of its good intentions. Johnson believed that Hopkins did not have "what it takes" to fake or foster graft and politics. There was, in his opinion at that time, neither graft nor politics "upstairs." WPA had its orders—that he knew from having been in the organization—and those orders were to "keep WPA's nose clean." Johnson maintained the critics of WPA would do far better to watch for extravagance, inefficiency, and ineptitude on individual projects than to play politics with human misery by making false or unfounded charges which had not been verified.[45]

Hickman Powell, one of the reporters most familiar with Hopkins' work, noted in January, 1939, that "Hopkins has made many enemies in his work, and it is a question whether he made more enemies by keeping politics out of WPA or letting them get in. He has never been popular with practical polticians." Hopkins, he thought, had obtained pretty much what he wanted from Congress, but he was not sure that congressmen had secured all they wanted from Hopkins, and "among the criticisms thrown at him have been a certain number of sour grapes." Raymond Clapper believed part of the difficulty in 1938 was Hopkins' lack of interest in the WPA program and his absence from WPA headquarters for several months because of ill health. Nonetheless, states Clapper, Hopkins was willing to aid the President in the attempted purge of conservative Democrats and he was willing to make political speeches. He observed that Hopkins believed, in January, 1939, that Administrator Hopkins, in the summer of 1938, could have cracked down a little harder on those who engaged in politics in behalf of WPA, and that Administrator Hopkins should not have made the political speeches that he did. Aubrey Williams believed that Hopkins did tire of WPA, did not care to bother himself with the details of the program after his first serious illness in the winter of 1937–38, and was looking to bigger things in connection with the New Deal program.[46] Mrs. Roosevelt believed that the decision of her husband to attempt the purge and to have Hopkins play a leading role must be considered in evaluating Hopkins' actions during 1938. She believed, also, that the death of Barbara Hopkins, his second wife, with whom he had a very satisfactory relationship, deeply affected him. His own illness, said Mrs. Roosevelt, was an important factor. Thus, as a means of escape, after partial recovery in 1938, he turned to a social life unlike that before 1938.[47]

During 1938, 1939, and 1940, WPA and related activities of the New Deal were investigated by two congressional committees. The more important of the two, as far as Hopkins was concerned, was the Senate committee to investigate politics in connection with WPA and senatorial campaigns. After hearings of several weeks and recorded testimony of several hundred pages, the committee came to no startling conclusions. It noted that politics had crept into the WPA and recommended that Congress correct certain weaknesses in the laws which had been apparent for some time. The record of the committee is full of specific charges of questionable activities in certain areas and on certain projects. There is no systematic theme, no basis for many of the charges which were later proven false, and many of the statements of a general nature appear to be open to serious doubts as to reliability. There is nothing in the hearings to indicate that WPA headquarters ever systematically attempted to make WPA a political machine. The committee was most careful to avoid discussion of such topics as the possible influence of confirmation by the Senate of administrators and officials receiving $5,000 or more. In its report the committee gave no indication of the extent of practices it criticized. It did not point out that the sum total of testimony showed clearly that most political activity was at the local level. While the hearings provided many interesting interpretations of the actions of WPA, nothing really constructive was accomplished.

The Woodrum-Taylor Committee, organized in the House in 1939 to study the activities of WPA, proved to be of little more help in understanding the political activities of WPA. It was interested mainly in the theater projects and possible influence of communists in the writing and presentation of plays. Once it had covered that subject, the committee turned to the question of how much WPA had benefited private property owners. In this investigation most of the leads for information came from WPA files and, in many instances, WPA had already started or completed action against officials and others. The net result of this investigation, other than a few headlines, was the stopping of most of the federally sponsored art, theater, music, and writing projects. In earlier laws Congress had already started the practice of making these illegal for sponsorship by WPA itself. Local sponsors could still secure funds for them and did so. The committee also found that the non-contract system proved to be more expensive than the contract system, but then, as Colonel Brehon Somervell, head of WPA in New York City, pointed out, much of the cost of the non-contract method resulted from the way the acts were written and not from poor administration. As to politics, Congressman Woodrum said on the House floor that his committee found nothing to raise "any question upon the personal character or integrity of any high WPA official in Washington." Colonel Harrington, the new WPA administrator, pointed out that in four and one-half years there had not been one case of a really responsible official of the WPA who had gone crooked. The highest level on which a person had been involved in dishonesty was that of a district manager.[48]

Evidence indicates that if it had not been for local politics, the average employable person on relief would not have needed political endorsements for appointment to WPA projects. Indeed, in many instances, even with local politics entering into the picture for the majority of workers, this was not necessary. It is true that supervisory personnel and administrative officials were subjected to political pressures. Officials who served under Hopkins in both the FERA and WPA programs have stated that requiring Senate confirmation of administrative personnel marked the real beginning of political pressures upon the administration of the relief and work relief programs. Impartial observers have also held that Senate confirmation opened the door to forces that were inimical to sound administrative practice and that it was largely responsible for such politics as may have crept into the program.[49]

According to Aubrey Williams, up to the time WPA administrators were confirmed by the Senate there was very little politics in any of the agencies headed by Hopkins. Hopkins had not allowed James Farley to have "anything to do with the selection . . . of the personnel of any of the agencies under him." Hopkins, said Williams, neither desired nor attempted to appoint men hostile to the senators, but "he refused to accept mediocre people no matter who tried to get him to." Once the Senate decided that it wanted to approve the top men in WPA, "Hopkins lost control of the organization. He fought passage of such a law. . . . He resisted some of the worst suggestions. Those of Bilbo, McKellar, and Guffey of Pennsylvania as well as Byrd of Virginia, who was one of the worst. But in the end he yielded." At one time, Williams recalled, "he and I took a drive . . . when he was asked to make a terrible appointment. Hopkins seriously considered resigning at that time. But his loyalty to the President was too great; he gave in for the President. He shielded the President and took many public beatings for senators and the President." [50]

The pressure of politics thus corrupted the former idealistic social worker to some extent. He used some of his power to serve both the Democrats and his benefactor, Franklin D. Roosevelt. Evidence indicates, however, that Harry Hopkins should have had a clearer conscience about politics in the Works Progress Administration than many local officials and several senators and congressmen.

This bill is simply a starter for Hopkins. . . . He has his eye on the presidency. —SENATOR DICKINSON OF IOWA

X. Presidential Aspirations

The interweaving of the New Deal, the Democratic party, agencies such as the WPA, and the political ambitions of top New Deal administrators intensified with each additional year of legislation and political experience. The political maneuvering, typical of our federal and political systems, linked outstanding government leaders like Ickes and Hopkins with the success of their own projects, the power of the political party to which they were attached, the whims and desires of the President, and the likes and dislikes of senior congressmen. Where did personal ambition end or the desire to have a top-notch program begin? Was everything political?

Hopkins and the WPA were certainly in the middle of the Washington political arena. Hopkins and other key WPA personnel learned at first hand the importance of political log-rolling. Hopkins knew the best way to continue with his relief and work relief programs was to have Roosevelt and the New Deal continue in power in Washington; therefore, the New Dealers had to dominate the Democratic party. Conservative leaders like Farley, George of Georgia, and Byrd of Virginia had to be pushed into a secondary role before 1940. Coupled with this were Hopkins' own ambitions to increase his power and prestige. Hopkins, by his own admission, failed to keep his personal ambitions from interfering with his administrative responsibilities. Thus, particularly in 1938, as previously noted, WPA, the attempted purge of conservative Democrats, and Hopkins' interest in a cabinet post or the vice-presidency or the presidency itself tended to become inseparable.[1]

At the request of President Roosevelt and because of his own personal interest, Hopkins had his field representatives and others report to him during 1936 on political conditions. Hopkins evaluated these reports and sent information to the President about the loyalty of such Democratic organizations as the Davey-Roosevelt Clubs in Ohio. Many of the reports from field representatives related directly to Hopkins. Lorena Hickok reported that in New York State Hopkins and the work program, particularly WPA, were to be the center points of attack by the Republicans. "Waste" and "graft" and "inefficiency," she said, were their key words. They considered Hopkins honest and sincere and a "darned good social worker," but not a good administrator because "you're not a businessman." [2] Lawrence Westbrook, one of Hopkins' administrative assistants, told Hopkins that he must get out and tell the people about WPA even if the money had to be taken "out of administrative expenses," for they should know the truth. Hopkins made one major trip in the fall of 1936, a swing through the West.

Robert Sherwood points out in his account of Hopkins' political activities that James Farley cared little for Hopkins' campaigning, and this was partly responsible for Hopkins' silence during the latter days of the campaign. Be that as it may, Hopkins did do effective work during his Western tour, if the materials in his files are a reliable indication. Letters to Farley and to Hopkins indicate Hopkins' sincerity convinced many people WPA was not the monstrosity the Republicans claimed it was. E. J. Griffith of the Griffith Transport Company, located in Portland, Oregon, reported that even Republican newspapers were giving Hopkins "favorable first page publicity." Reports from California were also favorable. Some wrote asking specifically that Hopkins be kept in the campaign to the very end, for his "simple, sincere way of expressing the facts about WPA" would help overcome the resistance to President Roosevelt. One gentleman reported that "until I heard him [Hopkins] I was disposed to be quite critical of some of the W.P.A. activities, but after I heard him I became a thoroughgoing friend and supporter of his. In my opinion arrangements should be made to have Hopkins go on several nationwide hook-ups to explain to the people what has been accomplished and the method and policies that have controlled the organization." And another told Farley that he would be missing a "real bet" if Farley did not have Hopkins repeat over radio networks his speech given before the Commonwealth Club of San Francisco. In reference to this, Hopkins received two written brief messages from Farley. On the 20th of September, Farley wrote, "I want to talk to you about your trip when you return. Frankly, I think your trip was very very helpful." And on October 5, 1936, Farley told Hopkins that he had been "in touch with Tom Stork and he advises me that you made a very good speech in Los Angeles." [3]

The speech at Los Angeles was one of Hopkins' best. It was largely his own. It revealed a philosophy and feeling which was really Hopkins but too often covered over with his cynical and sarcastic cracks. Hopkins hit hard at his critics. He said he was "getting sick and tired" of people on local relief rolls and on WPA being called "chiselers and cheats." They were, stressed Hopkins, "just like the rest of us." They "don't drink any more than the rest of us, they don't lie any more, they're no lazier than the rest of us—they're pretty much a cross section of the American people." Hopkins emphasized the fact that "with our capitalistic system" it was an outrage that we should permit hundreds and hundreds of thousands of people "to be ill clad, to live in miserable homes, not to have enough to eat; not to be able to send their children to school for the only reason that they are poor." We in America, said Hopkins, were not going to permit things like that to happen again. People are not poor because "they are bad. I don't believe it. A system of government on that basis is fallacious." Hopkins believed "this economic system of ours is an ideal instrument to increase this national income of ours, not back to 80 billion where it was, but up to 100 billion or 120 billion. The capitalistic system lends itself to providing a national income that will give real security for all." Hopkins admitted that he and his staff might have made mistakes, but they did not intend to apologize for them for they were honestly made and made in the "interests of the people that were broke." In conclusion he said in reference to his own role:

> When this thing is all over and I am out of the Government the things I am going to regret are the things I have failed to do for the unemployed. I don't know whether you would have liked the job. Every night when you went home and after you got home and remembered there was a telegram you didn't answer, the fact that you failed to answer the telegram and the telephone call may have resulted in somebody not eating. That is the kind of a job I have had for the last three and a half years, and still have. When it is all over, the thing I am going to be proudest of are the people all over America, public officials, volunteers, paid workers, thousands of people of all political and religious faiths who joined in this enterprise of taking care of people in need. It has been a great thing. I am not ashamed of one of them and I hope when I am through they are not going to be ashamed of me, and as I go around this country and see the unemployment and see the people who are running this show of ours, I am tremendously proud of this country of ours and I am tremendously proud that I am a citizen of it.[4]

On October 17, 1936, Hopkins made his first major radio campaign speech. Entitled "Jobs vs. Jibes," it was aimed primarily at Governor Landon's remarks on relief, with a brief reference to President Hoover's relief program. He called attention to the fact that, although Landon said during the campaign that "the ugly fact is that this Administration has condemned one-sixth of our people to live in a separate economic world," Landon had written President Roosevelt in January of 1934, "I have felt that this Civil Works program is one of the soundest most constructive policies of your Administration, and I cannot urge too strongly its continuance." Hopkins then went over Landon's remarks point by point. Landon favored, stated Hopkins, a system whereby local communities would determine the nature of the work programs in their area. Hopkins pointed out this was the way it was being done under WPA. The governor of Kansas stressed local contributions. Hopkins claimed that in 1936 they were contributing 20 per cent of the total costs. Landon stated that WPA workers were isolated in another world and could not transfer back into normal employment. Hopkins called this "ridiculous," stating that 3 per cent of all WPA employees returned to private jobs every month. As to charges of politics made by Landon, Hopkins said that after all the false charges were eliminated, the total would be no more than "one one-hundredth of one per cent of the people in our program. That makes us 99.99 per cent pure." Hopkins gave figures indicating the administrative cost of relief in Kansas and of WPA had been and was, in the fall of 1936, noticeably higher than the national average.[5]

Once the campaign was over, Hopkins participated more vigorously in New Deal activities. He now knew WPA was not the political liability to Roosevelt that many had claimed. The election convinced Hopkins, if not all Democratic leaders, that Roosevelt and his more liberal policy of 1935 and 1936 had the support of the people. He actively supported Roosevelt's attempt to change the personnel of the Supreme Court in the spring of 1937. And upon the death of Senator Joseph Robinson, majority floor leader in the Senate, Hopkins backed Roosevelt's effort to make Senator Alben Barkley of Kentucky majority leader rather than Senator Pat Harrison of Mississippi.

Louis Howe, the President's former close adviser and personal friend, had died a few months earlier. The time came, as Mrs. Roosevelt has written, when Roosevelt was to find in Hopkins some of the "companionship and loyalty Louis had given him, but not always the political wisdom and careful analysis of each situation." The hard work and loyalty Hopkins gave the President in the years from 1932 to 1936 was now to materialize into an even closer relationship between the two men. Hopkins was younger than Roosevelt and an amateur at political maneuvering. He considered the President a master politician, and was grateful to him for having backed the work program. He confided to friends that he could not ever be satisfied with being a social worker again. His role in dramatizing the one-third of the nation that was ill-clothed, ill-housed, and ill-fed, and his increasing desire to play a bigger role in the New Deal program, increased his efforts to be close to the President. He found in Roosevelt, as Roosevelt did in him, a source of strength for the humanitarian approach each had and which was severely criticized by their opponents. Hopkins, younger and less experienced, could not act as a counterbalance on Roosevelt as Louis Howe had. He worked as a loyal servant of the President rather than a senior adviser. Thus, from 1937 through 1940, he became a willing tool of Roosevelt on two scores—a fellow congressional purger in the congressional campaigns of 1938, and an unannounced candidate for the presidential nomination of 1940. While this led Hopkins into some questionable activities as administrator of relief, it also gave him a further understanding of the President, his moods, his likes and dislikes, and his need for a man to serve him loyally at all times.[6]

Several sources indicate that by 1937 Hopkins was in the running for the Democratic presidential nomination in 1940.

General Hugh Johnson wrote that Hopkins had now become "the No. 1 boy in the inner circle of the New Deal economists." Johnson also claimed that Hopkins' personal staff had filled his head "with the ineffable nonsense that he has political possibilities." [7]

How soon Harry Hopkins began to look upon himself as a presidential candidate is not clear. There is some evidence to indicate that it might have been quite early in his Washington career. The reluctance of Congress to go along with Hopkins in the amount requested for WPA in 1936 and again in 1937 was partially due to the belief that Hopkins would become, if indeed he had not become already, a powerful political opponent of some members of the Senate and House. Senator Dickinson of Iowa claimed that if Congress gave Hopkins the money he sought, "we will be raising an American Caesar in our midst. This bill is simply a starter for Hopkins. . . . He has his eye on the presidency." Senator Dickinson's observation was correct.[8]

Hopkins had political support outside WPA and the White House. The editor of the *Aberdeen* (South Dakota) *News* wrote that Hopkins was "the only prominent New Dealer who came to Washington in 1933 who had done a good enough job of his difficult assignment to keep from embarrassing his superior. . . . Who then, at this early stage, has any better right for consideration as a candidate than Mr. Roosevelt's right-hand man—Harry Hopkins?" The (Jackson, Mississippi) *Jackson Daily News* told the public and Harry Hopkins, "You are, Harry Hopkins, our candidate for the next President of the United States." In December, 1937, Raymond Clapper wrote that many of Hopkins' friends had talked to Hopkins about the presidency. Herbert Swope, Rex Tugwell, Representative John M. Coffee of Ohio, and Mayor LaGuardia all wrote or talked to Hopkins about his candidacy. The colorful mayor of New York City on one occasion wired Hopkins, "Many happier returns of the day. I thought you were younger but judging from the age given in the papers today you will not be the youngest President of the United States. At any rate good luck." Hopkins told LaGuardia in a return message to "give up crystal gazing and stick to the mayor business." [9]

In the spring of 1938 Hopkins conferred with Roosevelt. What were Hopkins' chances for 1940? Undoubtedly Hopkins had a strong interest in the vice-presidency if Roosevelt decided to run for a third term. This discussion involved several possible candidates for 1940. President Roosevelt had reservations about Cordell Hull, Henry Wallace, Harold Ickes, Paul McNutt, Frank Murphy, and George Earle. These men were leading cabinet members (Hull, Wallace, Ickes) or better-than-average state governors. Attention was also given to James Farley. Hopkins found that the President believed he had several assets which made him a likely possibility, and later told a few of his close friends that Roosevelt had given him the green light. For several months during 1938 Hopkins seemed to take seriously suggestions that he was a likely prospect for the Democratic party presidential nominee in 1940, but it is doubtful how intense Hopkins' presidential aspirations were. In April, 1938, Hopkins wrote to Herbert Swope:

> I find your note awaiting me on my return. I have no idea whether the Reorganization Bill will pass or not and, if it does, what my fate will be. It really isn't very important. The last few months have made me revamp my point of view about what is important in this life, and I find that warm and understanding friends are at the top.[10]

A duodenal ulcer had caused Hopkins real trouble beginning in 1935. It forced him to follow a rather rigid diet. Hopkins' telephone conversations during the summer and fall of 1936 reveal that those who were close to him were aware he was not well. Senator Robert LaFollette on one occasion asked Hopkins how he was feeling, and Hopkins replied, "Just so-so, and that bothers me a lot." By 1937 he not only had the problem of his own health to deal with but also that of his wife, who was suffering from cancer. Within a few months following a last big holiday for her at Saratoga Springs, New York, she died. It was shortly thereafter that Hopkins' own fears that he too was suffering from cancer were confirmed. In December, Hopkins entered the Mayo Clinic and by January 1, 1938, was slowly recovering from an operation during which a large part of his stomach was removed. From that time until the spring of 1938, Hopkins spent little time at WPA headquarters. He did not feel like returning. Further, he had specific orders from his doctors at the Mayo Clinic not to do so. During these months Hopkins spent some time at the homes of friends—particularly Joseph P. Kennedy's Florida residence. By April he was reporting to friends that he had never "felt better in years" and he realized "how fortunate" he had been to get to the Mayo Clinic in time.[11]

In contrast to these facts, which seem to indicate that Hopkins' hopes for a bright political future were stopped while only budding, is material in his correspondence and records which indicate that at least some persons thought his name should be kept before the public as a presidential candidate. Whether in an effort to keep in the public eye or out of loyalty to the President, Hopkins jumped into the congressional elections of 1938 with great vigor considering his recent illness. In May, 1938, he told newspapermen and others that if he were voting in Iowa in the primaries, he would not vote for Senator Guy Gillette. He gave his support to Otha Wearin. This caused a stir in both Washington and Iowa. Republican party leaders and the Republican press immediately claimed Hopkins was playing politics with WPA. Senator Champ Clark of Missouri said Hopkins' remarks were like telling WPA workers "if you don't vote for Wearin you'll lose your jobs. If you vote for Gillette your families may go hungry." The Pittsburgh *Post-Gazette* called this a "glaring example of the low estimate Hopkins puts upon the public intelligence." Incidentally, this editorial also referred to the "too damned dumb" phrase in that famous statement of Hopkins in the spring of 1935. In the primary race Wearin was soundly defeated by Senator Gillette. Hopkins' comment was that it proved that WPA voters knew they were free to vote for whom they pleased.[12]

Within a few weeks Hopkins became involved in further political controversies. In July, Hopkins reportedly said that 90 per cent of WPA workers would vote for Roosevelt in the election, meaning for the candidates that Roosevelt chose to support.[13] The Portland *Oregonian* observed that Hopkins was probably right, as most workers "cleave to the source of supply." The *Oregonian* thought, however, that there was only one way Hopkins could have obtained the information for his statement and that was to have had someone ask them in large numbers. That "is political exploitation," said the paper, and supposedly WPA does not allow that. "Now we have it on authority no less than Mr. Hopkins himself that the charge often made in and out of Congress is true." It concluded that perhaps "there is exploitation and there is regimentation of human misery to make votes for new dealers."

Such attacks by the opposition, now rather old stuff to Hopkins, did not hamper his efforts in behalf of what he knew Roosevelt wanted done. In a speech at Boston late in August, 1938, Hopkins hit hard at the critics. He was taking one of the leading roles in "clearing away the cobwebs and the confusion and making the issues plain before the voters." Hopkins, along with Tom Corcoran, Harold Ickes, and other New Deal associates in whom the fire for reform and change still burned, was willing to battle the Southern wing of the Democratic party. These Democratic liberals lost several of the contests in 1938 as senators Tydings of Maryland, George of Georgia, and Gillette of Iowa were re-elected. Actually, the only victim of the purge of any note was John O'Connor of New York, chairman of the House Rules Committee. The battle for control of the Democratic party increased as the time approached for the 1940 conventions. Roosevelt wanted Hopkins to be in the thick of the fight. He was soon to appoint him to a more politically respectable position. He encouraged Hopkins to give a series of speeches in the summer of 1938. Several were delivered at the Chautauqua Institution. It became obvious to discerning newsmen that either FDR still believed Hopkins could be a candidate in 1940, or else he wished to use Hopkins to keep other candidates from building a solid block of support. Hopkins could temporarily, until the President made up his mind whether to run for a third term, hold some liberal Democratic support which could be given to Roosevelt when the time came.

By the time Roosevelt announced his appointment as Secretary of Commerce in December, 1938, any favor Hopkins might have gained with business interests by his speeches or his press conferences was largely offset by a story reported in September of that year. Arthur Krock gave it most publicity, but Frank Kent, Joseph Alsop, and Robert Kintner also reported that Hopkins had said, "We shall tax and tax, and spend and spend, and elect and elect." Max Gordon, successful New York theatrical producer, was the source of the quote which Hopkins persistently denied. He wrote the editor of *The New York Times*, "I never made such a statement and there is no basis in fact for such a quotation."

Heywood Broun, the columnist, and Daniel Arnstein, the transportation expert, were with Hopkins at the time he was supposed to have made the statement, and both denied that he had. Krock maintained that whether he had actually said it or not, it seemed to him "a concentrated gem of Mr. Hopkins' philosophy." [14] Sherwood in his account leaves the impression that Hopkins probably did not say it as quoted. It was not in keeping with his other comments on taxes in relation to spending. He was from the start of his Washington career worried about local relief efforts being such a burden that property taxes would become injurious to owners. In 1937 he told a group of state administrators that it was time to bring expenditures into proper balance with the possible taxation levels. In October and November of 1937, Hopkins was reported to have favored a revision of taxes in a manner helpful to business. Hugh S. Johnson claimed that Hopkins was "too smart" to think that "spending and taking" could go on forever. Hopkins had clearly indicated to him that he knew the economic "necessities" of our free economy.[15]

Hopkins' own staff continued to support him for the Presidency despite the results of the unsuccessful purge in 1938. Howard Hunter informed Hopkins shortly after the fall elections that Mayor Kelly of Chicago would "go all the way down the line" and would soon confer with the President concerning the "delivering of the goods." He suggested Hopkins contact Frank Hague of Jersey City at once, and he also made some suggestions for gaining support in Minnesota. Hunter informed Hopkins that Frank Murphy was willing to cooperate in Michigan and to take action against those Democrats who hoped to "get their finger in the Federal pie through J. F." A short time later Hunter revealed to Hopkins that a meeting held in Chicago was called by Farley to build strength against the possibility of the nomination of Hopkins or "any other liberal candidate." The whole tone of the meeting, reported Hunter, was to arrange for the re-election of the worst reactionary state and county groups in North Dakota, Wisconsin, Iowa, and Michigan. In Wisconsin, Farley was, said Hunter, even making attempts to get hold of the WPA personnel. In all of this correspondence it is impossible to tell from the wording whether Hopkins is the candidate concerned, or whether Roosevelt is also involved. In New Jersey, as well as other states, Hopkins received cooperation from some of the senators and representatives who had benefited from the work relief program and who were New Dealers anxious to see men like Hopkins dominate the scene.[16]

Albert Warner reported in November, 1938, that Democratic leaders of 21 eastern and southern states meeting with Farley had concluded that Hopkins was at that time Roosevelt's choice for a successor. They returned home with the set conviction that Hopkins would be nominated "only over our dead bodies." Public opinion polls early in 1939 and throughout that time until the spring of 1940 never showed Hopkins as one of the leading contenders for the nomination. A poll taken when there were serious rumors that Hopkins was to become Secretary of Commerce showed that Hopkins was considered by 40.9 per cent of those expressing an opinion to have done a good to fine job as relief administrator, with 27.5 per cent of those expressing an opinion believing he had not done the job well enough and should retire to private life.[17]

It is likely that Hopkins and Roosevelt both felt by the end of 1938, and knew certainly once he became seriously ill again after becoming Secretary of Commerce, that Hopkins could not be a candidate in 1940. Hopkins probably remained a prospective nominee as long as he did because of a natural desire for revenge, although normal hunger for power and glory was part of the impelling motive. Hopkins liked to appear as a tough-skinned person who was not upset by the attacks of his critics; however, Hopkins was not like this, nor was he like that while administrator of relief. Hopkins' pride had been hurt by those who claimed he was a liability to Roosevelt. Sherwood believed Hopkins was actually an idealistic social worker, with an Iowan concept of the purity of the democratic process, who underneath suffered from honest disgust with the pork-barrel attitude of many congressional leaders.[18] Hopkins was not willing to run from his opponents. He fought back and was now making an effort to clean out some of the venal politicians who had interfered with his original honest efforts to help feed, clothe, and shelter those in need. In his mind, it was his turn to play politics. He thought he could do so without doing serious harm to his efforts as administrator of the relief programs. Years later Hopkins was to conclude that this concession to his own candidacy was one of his major mistakes.

> The value is the point. There are three items in this book of values. The first one is the vital need of millions of destitute people. I make no apology for ranking it first, and I can not conceive that in any civilized nation it could occupy a secondary position. The second item is the preservation of the ability of these people to work; and the third is the tremendous actual and social value of the community benefits they are building.
>
> —HARRY L. HOPKINS

XI. The Task: Well Done?

The Roosevelt administration gave more time, effort, and money to WPA than to any other of the relief and work relief agencies. Throughout the nation WPA received the most praise and the most criticism of any of the relief agencies, partly because it was the most extensive. The previous four chapters described the development of the WPA program and the highlights of its organization. The role of politics was emphasized. Little attempt to draw any basic conclusions was made. Conclusions and keener evaluations must be made, however, to determine the general areas of successes and failures of the WPA.

A logical analysis of the administration of the WPA program by Hopkins and his staff centers on three main topics: first, its integration with other agencies with which it worked on national, state, and local levels; second, the efficiency with which the WPA operated; and third, both the adequacies and inadequacies of WPA as a relief agency.

The integration of WPA with other federal agencies was not as successful as it could or should have been. Haste in starting the program was one factor limiting cooperation. Haste in itself can at times be helpful, indeed, necessary. It is difficult, and some claim impossible, to prove that the haste in starting WPA was necessary. It occurred because of President Roosevelt's failure to designate in the early spring of 1935 the nature of the work program being initiated. The President, plagued by many problems, was slow to indicate whether he favored primarily a vast public work program, or a work relief program. If he wanted both, as he did, a decision as to the relative weight to be given each should have been made. The strong personalities of Hopkins and Ickes, and the firmness with which each stood his ground, undoubtedly made any decision by Roosevelt very difficult. The vital emphasis given the program, coming in September, 1935, forced the WPA staff to rush the launching of projects before winter set in.

The entire organization of WPA made proper relationships with other agencies of the federal government essential if it was to be successful. These relationships existed in three areas: welfare activities like the Farm Security Administration; agencies giving technical assistance, such as the Public Health Service; and agencies actually assisting WPA in its own operations, i.e., the Treasury Department and the United States Employment Service.

Lack of adequate cooperation between the WPA and other federal agencies providing welfare services resulted in several thousand persons' receiving inadequate aid. An example is the failure of the Resettlement Administration (Farm Security Administration) and the WPA to agree on areas of activity. The WPA preferred to deal with the unemployed in populated areas, cities of 2,500 or more. The Resettlement Administration wanted to avoid being a relief agency, for its primary function was rehabilitating farmers to a point where they could carry on productive farming. People in need of relief and work who were caught in the gap of inadequate coverage, suffered even more than usual during the summer of 1935 when the WPA was not in full swing and the state FERA agencies were inadequately supplied with money. A definite decision as to who was responsible for these people was needed but never given.[1]

Part of the inefficiency in the WPA functions can be

attributed to the failure of the Office of the Comptroller General and the Treasury Department to expand their own staffs with sufficient speed during the summer and fall of 1935, and the failure of these central offices to decentralize and make appropriate changes in accounting and control procedures. These important federal offices, as staff offices having traditional practices and legal responsibilities to the President and Congress, found it difficult to move with the same flexibility as did WPA. Undoubtedly they should not have, for their functions and purposes were different. The administrators of these federal agencies and their staffs did not receive adequate direction from the President. Wanting to cooperate in the processes of procurement, payrolls, and accounting, they nonetheless had officials who seemed more interested in maintaining traditional procedures than adapting to new organizational patterns. Thus, the comptroller general eventually doubled his staff to assist in the expansion of the work program, but he refused to establish state offices to handle the great bulk of WPA records which had to clear through the comptroller's offices. Therefore quantities of records had to be sent from state WPA offices to the comptroller general's office in Washington to be processed in a setting remote from people who had pertinent answers to questions which arose as the staff worked with the forms. Had the General Accounting Office, under the direction of the comptroller general, established a staff member to work directly with WPA and treasury staff at the state office level, processing of projects could have been handled with more efficiency and speed.

In many instances the Treasury Department made efforts to decentralize and to expand as the work program expanded and as other federal agencies made additional calls for its service. Its traditional responsibility, and indeed a specific function for the President in this case, was that of providing an accurate record of expenditures and obligations.

The Treasury Department did carry out some decentralization, setting up state offices to work with the state WPA officials; however, it was for many months insistent in maintaining an elaborate accounting system duplicating in large measure the work of WPA accountants. For district offices within a state, the state treasury department office was too distant to secure the immediate facts needed in the day-by-day supervision of projects.

Other newly established federal agencies, the PWA, the RA, and offices in the Department of Agriculture, had difficulties working with the General Accounting Office and Treasury Department. Despite traditionalism and inertia, many staff members of these agencies did pitch in and attempt to meet the task. Many personnel of the General Accounting Office and Treasury Department worked extra hours to process WPA records. Key officers succeeded eventually in adjusting many procedures as a means of making the machinery meet the challenge. While major defects existed, all was not negative. Much was done in procurement and accounting which proved valuable to the WPA staff.

The uncertainties concerning the actions or possible actions of WPA and other agencies permeated functions at the state and local levels. Here, of course, the problems were of a slightly different nature. One of the most difficult problems for local and state relief officials was that of gauging how extensive WPA's operations were to be in any given week or month. If the rolls of WPA were expanded, then state and local relief agencies could often count on a lighter relief load. If WPA curtailed its operations, their load would become heavier unless economic conditions improved enough to offset the cuts made by WPA. Local and state relief agencies had the task of determining what local and state relief needs might be as determined by economic conditions, the impact floods, drought, or hurricanes might have, and what portion of the unemployed employables they must care for. President Roosevelt had said, when announcing the new work program, that only the federal government had sufficient power and credit to meet the unemployment situation and that it was assuming the task of placing unemployed employables at work.[2] The federal government was never able to do this completely. Records kept and published at the time show there were always 3,000,000 to 5,000,000 more workers unemployed besides those used by WPA. Later this situation as it relates more directly to the adequacy of WPA will be analyzed.

Time and money were, of course, important factors in coordinating and integrating the program on federal, state, and local levels. How long was the program to last? One year, two years, or a period of four or five years? No one could, would, or did say. As noted previously, it can be seen in retrospect that a program planned on a basis of three to seven years would have been more realistic. Limiting factors, including budgetary and political situations, determined that WPA would operate on a twelve-month pattern.

A natural result of short-term planning was that local and state relief officials and social workers accused WPA of indefiniteness in planning. The WPA staff was at times at fault, but uncertainties it faced made it difficult to provide definite information for state and local offices. Some local and state officials lacked the ability to judge what WPA might do in the next several months even though the amount of money WPA might have to spend over the nation was known. Had WPA been strictly a work agency rather than a relief and work agency, the Washington staff of WPA could have provided state WPA officials and local and state staffs better forecasts of its expenditures.[3]

The change from FERA to WPA in 1935 disrupted local relief organizations and their work. The procedures and techniques developed under the FERA had to be readjusted to state and local attitudes and influences. Confusion was added to a system which was only then emerging from a trial-and-error period. It is for this reason that some people felt Roosevelt and Hopkins made a serious mistake by launching WPA largely separate from local and state agencies and without adequate plans for liquidating FERA. Josephine C. Brown, an outstanding authority on local and state relief efforts as well as federal relief activities, refers to the period of transition in which relief was being turned back to the states as "a time of confusion and near chaos in the history of public relief." It was a time of uncertainty, insecurity, and even terror for the relief client who could secure no work relief and who had no sure niche in the developing categorical programs (social security, rural resettlement, or local relief). Suffering was acute in many sections of the country as funds for general direct relief were "inadequate or entirely lacking" in state after state.

The lack of an acceptable definition of an employable person caused serious difficulties in federal-state-local relationships. What was an employable person? Each individual could have his own opinion. Local relief offices often declared an applicant to be able-bodied and therefore not acceptable for relief. WPA officials might find this same person unemployable, however, if he or she could not fit into the WPA work program. Certain psychological handicaps resulted from labeling a man as unemployable. Governor Alfred Landon once said of this, "That is a terrible thing—arbitrary drawing of the line and branding a man as unemployable. That does something to that fellow." C. M. Bookman, himself at one time on the staff of FERA, said doing that killed "what little hope is left in the hearts of thousands of men that some day they may be once again independent workers providing for their own families." The answer to this problem did not lie, as some claimed, in not providing work; to employables and the able-bodied that would have been a more serious blow to morale than what did occur. The answer, without considering other factors, would have been to respond to the need, increasing expenditures to a level making possible work for all able-bodied who wanted work. Could you keep a man's morale high by telling him he was employable and not giving him anything to do? Many did not think so. Hopkins preferred to do away with means tests and with basic eligibility checks, putting those who could not find jobs in private employment at work on useful projects. If such an approach could have been used, much of the red tape in the administration of WPA would have been eliminated.[4]

Another vital factor in the relationships within WPA from the Washington staff down to the local level was politics. The opponents of WPA claimed federalization of WPA meant more politics than under locally administered relief. This attitude, summarized by Senator Frederick Steiwer of Oregon on one occasion, held that if relief were controlled locally, public money would be used to "feed hungry mouths and not to feed hungry political manipulators."

In practice it apparently makes little difference whether such a program is administered federally or locally. Politics operate in both systems. As previously pointed out, Hopkins did not have his major difficulties with politics at the top level until senatorial confirmation of key administrative officials was required. The accusations of political activity in WPA dealt mostly with politics at state and local levels. Politics in state and local relief offices under the grant-in-aid system of the FERA became so bad that in six states Hopkins and his staff took over administration of the relief agencies. The American Public Welfare Association discussion group observed in 1939 that in many local areas there was "inevitably . . . the worst kind of partisan manipulation of relief." This group cited several examples of maladministration. In the state of Pennsylvania, where some of the worst violations of WPA political regulations took place, state and local politicians had misused relief funds in 1932 and 1933. The handling of funds under the First Talbot Act passed in 1932 had resulted in large amounts of waste and graft and much political activity.

William H. Matthews, director at one time of the Association for Improving the Condition of the Poor, stated in reference to politics in relief: "The grossest irregularities that have been written of from time to time, not only as to relief of the unemployed but also in connection with the administration of the old age assistance act in certain states, have been due to the deviltry and dishonesty of local rather than federal administration." Use of public funds for political purposes seems to be not a problem of the level of administration, but of the honesty and integrity of individuals having a hand in the use of those funds. Fear of politics in a program sponsored by the federal government, if held in right proportion to other factors, can serve to keep the citizenry awake to possible exploitation by dishonest politicians. It is doubtful that undisputable facts clearly point toward the elimination of federal programs simply because there will be more (or even as much) politics in them as in state and local programs.

The second major area to be considered here in evaluating the administration of WPA is that of WPA as a work agency. Were the charges of inefficiency as true as its opponents would have people believe? Was WPA as efficient as its staff claimed? Were the projects reasonably well done? And what did WPA actually accomplish during the time Hopkins headed it?

The American people assumed up to 1933, and rightly so, that the most return for their tax money when used by government for public works would be obtained by certain traditional procedures.

The federal government used the contract bidding and letting system for public works projects. This was the typical pattern in private construction work as well. Government specifications and inspection helped govern the quality, making certain taxpayers received an adequate return on their investment in construction projects. As noted earlier, WPA did not use the contract system. Even if it had, the results could not have been the same as on other government projects. WPA, by the very nature of its assignment, used a high percentage of the unskilled and semiskilled, many of whom had had no previous experience doing the jobs assigned to them. Labor-saving equipment was not used to the same degree as on private or regular government construction projects handled by private contractors. It is evident, therefore, that although WPA workers were not as inefficient as many people claimed, a higher caliber of projects completed could be achieved best by such agencies as PWA or through a private contract letting system. WPA's particular function must be kept in mind: employment of people on the relief rolls.

WPA workers were not as inefficient as many claimed; however, if a higher caliber of projects and more efficiency in construction were the major objectives, public works sponsored and conducted by agencies such as the PWA would have been more logical.[5]

Many of the workers on WPA projects were honest, industrious workers, including many doing precisely the same type of work they had done most of their lives, but their efficiency was low because of some limiting factor, such as age. These the private contractors did not want to use, and did not use. An additional consideration is that much of the WPA work involved projects not normally handled by private contractors but by county and local government work crews or state employees not operating under a contract system. This type of work often appears to be less efficiently done than regular construction projects. Opponents of WPA often pictured the WPA worker posed leaning on a shovel. That some WPA workers deserved this is true, but to imply that the WPA workers were in most instances lazy and indifferent is to exaggerate. Colonel Harrington reported that in his twenty-five years of engineering experience WPA workers were as willing as any he had seen. Frequently, local officials reported the efficiency of WPA crews was higher than that of their own local public utility crews or civil service employees.

There were certain barriers inherent in the WPA program which prevented workers from being as efficient as they might have been in private employment. There was no hope of advancement for the majority of the workers, although some were selected for positions as supervisors and foremen, and others eventually returned to private employment. Supervisors often saw possibilities of positions in private employment; therefore, incentive was fairly good for some of these men. The workers were always fearful because of WPA's lack of sufficient funds to employ all the unemployed. There was no guarantee of a job. Thus, if workers knew funds were scarce in their locality, knew there had been talk by their superiors of no new projects being initiated, from a selfish point of view it was time to make the job last so they could have additional income for themselves and their families. The desire not to return to direct local relief was also a factor in workers' attempting to keep the project going.

The turnover of supervisory personnel impaired the efficiency of WPA. From the over-all point of view, turnover was a good indication; it meant the men of better caliber were going to positions in private employment. This gave WPA an opportunity to train new men for such positions. From these advancements came both good and bad situations. The efficiency of WPA projects often decreased, making them appear poorly organized. For the one leaving WPA, the new position might have been gained because of his experience and success on a WPA project. In essence, WPA always faced a shortage of competent supervisors because it could not draw them away from private employment by offering higher salaries. In all work relief activities the problem of proper supervision was one of the most difficult.[6]

Restrictions placed on supplies and equipment limited the efficiency of WPA. The National Appraisal Committee found in its study that if ample material and equipment were available, WPA workers kept busy.[7] Representative K. E. Keller pointed out that no worker could do efficient work without the proper materials and equipment. "It is nonsense to expect a different result" from WPA workers.[8] Some WPA authorities estimated that the costs of many WPA projects could have been cut by two-thirds if machinery normally used by contractors on such projects could have been used. WPA itself did not set the low material to labor ratio for its program, although it might have done more to oppose it. Congress, and the nature of the program as conceived at its beginning, determined the cost of materials and equipment per man per month. This situation was more acute in instances where local sponsors of projects agreed to provide all materials and equipment but did not do so. The severest critics of WPA, engineers sent out by congressional committees, agreed the construction work WPA workers had done was largely well done even if not completed as quickly or handled as efficiently as regular contract work.

Considering the obvious fact that much of the work was not of the best, the net results were and are yet today of lasting value to this nation. In places such as Fairmont, West Virginia, and Orland, Indiana, parks are still in use which were developed and made usable by WPA labor and funds. Millions of fish placed in this nation's streams and lakes since the mid-thirties have been hatched in WPA-built hatcheries. Since 1936 people have lived in houses along the river fronts in Cincinnati, Ohio, Evansville, Indiana, and other Ohio River towns in safety from floods which once ravaged their homes periodically. WPA-built flood control levees have in many instances more than paid for their cost. Doctors, lawyers, school teachers, and thousands of other professional people living today once attended schools built by WPA. Frequently some of the teachers were in the classroom because WPA assisted in the educational program of the community. As students in these schools these people were recipients of money earned as participants in the NYA program. Each year since 1936 thousands of Americans enter and leave post office buildings built by WPA. In nearly every county in the United States in the year 1942, one or more WPA projects of merit received daily use by residents of the area.

The third criterion which can be used in evaluating WPA is its adequacy as a relief agency. How much of its inadequacy was caused by poor administration? How much of WPA's failures were the result of the nation's not meeting fully the needs of the WPA staff? To those who maintain WPA was inadequate, those defending it say WPA progressed considerably from the system of traditional relief, and that it was not by any means what they would have liked to see accomplished. Hopkins and his staff could not control all the factors which made the program inadequate; nevertheless, basic policies were set forth by staff which had their effects on the efficiency of administrators throughout the entire organization.

WPA was inadequate in that it did not employ all the unemployed employables. At all times there were 350,000 to 900,000 unemployed certified for WPA employment but not used by WPA because of insufficient funds. Another

1,500,000 to 2,300,000 people were on relief, but not certified for WPA employment. Greater efficiency in operating WPA would have made more money available for placing more certified workers on projects. At most, however, this would have meant only a small increase in additional workers used as compared to the total wanting WPA employment. Additional funds were what WPA really needed to employ more people. Both Congress and the New Deal leaders were cautious in appropriations, desiring to keep expenditures within reason, and usually hoping the economy of the nation would improve sufficiently to eliminate federal work relief.

Many WPA workers did not earn the annual income intended by WPA administrators. Poor weather conditions, shifting of personnel from one project to another, and illnesses of the workers contributed to the failure of the pay scale to equal in many instances the budgetary deficiency standard set by relief authorities. Particularly for the semi-skilled, the total wages per year were often only 65 to 70 per cent of that originally intended. In the South the percentage was much lower. There the workers often received only 30 to 40 per cent of their total needs. Hopkins said in 1935, when defending the low wages agreed to for WPA: "You must remember that we are guaranteeing this wage—that is, the men and women will be paid whenever they show up for work, in spite of weather or other things that may hold up a project." This policy of paying WPA workers for time lost for which they were not responsible lasted only one year. During the time the prevailing wage was in effect (1936 to 1939) and workers were not paid for time lost for which they were not responsible, the idea of a security wage sufficient for family needs passed out of existence.[9]

Hopkins believed that "all families should receive the

same wages regardless of their size." [10] In other words, each WPA worker, no matter what the size of his family, received the same pay for his work as his fellow worker doing the same kind of job. One worker might have four dependents, the other six. Such a system was traditional in the United States, and WPA kept this approach as one means of making the WPA job seem like private employment. In this sense the policy was held by many to be correct. But WPA was not strictly a work agency. Thus, relief per case, as opposed to actual wages paid, was not well distributed. The emergency budget standard for relief needs was based on a family size of four. This was about all unskilled and semiskilled workers on WPA projects ever earned. As of June 15, 1940, an analysis of WPA workers showed that 47 per cent had families or dependents numbering more than four. On the other hand, many skilled WPA workers earned more than they needed for family needs, and they did this often in only a three-week working period, leaving the fourth week of the month free for loafing, for personal business, or for part-time employment.

Was it more important to maintain the principle of pay for work done rather than giving relief based on the size of the family? Many said the principle was more important, but Allen T. Burns, executive vice president of Community Chests and Councils (1942), and other representatives of the workers argued that since WPA was partly a relief organization in existence to aid the unemployed, fulfillment of basic needs of each family represented by a worker was the key objective.[11] Representative C. A. Woodrum of Virginia commented, in reference to the inadequacy of WPA wages, that they were like Billy Sunday's description of a guinea pig, "neither guinea nor pig." Similarly, said Woodrum, "security wages" was a misnomer "because a man on a WPA job could not possibly be in a more insecure position and I do not believe we can seriously dignify the amount of money that is paid him as wages."[12]

The seriousness of the defects in the WPA program vary. To an unemployed employable not securing work on WPA projects when he needed work, the lack of funds was serious. To a person declared ineligible because he was an alien, the eligibility requirements were unfair. To a person who honestly could see no value in giving work rather than cash relief, the extra expense of providing work relief was an administrative mistake by Hopkins and the President. To workers who did not receive sufficient amounts from WPA to meet family needs and could not receive aid from local relief stations because they were on WPA, the lack of proper wages was an administrative inadequacy. To workers who went without pay checks a few weeks in the New York City area because WPA decided to change the method of payment, another defect in administration was obvious. To those who thought the federal work program should place nearly every employable person on a project, the great reservoir of those in need who did not have work was real testimony to an inadequate program. To individuals who observed some of the inefficiency on WPA projects, there was poor supervision. But the WPA staff did get projects approved, did check quality of projects, and did place unemployed on projects in a sufficiently successful manner to make the total operation a success. Certainly if serious and widespread weaknesses had existed constantly, several developments would have resulted. They did not, which is evidence, although admittedly of a negative sort.

If WPA had been a failure, one of the first results would have been the insistence by the majority of congressmen that the program be curtailed and eventually brought to an end. This did not occur until the effects of World War II reduced the number of unemployed workers to a reasonable percentage of the working force. Second, the program would have served as a major campaign issue in 1940. WPA was the victim of many a campaign joke and jest; the opposition party did not recommend, however, that federal relief be abolished. Instead, the Republicans emphasized their view that after nearly eight years of New Dealism there was need for improvement in approaches to providing relief. Third, the reaction against WPA by the American public would have been stronger. At no time during the first five years of WPA's existence did a majority of the people indicate a desire to abandon WPA. Usually from 54 to 90 per cent thought WPA should continue. In a poll in 1937, in no section of the nation did more than 25 per cent of the people believe WPA should be eliminated. After WPA's first year of existence, 54.2 per cent of the people apparently believed WPA was "doing useful work." Only 13.5 per cent said it was not doing "useful work." [13] The National Appraisal Committee reported in 1939 the feeling about WPA in communities throughout the nation.

93 per cent: the work performed was badly needed and was of benefit

90 per cent: the work was of permanent value

79 per cent: their own local fiscal situation was improved as a result of WPA's activity

80 per cent: the work had maintained the skills and employability of many workers

85 per cent: the quality of the workmanship was good

75 per cent: the quality of the administration had been good [14]

Fourth, Congressional investigating committees would have found serious defects in the WPA program. The investigation of WPA by Congressional committees during the years 1938–40 did not result in well-documented, reliable charges of defective administration. Nor did these committees find any sizable scandal such as those which had occurred during the Grant and Harding administrations.

Fifth, scholars studying the administration of WPA would have concluded that it was poorly administered. They have not. Weaknesses have been noted in the over-all work program, and detrimental aspects of the WPA program have been revealed and analyzed. Two major studies indicate the program was "well administered." A third states the "WPA program . . . in light of evidence presented . . . appears to have been more efficient, more humane and less 'political' than if local and state authorities had been given a larger voice in its conduct." [15] A fourth study is much less favorable to WPA but questions the philosophy behind the WPA program rather than the administration of it. The only contemporary article of fundamental value was one published in *Fortune* in October, 1937. The authors of this article said WPA was administratively sound from the efficiency angle, but did not care for the worker adequately. They also noted the public had many misconceptions about WPA and its effect on the nation.

The evidence available makes clear that work relief was a controversial method of providing jobs and relief. It probably always will be. Work relief has a dual role—providing relief and jobs. Efficient relief and efficient work programs are incompatible in many areas of purpose and function. In attempting to administer this combination program, Hopkins and his staff made both minor and major mistakes, many through lack of foresight not uncommon in the direction of the activities of large government agencies and large corporations. Only a few defects or mistakes occurred because of political decisions or personal ambitions.

"Mr. Hopkins, lean, restless, imaginative former social worker, hard-boiled and sentimental at once, beloved by all who know him well, burning himself out on the altar of humane service."

—DELBERT CLARK

XII. Hopkins' Imprint

Harry L. Hopkins had more impact on relief in this nation during the 1930's than any other individual, including the President of the United States. Granting that Hopkins inherited an economic and social situation which prepared this nation psychologically for federal relief programs, and that he had supporting him a President who possessed an understanding of much he was trying to do, the fact remains that it was Hopkins who took the leading role in this nation in winning and keeping support for federal relief and work relief. Hopkins sifted through the many proposals for aiding the unemployed, particularly the unskilled, semiskilled, and white-collar workers, secured Roosevelt's support, implemented the programs, and administered them with a competent staff. Through his more modern social work approach he brought new concepts and procedures into being in local and state relief programs, making these agencies more humane than in the past. And it was Hopkins who bore the brunt of the political battles with Congress to secure funds for work relief programs in which he believed. Hopkins hated the "handout," the dole. He believed most Americans wanted to contribute to their nation's well-being. The federal government, if it represented the people, should assist in developing the means for our people to contribute to the growth of our economic life and the elimination of our social ills. To have had at the head of the federal relief administration a man without vision, determination, understanding, and sympathy would have been disastrous for millions of our people.

Hopkins arrived in Washington in 1933 believing a federally administered relief program could be as efficient as state and local relief programs, and as humanitarian. He wished to provide adequate relief, relief not limited to the prevention of starvation or mere subsistence. FERA raised the standards of relief throughout most of the United States, although at some stages in its development this was not the case. By the end of the thirties almost all public relief programs in the nation were more adequate in operation than they had been a decade before. Hopkins and federal relief performed a vital role in this development, providing a yardstick (FERA) against which to measure state and local relief standards. With the development of war production in the early forties and the resultant decrease in unemployment, relief programs became less common. WPA ceased operations in 1943. By this time Hopkins was busily engaged in the war effort, continuing to serve as a confidant for the President and as a troubleshooter carrying different titles from year to year.

Hopkins did not believe the threat of graft and politics in a federal relief program would be any worse than what he had known, heard of, or seen at the state and local levels. Many a man would have considered that on the federal level there would be a greater possibility of scandal which might ruin his career; Hopkins' attitude was that the job had to be done, whether the relief agencies were administered by local or state or federal authorities, or by all three. He also believed that honest people were essential to honest operation of any program or agency. Hopkins and his staff in Washington, working with hundreds of state and local administrators, showed a devotion to their task seldom equaled by any agency of our government.

Besides helping to put the federal government into relief work, Hopkins had much to do with the nature of the programs. First, his firm belief in work relief eventually dominated the entire character of the federal relief efforts. This was an important achievement. There was much vocal opposition to this approach, although the public did prefer it to the dole system. Second, Hopkins had a strong desire to have a variety of projects. He could see the need for (and, more important, was willing to risk the criticism involved) projects in art, music, and other areas of intellectual activity. He could not accept the idea that every unemployed person should dig with a shovel or push a wheelbarrow. One of the goals of the relief agencies became that of aiding men in keeping their skills and upgrading unemployed workers so they could serve society once they were back in private employment. Third, Hopkins, as much as any person other than Mrs. Roosevelt, kept Roosevelt's ear tuned to the one-third of the nation that was ill-housed, ill-fed, and ill-clothed. Hopkins' humanitarianism, which first attracted him to social work, never left him.

Many of Hopkins' critics charged that he was an opportunist who rode the Roosevelt bandwagon for whatever benefits he could reap. Others claimed he was nothing more than a playboy who liked to hobnob with the rich. Numerous newspaper columns during the thirties stressed Hopkins' liking for poker (with money bets), his "love" for the horses, and his spending time on Long Island and elsewhere at the estates of the known aristocracy of the nation. Hopkins, the poor boy from Iowa, the low-paid social worker, obviously did have a facet of personality and character that made him like these experiences. His involvement in them increased after the death of Barbara Hopkins in October, 1937. Heywood Broun, who wrote a few columns in which he referred to Hopkins as a race-horse fan and playboy, observed later, when Hopkins was named Secretary of Commerce, that he and other columnists had probably overplayed this aspect of Hopkins' life.[1] Actually, Hopkins spent a minor portion of his time and energy in these activities.

In fact, during the years 1933 to 1937 it would have been better for his own health had he done more relaxing and less work with long daily hours. It is easy to see, however, that some of Hopkins' social activities, his association with wealthy friends, and his candor in speaking caustically of his critics, worked to his disadvantage. Unfriendly columnists and editors depicted him for their readers in ways not conducive to his popularity. And by Hopkins' own admission, the fact stands that his political ambitions marred his work, during the year 1938 particularly. Typical of the many cynical and sarcastic evaluations of Hopkins is one which appeared in the Charleston (S.C.) *Daily Mail* as he was leaving the WPA. This editorial reads:

> A long and distinguished career as a member of the Socialist party, as an obscure social worker and finally as the head of the works progress administration which he brilliantly succeeded in converting into one of our national scandals eminently fits Mr. Harry Hopkins for his new position as secretary of commerce. Mr. Hopkins, however, has abundant reason to be thankful; he has been removed from the WPA and Colonel F. C. Harrington, an extremely able and honest official according to reports, has been appointed in his place.
>
> As a man who was second only to Mr. Harold (Honest Hal) Ickes in abusing business and private initiative, Mr. Hopkins is further fitted for a cabinet position that is closely identified with the nation's business. . . . As a man who said that his philosophy of government was to spend and spend, tax and tax, elect and elect, the new secretary of commerce undoubtedly will be a shining light restoring business confidence in cooperation with the . . . National Manufacturer's Association.[2]

In contrast to Hopkins' so-called playboy activities was his pervasive concern through all his years with the fulfilling of our responsibilities to society. Hopkins stressed this in his own life, to his staff, before charity organizations, in comments during many of his press conferences, and in several of his major addresses during his career. Success, leadership, and attainment of worthy goals did not depend on making the "fast buck" or engaging in frenzied and destructive competition. Hopkins told the 1937 graduates of Babson Institute:

> Most of your futures are assured. You have been favored with the destiny of leadership. How far you will go toward really achieving it depends on the way in which you meet your responsibilities.
>
> All over the country, this month, thousands of bewildered students are finishing college and university courses with no jobs to go to. For them, also, it is called "Commencement." Commencement of what? Perhaps of an endless round of futile interviews, ending in a breadline or on a WPA project.
>
> As you move from this institution into junior executive offices, what are you thinking about these other fellows? They have worked just as hard as you have—perhaps, in many cases, harder.
>
> You can tell them, "Root, hog, or die." You can deny moral responsibility. You can—but I don't believe you will. I believe you will recognize the barriers which this system built by your fathers has placed in front of them, and that you will come half-way. . . .
>
> To what higher purpose could you use your excellent training than the adjustment of this American system so that a decent minimum of its comforts is available even unto the least of its people.
>
> There was a certain carpenter of Galilee who had some very important ideas along this line. If you need guidance in the big job you face, I would recommend His teachings

> and philosophy. They are as good as new, they have been used so seldom.[3]

Hopkins' concern for his fellow Americans who were struggling for certain social equalities is also revealed in his sincerity, apparent to those who worked closely with him and to those who heard him talk. The intensity of his convictions made it difficult for him to follow his manuscript when giving speeches. President H. C. Byrd of the University of Maryland, certainly no close friend or great admirer of Hopkins, paid him a compliment in a letter.

> May I say further to you that instead of looking at you askance, the public, poor and rich alike, in reality believe in your sincerity and honesty of purpose. Some of the wealthy may say you have spent too much money, but not one have I heard ever express any question as to your ideals and sincerity. Several of my very rich friends have said, without approving all that you have done, "You can have confidence in Harry Hopkins as a man." [4]

In May, 1939, Hopkins spoke at the Governor's Day dinner held in Indiana. Eugene Pulliam, editor of the Republican Indianapolis *Star*, wrote Hopkins a short time later to this effect:

> The reaction to your talk has been amazingly onesided. Republicans and conservative Democrats in that group have been just as vocal in their praise and appreciation for your frankness as have your own liberal friends. I never saw a man completely convince a crowd of his sincerity as well as his keen sense of humor, as you did, and knowing what I do about you, I feel sure you would rather have left the impression of sincere devotion to your work and your ideals than anything else.[5]

Aubrey Williams pointed out to this writer that one of the prime requirements for any successful administrator in Washington is that of a tough, first-class mind. Hopkins had this. He was keen, sharp, wary, and had the ability to ferret out the important elements of a problem. He was, within his frame of reference, a great analyzer. He was not one to be stymied by traditions, regulations, and the like. He could, as Mrs. Roosevelt has said, come up in twenty-four hours with three or four fresh ideas for President Roosevelt in instances where other men would have little or nothing to offer except traditional thoughts. Along with creativity and originality went a personality which could be used to persuade people of the rightness of his concepts. He was a charmer in some instances. He knew the value of the psychological approach. He could also be direct and blunt when occasion demanded it.

Hopkins was able to delegate authority. He liked to put men on their own and to make them responsible. He did not believe it was his job to be a checker of assignments. As Aubrey Williams told this writer, Hopkins would "give you something to do and that was the last he had to do with it unless you got into trouble. . . . And if you got into too much trouble he would replace you." One of the greatest weaknesses an administrator can have is the inability to delegate authority, keeping himself too busy with details day in and day out. While Hopkins obviously fell victim to situations in which too many small items took his time, he did succeed through the years in concentrating on the larger aspects of his programs.

Probably Hopkins was better at organizing or launching an idea than at the actual day-by-day administration of it. He was more the originator who sparked the idea and got it going well enough so those who had the ability to run the day-by-day operation could work out the rough spots and have a smooth-running program. The importance of the ability to find new approaches and to devise new means of meeting new situations was crucial in the thirties, in the midst of this nation's worst depression. Many men would have been swamped by the magnitude of the situation, by political opponents, by doubts of personal ability, and would have twiddled their thumbs and sat about not knowing in what direction to go. This Hopkins did not do. He was a man of ideas and action.

In contrast to the criticism of Hopkins and the WPA which appeared in many newspapers throughout the country, there were several newsmen active on the Washington scene who held Hopkins and his administrative ability in high esteem. These men considered Hopkins one of the "finest public officials" Washington had seen in years, or as another said, "one of the best administrators of his generation." There are literally hundreds of similar comments scattered throughout the press of the day. They reflect the fact that Hopkins was certainly, in their opinion, more than an average administrator.[6]

Hopkins had the loyalty of his staff. His leadership was largely inspirational and personal. Most of the men and women believed in the programs they administered, but even more, they believed in Hopkins. Most of them had a deep, sincere admiration for him. There were petty jealousies among them at times. There were on occasion outright disagreements based on principles or on personality differences. Because of his sincerity and his own personal ability to achieve harmony, Hopkins managed to keep a highly capable staff together over a period of several years.[7] This was no small feat, since most of the top echelon could have had jobs with private concerns at salaries of two or three thousand dollars more per year (and in some instances even more) than they received while working with the government. Stanley High, after talking with many of Hopkins' staff, concluded it was in large measure Hopkins' own ability and his enthusiasm for his job which kept his organization running smoothly. Hopkins instilled devotion to the job which many administrators never develop in their subordinates. Without this type of leadership no organization can keep moving into new areas of endeavor and have continued vitality. As long as Hopkins was in good health, his organization in Washington was without doubt one of the best of all the prominent government agencies.

Hopkins was basically an honest administrator. There was no major scandal during his administration of the relief programs. He and his staff spent nearly $9,000,000,000 during the five years from 1933 to 1938. There were many cases of local and state manipulations which had to be taken to court or where the threat of legal action had to be used to correct the situation. But no major staff member in Washington ever had to resign because of fraudulent activities or graft. And, as noted earlier, the really nasty situations occurred where the influence of senators had resulted in weak appointments or where the pressure for dishonesty came from outside sources.

Hopkins was able to work effectively with his superior, Franklin D. Roosevelt. Those who have had no administrative experience may accept this fact without realizing its importance. It is one of the most important elements in administrative success, but often one of the most difficult to maintain. Hopkins seldom did anything which seriously jeopardized the New Deal program, even though Ickes, for example, argued at the time that Hopkins would cause the downfall of Roosevelt. At the same time, Hopkins did take criticism from the President, and on occasion he got negative responses from Roosevelt which he resented; however, his feelings were disciplined well enough so that usually he did not make a public issue of it. While Hopkins did have trouble with Ickes, and just lukewarm relationships with several other key administrators of the Roosevelt administration, Hopkins' relationship with other members of the Roosevelt team was of the type which caused Roosevelt little difficulty. In addition to this was the fact that Hopkins exhibited a deep loyalty to the President. He took many criticisms of his programs or actions at times which were the result of directives or requests from the President. This is difficult to do without complaining openly, particularly when the criticism is carried by papers and radio to the entire nation. Through the years Hopkins became more and more a personal adviser to the President, although, as Mrs. Roosevelt has said, he never enjoyed the relationship that Louis Howe did. Hopkins did not criticize Roosevelt in the same way Howe had done, and was more prone to do what Roosevelt desired without question, although by the late thirties on some occasions Hopkins stuck very strongly to his views even though they differed from those of the President.[8]

Charles C. Stillman, head of the FERA in Ohio for a time, and Director of the School of Social Administration at Ohio State University, wrote Hopkins in November, 1935:

> You seem to have, in great measure, some particular quality that can't well be described or defined, but which commands whole-hearted loyalty of those who are associated with you. . . . As a "boss" you have been exacting to the point of keeping us on our mettle. . . . On the other hand, you have always had such a keen appreciation of the difficulties your associates have to meet when they are out in the field that your judgments have been notably charitable. I count it the richest experience I have had in my life to have worked with you during these very trying times.[9]

These words help signify the importance of Hopkins and his administrative leadership. Only a man with above average ability and personality could shape major programs in the manner Hopkins did. His strong convictions were vital in giving direction to federal relief.

Today, in America there are literally millions of persons whose lives have been better physically and mentally because of the relief programs fought for and set forth by both Roosevelt and Hopkins. The fact that for a period of a few years they did not suffer further in loss of physical health, in discouragement over not having any type of work, is an important aspect of our national life which cannot be accurately measured, but which certainly contributed positively to this nation's social life. When one looks at the billions of dollars loaned abroad in the twenties by the large financial firms of this nation, and later the vast amounts spent during and after World War II and the resultant government debts the people of this nation have carried ever since, the money spent during the thirties for relief, work relief, and public works can scarcely be called a poor investment. Waste there was at times, and there were wrong decisions made. But to farmers using farm-to-market roads which were first made usable the entire year by WPA labor, to children who were taught by teachers paid for out of FERA or WPA funds, for towns and cities whose streets were repaired and improved, for the people in many areas across the land who since the thirties have ceased to suffer from floods, for the blind who learned to read from materials and teachers financed by the FERA and the WPA, for the high school and college youth who received additional education as a result of the NYA, for all of these and hundreds of thousands more, the money spent for relief and work relief was not a waste of the financial resources of this nation.

The federal government extended, largely through the efforts of Hopkins and his staff, a helping hand to the unemployed and the needy. The people did not lose faith in democracy and turn to other political ideologies. In those discouraging years when trained engineers, lawyers, teachers, businessmen, and in instances even medical doctors could not find employment, the powers of our federal government became visible to millions of Americans. Hopkins succeeded very well in extending encouragement and hope through our federal government to the unemployed. He made real something he strongly believed, that the federal government was theirs and that it could be used to aid them. If it can be held in retrospect that Alexander Hamilton, through his financial plans, kept the aristocracy of America aligned with our central government, it can also be said that Harry Hopkins served his nation well by originating and administering effectively programs which kept our unemployed in the thirties aligned with our federal government and loyal to our democratic way of life.

Notes

I. THE DIE IS CAST

1. Broadus Mitchell, *The Depression Decade* (New York: Rinehart & Co., 1947), pp. 97, 98; Basil Rauch, *The History of the New Deal* (New York: Creative Age Press, Inc., 1944), pp. 7, 8; Harry L. Hopkins, *Spending to Save: The Complete Story of Relief* (New York: W. W. Norton and Co., 1936), pp. 80, 81; Herbert Hoover, *The Great Depression, 1929–1941* (New York: The Macmillan Co., 1952), pp. 43, 44; W. S. Myers, ed., *The State Papers and Other Public Writings of Herbert Hoover* (Garden City: Doubleday, Doran, and Co., Inc., 1934), I, 133, 134; R. L. Wilbur and A. M. Hyde, *The Hoover Policies* (Charles Scribner's Sons, 1937), p. 370.

2. Cited in *Time*, XVII (February 9, 1931), 12.

3. *Time*, XVII (February 23, 1931), 12.

4. Hoover, *Great Depression*, pp. 55, 56; Myers, *State Papers . . . Hoover*, I, 412.

5. E. P. Hayes, *Activities of the President's Emergency Committee for Employment* (Concord: The Rumford Press, 1936), p. 43; Wilbur & Hyde, *Hoover Policies*, pp. 376, 377; W. S. Myers and W. H. Newton, *The Hoover Administration: A Documented Record* (New York: Charles Scribner's Sons, 1936), p. 112; *Time*, XVIII (August 10, 1931), 12.

6. *Time*, XVIII (August 31, 1931), 9.

7. *Time*, XVIII (October 19, 1931), 10, 11.

8. *Time*, XVIII (August 17, 1931), 7.

9. Hopkins MSS.

10. Hopkins, *Spending to Save*, pp. 56, 57; Edward A. Williams, *Federal Aid for Relief* (New York: Columbia University Press, 1939), p. 25; *Time*, XVIII (August 17, 1931), 7; T. G. Joslin, *Hoover Off the Record* (Garden City: Doubleday, Doran & Co., 1935), pp. 155, 156. The Hopkins manuscripts contain many reports pertaining to the Hoover relief program.

11. Herbert Hoover, "My White House Years: The Great Depression," *Collier's* CXIX (May 17, 1952), p. 36; Arthur Schlesinger, Jr., *The Age of Roosevelt* (Boston, Houghton Mifflin Co., 1958), I, 232.

12. Hoover, *Great Depression*, pp. 146, 147.

13. Wilbur and Hyde, *Hoover Policies*, pp. 279, 381, 384; Schlesinger, Jr., *Roosevelt*, I, 240.

14. Mitchell, *Depression Decade*, p. 110; William Leuchtenburg, *The Perils of Prosperity* (Chicago: University of Chicago Press, 1958), pp. 262, 263.

15. New York *Times*, August 29, 1931, 1:8; Daniel R. Fusfeld, *The Economic Thought of Franklin D. Roosevelt* (New York: Columbia University Press, 1956), pp. 177, 178.

16. Samuel I. Rosenman, ed., *The Public Papers and Addresses of Franklin D. Roosevelt* (New York: Random House; Macmillan Co., 1938–50), I, 625.

17. *Ibid.*, I, 646.

II. MEETING IMMEDIATE NEEDS

1. Robert E. Sherwood, *Roosevelt and Hopkins: An Intimate History* (New York: Harper & Brothers, 1948), pp. 14–37.

2. *Ibid.* p. 49; Raymond Clapper, "Who Is Hopkins?" *Forum*, XCVIII (December, 1934) 283–87; TC, W. W. Norton and Harry Hopkins, Hopkins MSS; Thomas Sugrue, "Hopkins Holds the Bag," *American Magazine*, CXXI (March, 1936), 27.

3. Washington *News*, October 26, 1935.

4. Lewis Meriam, *Relief and Social Security* (Washington: The Brookings Institution, 1946), pp. 9–11; Josephine C. Brown, *Public Relief, 1929–1939* (New York: Henry Holt & Co., 1940), pp. 1–38; FERA, *Unemployment and Relief Census* (Washington: Government Printing Office, 1934), pp. 1–17.

5. Williams, *Federal Aid for Relief*, pp. 72–96.

6. Sherwood, *Roosevelt and Hopkins*, pp. 22–37; Brown, *Public Relief*, pp. 145–49, 184–87; *Fortune*, XII (July, 1935), 64, 126; Williams, *Federal Aid for Relief*, pp. 67, 72–76, 88, 92, 93; FERA, *Monthly Report of the FERA* (May 22–June 30, 1933); Gertrude Springer, "The New Deal and the Old Dole," *Survey Graphic*, XXII (July, 1933), 348.

7. Hopkins to Roosevelt, printed in the *Monthly Report of the FERA* (December, 1933), pp. 8, 9; Williams, *Federal Aid for Relief*, pp. 189–95, 200, 201; File of Field Representatives, Hopkins MSS; New York *Times*, May 23, 1937, Sec. IV, 3: 4–6.

8. Press release, The White House, June 14, 1933, Hopkins MSS.

9. Cited in Dorothy Carothers, *Chronology of the Federal Emergency Relief Administration* (Washington: Works Progress Administration, 1937), p. 12.

10. Cited in Williams, *Federal Aid for Relief*, p. 188.

11. Hopkins to Roosevelt, July 7, 1933, and Roosevelt to Lehman, Roosevelt MSS, Official File 444.

12. Cited in the *Christian Science Monitor*, July 25, 1933.

13. *Expenditure of Funds, FERA*, Senate Document No. 56, 74th Cong., 1st Sess., p. xix.

14. Williams, *Federal Aid for Relief*, pp. 206–14; *Expenditure of Funds, FERA*, Senate Document No. 56, 74th Cong., 1st Sess., pp. xii, xiv.

15. Washington *Herald*, April 30, 1935; New York *Times*, May 1, 11, 1935; Washington *Post*, May 3, 1935; Chicago *News*, May 24, 1935; Cleveland *Plain Dealer*, May 25, 1935.

16. Chicago *News*, April 29, 1935.

III. TRIAL BALLOON: THE CIVIL WORKS ADMINISTRATION

1. Richard Hofstadter, *The Age of Reform* (New York: Alfred A. Knopf, 1955), p. 305.

2. Schlesinger, Jr., *The Age of Roosevelt*, II, 1–27; Rexford G. Tugwell, *The Democratic Roosevelt* (Garden City: Doubleday and Co., 1957), pp. 319–23; Edgar E. Robinson, *The Roosevelt Leadership, 1933–1945* (New York: J. B. Lippincott Co., 1955),pp. 25–138; Sherwood, *Roosevelt and Hopkins*, pp. 50–52; Robert Post, "Grappling With the Vast Problems of Relief," New York *Times*, July 8, 1934, Sec. VI, pp. 3, 18; Paul W. Ward, "Dirge for Mr. Hopkins," *The Nation*, CXL (May 22, 1935), 594–96; Aubrey Williams to me, October 16, 1952; interview with Lorena Hickok, July 16, 1958.

3. New York *Times*, November 26, 1933, Sec. IV, 1.

4. Lorena Hickok to Hopkins, November 11, 25, 1933, Hopkins MSS.

5. New York *Times*, December 1, 2, 1933, 1.

6. C. Gill, "The Civil Works Administration," *Municipal Year Book*, IV (1937), p. 426.

7. *Ibid.*, pp. 426, 427; *Expenditure of Funds, FERA*, Senate Document No. 56, 74th Cong., 1st Sess., p. ix.

8. Hopkins' testimony before Bureau of the Budget officials, January 22, 1934, Hopkins MSS; Williams, *Federal Aid for Relief*, p. 120; Gill, *Municipal Year Book*, IV (1937), 422–24; Marvin H. McIntyre to Congressman A. W. Edmonds, January 29, 1934, Roosevelt MSS, Official File 444; Walter Wilbur, "Special Problems of the South," *The Annals*, CLXXVI (November, 1934), 53; *Fortune*, X (October, 1934), 146.

9. Mitchell, *Depression Decade*, p. 317; statement by Hopkins, staff meeting, December 6, 1933, Hopkins MSS.

10. February 12, 1934, Hopkins MSS.

11. Costigan to Hopkins, November 13, 1933, Hopkins MSS.

12. Hopkins to Pierce Williams, July 5, 1933, Hopkins and P. Williams, TC, July 8, 1933, Most Reverend Edward J. Hanna of San Francisco to Hopkins, July 5, 1933 (in support of Branion), Mary Barnum to Mrs. Harold Ickes, December 14, 1933, Lorena Hickok to Hopkins, June 27, 1934, P. Williams to Hopkins, July 11, 1933, telegram, McAdoo to Farley, July 11, 1933, P. Williams to Hopkins, December 28, 1933, all in Hopkins MSS.

13. New York *Times*, January 21, 1934, Sec. IV, p. 6; Lorena Hickok to Hopkins, TC, September 9, 1934, Hopkins MSS; Hopkins to M. H. McIntyre, July 2, 1934, Roosevelt MSS, Official File 444; Branion and Hopkins, TC, June 23, 1934, Hopkins MSS; Los Angeles *Examiner*, October 9, 1934; Branion and Hopkins, TC, June 23, 1934, Hopkins MSS; Alan Johnstone and Hopkins, TC, November 6, 1934, Hopkins MSS; Williams, *Federal Aid for Relief*, p. 157.

14. J. Edmonds to Hopkins, December 30, 1934, Hopkins MSS; Howard O. Hunter to Hopkins, December 19, 1933, Hopkins MSS; Harold Ickes to R. J. Dunham, March (n.d.), 1934, Hopkins MSS; Johnstone, report to CWA officials in Washington, February 3, 1934, Hopkins MSS; Lorena Hickok to Hopkins, November 24, 1933, Roosevelt MSS, Official File 444; staff meeting notes, December 11, 1933, Hopkins MSS; New York *Times*, January 23, 24, 25, 28, 1934; Baltimore *Sun*, January 23, 1934.

15. Broadcast, NBC, November 27, 1933, Hopkins MSS; CWA Reports, Press Release No. 423, Division of Information, WPA, National Archives; Roosevelt MSS, Official File 444.

16. *Time*, XXII (February 19, 1934), 12, 13.

17. Washington *Star*, February 1, 1934.

18. Hopkins' datebooks, Hopkins MSS; New York *Times*, February 8, 1934, p. 8; Baltimore *Sun*, January 23, 1934; Sherwood, *Roosevelt and Hopkins*, p. 56; Portland *Oregonian*, February 4, 1934.

19. New York *Times*, February 8, 11, 12, 1934; Rosenman, *Public Papers of FDR*, II, 458; Sherwood, *Roosevelt and Hopkins*, p. 56; Mitchell, *Depression Decade*, p. 318.

20. Original report, in Hopkins MSS.

IV. MATTRESSES, SAFETY PINS, AND POLITICS

1. *Time*, XXIII (February 19, 1934), 12; staff meeting report, August 8, 1934, Hopkins MSS; telegram from the American Association of Social Workers to President Roosevelt, May 14, 1934, Hopkins MSS; notations concerning mayors' conference, Hyde Park, September 24, 1934, Hopkins MSS; *Fortune*, X (October, 1934), 152; Brown, *Public Relief*, p. 241.

2. FERA, *The Emergency Work Relief Program of the FERA* (Washington: Federal Emergency Relief Administration, 1935), p. 1; Hopkins, *Spending to Save*, p. 105.

3. Press conferences, June 22 and July 20, 1934, Hopkins MSS.

4. A. Williams to Hopkins, July 25, 1934, Hopkins MSS; Detroit *News*, October 9, 1934; New York *Times*, October 9, 1934.

5. Press conference, April 4, 1935, Hopkins MSS.

6. April 6, 1935.

7. Harry L. Hopkins, "Boondoggling: It is a Social Asset," *Christian Science Monitor* (Magazine Section), August 19, 1936.

8. Memo, Roosevelt to Hopkins, March 6, 1935, Roosevelt MSS, Official File 444; Peters to Hopkins, April 13, 1935, Roosevelt MSS, Official File 444; Guffey to J. Farley, January 22, 1934, Roosevelt MSS, Official File 444.

9. December 31, 1934, Hopkins MSS.

10. August 3, 1933, Hopkins MSS.

11. June 22, 1933, Hopkins MSS.

12. August 9, 1933; report to Hopkins from A. Williams, August 16, 1933; Report of Professor Bond on Texas situation, Hopkins MSS.

13. Olson to Hopkins, October 16, 1934; Hopkins MSS; Hopkins to Olson, October 17, 1934, Hopkins MSS; Mrs. E. Roosevelt to Hopkins with an enclosure from Elizabeth Gardner, Assistant Professor of Sociology, University of Minnesota, December 6, 1934, Hopkins MSS; Washington *Herald*, March 21, 1934; *Kansas City Star*, March 28, 1935.

14. Mark Grossman to Hopkins, December 11, 1934; Grossman and Hopkins, TC, December 17, 1934, Hopkins MSS; Governor Davey and Hopkins, TC, January 19, 1935, Hopkins MSS.

15. Grossman and Hopkins, TC, December 17, 1934, Hopkins MSS; Charles Stillman and Kathryn Godwin (Hopkins' secretary), TC, February 1, 1935; Stillman to Hopkins, February 22, 1935, Hopkins MSS.

16. Davey to Hopkins, March 4, 1935, Hopkins MSS; Hopkins to Davey, March 8, 1935, Hopkins MSS.

17. March 7, 1935.

18. March 15, 1935, Hopkins MSS.

19. March 16, 1935, Roosevelt MSS, Official File 444.

20. *Ibid.*

21. Roosevelt MSS, Official File 444, Wyllie to Roosevelt, March 8, 1935, Francis W. Durbin to Roosevelt, March 8, 1935, telegram to Roosevelt from Ohio State Legislature, March 14, 1935.

V. A VARIETY OF INTERESTS

1. *Time*, XVI (October 4, 1933), 3; Roosevelt MSS, Official File 444, memo, Roosevelt to Henry Wallace, September 11, 1933, press release, September 22, 1933, memo, Hopkins to Roosevelt, August 3, 1933; Meriam, *Relief and Social Security*, p. 329.

2. Lorena Hickok to Hopkins, November 10, 1933, Hopkins MSS; press conference, June 22, 1933, Hopkins MSS; *Fortune*, X (October, 1934), 155.

3. Press conference, September 18, 1934, Hopkins MSS; Meriam, *Relief and Social Security*, p. 337; F. H. Walton to Jacob Baker, February 13, 1935, Hopkins MSS; minutes of the meetings of the FSRC, October 24, 1935, Hopkins MSS.

4. Hopkins, *Spending to Save*, pp. 133, 134; address, Hop-

kins, October 29, 1933, Hopkins MSS; Brown, *Public Relief*, pp. 260–62.

5. Hopkins, *Spending to Save*, pp. 130–36; press conference, August 15, 1935, Hopkins, MSS; Brown, *Public Relief*, p. 261.

6. Hopkins, *Spending to Save*, pp. 139–47; Lorena Hickok to Hopkins, April 7, June 7, 1934, Hopkins MSS; Washington *News*, February 28, 1935; press conference, October 26, 1934, Hopkins MSS; Hopkins to Roosevelt, March 13, 1935, Roosevelt MSS, Official File 444; A. Williams, press conference, July 20, 1934, Hopkins MSS; New York *Times*, October 6, 1934; Meriam, *Relief and Social Security*, pp. 284–86; H. Rutzebeck to Jacob Baker, May 31, 1934, Hopkins MSS; Hopkins to John N. Garner, June 24, 1935, Hopkins MSS.

7. Telegram, Osborn to FERA headquarters, July 9, 1935, Roosevelt MSS, Official File 444; Binghamton *Press*, February 8, 1936; file of reports on Matanuska Project, Roosevelt MSS, Official File 1779.

8. Hopkins, *Spending to Save*, p. 147; Atlanta *Journal*, October 10, 1934.

9. Hopkins, address, National Democratic Club, December 15, 1934, Hopkins MSS; press release, December 25, 1934, Roosevelt MSS, Official File 444; New York *Times*, May 30, 1934, II.

10. Hopkins' diary, entry of March 15, 1936, Hopkins MSS; radio address, Hopkins, March 16, 1935; Executive Order 6757, June 29, 1934, Hopkins MSS; report to President by the Committee on Economic Security, Roosevelt MSS, Official File 1086; Sherwood, *Roosevelt and Hopkins*, p. 63.

11. St. Louis *Dispatch*, August 23, 1934; press conference, August 24, 29, 1934, Hopkins MSS; Hopkins and Others, *Security* (December, 1934); *Time*, XXIII (February, 1934), 11; New York *Times*, July 20, 1934, p. 14; Sherwood, *Roosevelt and Hopkins*, p. 49.

12. Sugrue, *American Magazine*, CXXI (March, 1936), 150; John F. Carter, *The New Dealers* (New York: Simon and Schuster, 1934), p. 184.

VI. ANGLING, PLANNING, AND WRANGLING

1. New York *Times*, December 2, 1934, Sec. IV, 1.
2. Charles Beard, "Confusion Rules in Washington," *Cur-*

rent History XLI, 333; New York *Times,* November 9, 1934, pp. 1, 2; Arthur Krock, New York *Times,* November 18, 1934, Sec. IV, p. 1.

3. New York *Times,* November 20, 1934, p. 3, December 2, 1934, p. 1.

4. Rauch, *History of the New Deal,* pp. 137–39; see New York *Times,* November 18, 19, 20, 27, 1934; interview with Benjamin V. Cohen, December 30, 1958.

5. TC, Hopkins MSS.

6. Sherwood, *Roosevelt and Hopkins,* p. 65; Harold Ickes, *The Secret Diary of Harold L. Ickes* (New York: Simon and Schuster, 1953), pp. 194–201; Raymond Moley, *After Seven Years* (New York: Harper and Brothers, 1939), pp. 296–99.

7. Sherwood, *Roosevelt and Hopkins,* pp. 80, 81; Schlesinger, Jr., *The Age of Roosevelt,* III, 15–210.

8. *Cong. Record,* 74th Cong., 1st. Sess., Part I, 79: 94, 95.

9. Washington *Post,* March 24, 1935; Washington *Herald,* April 6, 1935.

10. *Cong. Record,* 74th Cong., 1st Sess., Part I, 79: 820.

11. *Ibid.,* Part I, 79: 1931.

12. U.S. Congress, Senate Committee on Appropriations, 74th Cong., 1st Sess., *Hearings on Emergency Relief Appropriation,* pp. 43, 44.

13. *Cong. Record,* 74th Cong., 1st Sess., Part II, 79: 2014, 2016.

14. *Ibid.,* Part I, 79: 1928.

15. *Ibid.,* Part I, 79: 825.

16. Based on summation of letters in the Hopkins MSS and the Roosevelt MSS, Official File 1435. See Walter Lippmann's column, New York *Herald Tribune,* February 28, 1935.

17. Roosevelt to John N. Garner, March 31, 1935, Roosevelt MSS, Official File 1435; A. W. Macmahon, J. D. Millett, and Gladys Ogden, *The Administration of Federal Work Relief* (Chicago: Public Administration Service, 1941), p. 64; hereafter cited as *Federal Work Relief.*

18. *Cong. Record.* 74th Cong., 1st Sess., Part I, 79: 820; Part II, 79: 1931, 1932, 2018.

19. Ickes, *Diary,* I, 264, 265, 266.

20. Hopkins' diary, entries of January 6, 8, 1935, Hopkins MSS.

21. Ickes, *Diary,* I, 286, 287, 293, 327, 328, 330, 337.

22. *Ibid.*, I, 338, 339; Early to Roosevelt, April 3, 1935, Roosevelt MSS, Official File 1435.

23. Ickes, *Diary*, I, 341.

24. Hopkins to Roosevelt, April 8, 1935, Roosevelt MSS, Official File 1435.

25. Roosevelt MSS, Official File 1435.

26. Ickes, *Diary*, I, 341, 342, 343, 355, 358; Sherwood, *Roosevelt and Hopkins*, pp. 69, 70; Schlesinger, Jr., *Age of Roosevelt*, III, 344–49.

27. Hopkins to Roosevelt, April 17, 1935, Roosevelt MSS, Official File 1435.

28. Hopkins to Roosevelt, July 25, 1935, Hopkins MSS.

29. Hopkins MSS; Ickes, *Diary*, I, 348, 352.

30. Draft of Speech, May 7, 1935, Hopkins MSS.

31. Ickes, *Diary*, I, 360, 361, 366, 370, 371, 378; Hopkins' diary, entry of May 14, 1935, Hopkins MSS.

32. New York *Times*, June 21, 1935.

33. Press conference, June 20, 1935, Hopkins MSS.

34. Ickes to Roosevelt, June 26, 1935, Hopkins MSS.

35. Roosevelt to Hopkins, June 28, 1935, Hopkins MSS; Ickes, *Diary*, I, 387, 388.

36. Ickes, *Diary*, I, 412, 413, 414, 420, 422, 424, 429, 434.

37. TC, September 10, 1935, Hopkins MSS; New York *Daily News*, September 11, 1935.

38. Ickes to Roosevelt, September 7, 1935, Roosevelt MSS, President's Secretary File.

39. Roosevelt MSS, President's Personal File.

40. Ickes, *Diary*, I, 438.

41. Hopkins MSS.

42. John M. Blum, *From the Morgenthau Diaries: Years of Crises, 1928–1938* (Boston: Houghton Mifflin Co., 1959), p. 248.

VII. THE WORKS PROGRESS ADMINISTRATION

1. Macmahon, Millett, and Ogden, *Federal Work Relief*, p. 212.

2. Newspaper clipping, Hopkins MSS.

3. Stanley High, *Roosevelt—And Then?* (New York: Harper and Brothers, 1937), pp. 134, 153; Macmahon, Millett, and

Ogden, *Federal Work Relief*, pp. 191, 192, 197, 212; A. Williams to me, October 16, 1952; Hopkins to assistant administrators, August 8, 1935, WPA-100, National Archives; Stone to Hopkins, October 30, 1935, WPA-100, National Archives.

4. *Proceedings*, Conference of State Administrators (June 17, 1935), Hopkins MSS; *Proceedings*, Staff Conference (June 16, 1935), Hopkins MSS; Macmahon, Millett, and Ogden, *Federal Work Relief*, p. 217.

5. *Ibid*., 197–99, 235, 236; WPA-64, September 30, 1935, WPA-600, National Archives; *Preliminary Instructions to State Works Progress Administrators, Bulletin No*. 3, June 24, 1935, WPA-600, National Archives; *Proceedings*, Field Representatives Conference (December 28, 1935); Donald S. Howard, *The WPA and Federal Relief Policy* (New York: Russell Sage Foundation, 1943), pp. 109, 110; hereafter cited as *The WPA*.

6. Macmahon, Millett, and Ogden, *Federal Work Relief*, pp. 212, 236–38; *Fortune*, XVI (October, 1937), 42.

7. Works Progress Administration, *Final Report on the WPA Program, 1935–1943* (Washington Government Printing Office, 1943), p. 10; Division of Information, WPA, 1939, National Archives; *Cong. Record*, 75th Cong., 1st Sess., Part I, 81:760; Howard, *The WPA*, pp. 121, 122.

8. New York *Times*, August 9, 1935; Hopkins and Mayor Kelley of Chicago, TC, September 19, 1935, Hopkins MSS; Hopkins to Roosevelt, July 25, 1935, Hopkins MSS; Macmahon, Millett, and Ogden, *Federal Work Relief*, pp. 95–100, 117, 118; see also articles by Robert S. Brown, Pittsburgh *Press*, last week of July, 1935.

9. Cited in Sherwood, *Roosevelt and Hopkins*, p. 80.

10. Lorena Hickok to Hopkins, December 21, 1935, Hopkins MSS.

11. Donald C. Stone to Hopkins, October 30, 1935, WPA-100, National Archives.

12. Macmahon, Millett, and Ogden, *Federal Work Relief*, p. 313; New York *Times*, September 22, 1935; *Bulletin No*. 33 (September 28, 1935), WPA-600, National Archives; telegram to state administrators, September 20, 1935, WPA-600, National Archives; letter to state administrators, September 30, 1935, WPA-600, National Archives.

13. National Resources Planning Board, *Security, Work and Relief Policies* (Washington: Government Printing Office,

1942), p. 39; *Bulletin No. 6* (June 28, 1935), WPA, Hopkins MSS.

14. Macmahon, Millett, and Ogden, *Federal Work Relief*, p. 126; *Proceedings*, Conference of State Administrators, June 17, 1935; Roosevelt to Congressman Sol Bloom, June 6, 1938, Roosevelt MSS, Official File 444-misc.; General Letter No. 193, Hopkins to state administrators, July 12, 1938, Hopkins MSS; Meriam, *Relief and Social Security*, pp. 367, 369; Bakke, *The Unemployed Worker*, p. 422; Howard, *The WPA*, pp. 486, 488; Hopkins, "The WPA Looks Forward," *Survey Midmonthly*, LXXIV (June, 1938), 195.

15. Bakke, *The Unemployed Worker*, p. 422; Meriam, *Relief and Social Security*, p. 379.

16. *Hearings on First Deficiency Appropriations Bill for 1937*, 75th Cong., 1st Sess. (1937), pp. 78, 79; press conference, April 28, 1938, Hopkins MSS.

17. Howard, *The WPA*, pp. 172–78, 216, 217; Macmahon, Millett, and Ogden, *Federal Work Relief*, pp. 133, 151; Mitchell, *Depression Decade*, pp. 323, 324; Executive Order 7046, May 20, 1935, Hopkins MSS; Gill to Hopkins, February 7, 1935, Hopkins MSS; Lorena Hickok to Hopkins, July 24, 1935, Hopkins MSS; press conferences, May 22, September 19, 1935, Hopkins MSS; Administrative Work Order No. 24, September 19, 1935, WPA-100, National Archives; *ibid.*, No. 33, November 9, 1935, WPA-100, National Archives; *Hearings on First Deficiency Appropriations Bill for 1936*, 74th Cong., 2nd Sess. (1936), p. 28; Committee on Unemployment and Relief, U.S. Senate, *Preliminary Report*, 75th Cong., 3rd Sess., Report No. 1625, p. 7; National Resources Planning Board, *Security, Work and Relief Policies*, pp. 177, 178.

18. *Administration and Operation of the National Youth Administration, June 26, 1935–January 1, 1937* (NYA, n.d.), pp. 1–11.

19. New York *Herald Tribune*, June 26, 1935; Washington *Herald*, July 7, 1935; Johnson to Roosevelt (n.d.), Roosevelt MSS, President's Secretary File; New York *World Telegram* and Washington *Times*, August 9, 1935; Hopkins and Johnson, TC, August 7, 1935, Hopkins MSS; Johnson to Roosevelt, September 13, 1935, Roosevelt MSS, President's Secretary File; memo, Johnson to Hopkins, October 26, 1935, Hopkins MSS.

20. Milford to Hopkins, April 16, 1936, Hopkins MSS;

Washington *News*, April 16, 1936; press conference, October 31, 1936, Hopkins MSS.

VIII. FLUCTUATING WPA ROLLS

1. Macmahon, Millett, and Ogden, *Federal Work Relief*, p. 23.

2. *Ibid.*, pp. 134, 135; General Letter No. 181, Hopkins to state administrators, June 27, 1938, Hopkins MSS.

3. New York *Times*, April 11, 1937, Sec. IV, p. 7.

4. Washington *News*, 1937; press conference, May 6, 1937, Hopkins MSS; New York *Times*, June 22, 1937, p. 22.

5. Appointment book, Hopkins MSS; New York *Times*, May 28, 1937, p. 14.

6. Daniel Bell and Hopkins, TC, May 25, 26, 1937, Hopkins MSS; Governor Earle of Pennsylvania and Hopkins, TC, May 26, 1937, Hopkins MSS.

7. Mayor LaGuardia of New York City and Hopkins, TC, June 15, 1937, Governor Leche of Louisiana and Hopkins, TC, June 16, 1937, Governor White of Mississippi and Hopkins, TC, June 16, 1937, Hunter and Hopkins, TC, June 15, 1937, all in Hopkins MSS.

8. New York *Times*, June 22, 1937, p. 22.

9. Roosevelt to Hopkins, August 29, 1937, WPA-100, National Archives; Dewey, address, March 28, 1940, as reprinted in *The Case Against the New Deal* (New York: Harper and Brothers, 1940), pp. 93, 94; T. S. Woofter and T. L. Whiting, *Summary of Relief and Federal Work Program Statistics, 1933–1940* (Washington: Government Printing Office, 1941), p. 48.

10. Mitchell, *Depression Decade*, p. 95; National Resources Planning Board, *Security, Work and Relief Policies*, pp. 129, 238.

11. *Report on Progress of the WPA Work Program* (June 30, 1938), p. 33; Hopkins' staff report to President Roosevelt, February 13, 1937, Roosevelt MSS; President's Secretary File; *Hearings in First Deficiency Appropriations Bill for 1937*, 75th Cong., 1st Sess. (1937), p. 76.

12. *Cong. Record*, 75th Cong., 1st Sess., Part I, 81:748.

13. New York State Temporary Emergency Relief Adminis-

tration, *Five Million People; One Billion Dollars* (Albany: New York State ERA, 1937), p. 15.

IX. POLITICS GALORE

1. *Roosevelt—and Then?*, pp. 135, 136.
2. Hopkins MSS.
3. Cited in the Wichita *Eagle*, December 11, 1935; *Proceedings*, Conference of State Administrators, June 17, 1935, Hopkins MSS.
4. *Hearings on First Deficiency Appropriations Bill for 1936*, 74th Cong., 2nd Sess., Part II, p. 230; James Roosevelt to Hopkins, June 1, 1935, Hopkins MSS.
5. Macmahon, Millett, and Ogden, *Federal Work Relief*, p. 270; Frank Kent, Salt Lake *Tribune*, June 22, 1935.
6. Macmahon, Millett, and Ogden, *Federal Work Relief*, p. 271.
7. *Ibid.*, pp. 271, 274.
8. December 13, 1935, Hopkins MSS; interview with Mrs. Eleanor Roosevelt, June 2, 1951.
9. Lorena Hickok's letters to Hopkins, many 10 to 15 pages, provide a wealth of information concerning social, economic, and political events during the years 1934 and 1935.
10. Hopkins to state administrators, March 13, 1936, Hopkins MSS.
11. General Letter No. 72, WPA, Williams to state administrators, September 1, 1936, Hopkins MSS.
12. General Letter No. 2, WPA, February 21, 1936, Hopkins MSS; General Letter No. 176, February 15, 1938; Hopkins and M. Miller, TC, January 2, 1936, Hopkins MSS.
13. Hopkins' address, "Politics and the WPA," May 8, 1938, Hopkins MSS; press conference, April 28, 1938, Hopkins MSS.
14. Macmahon, Millett, and Ogden, *Federal Work Relief*, pp. 281, 282.
15. Hinckley and Hopkins, TC, December 29, 1935, Hopkins, MSS; Washington *Times*, July 16, 1935; Portland (Maine) *Press Herald*, July 23, 1935; Hopkins to William Fray, secretary to the Postmaster General (James Farley), June 22, 1936, Hopkins MSS.

16. Roosevelt to Hopkins, June 11, 1934, Roosevelt MSS, Official File 444-c; M. Miller and Hopkins, TC, March 3, 1936, Hopkins MSS; Senator Bilbo to Roosevelt, March 27, 1937, marginal notation by MHM (Marvin McIntyre) on a memo, June 13, 1938, Senator Bilbo to Roosevelt, August 20, 1938, all in Roosevelt MSS, Official File 444-c.

17. Hopkins to editor of Reno *Evening Gazette,* August 4, 1938, Hamnel and Hopkins, TC, April 2, 1936, Jacobsen and Hopkins, TC, April 17, 1936, all in Hopkins MSS; New York *Herald Tribune,* April 19, 1936; Seattle *Post Intelligencer,* April 18, 1936; press conference, April 16, 1936, memo, Roosevelt to Hopkins, April 12, 1936, Hunter and Hopkins, TC, March 19, 1936, Don Abel and Hopkins, TC, May 23, 1936, Lorena Hickok to Hopkins, September 13, 22, 1935, and March 25, 1936, Hopkins and Joe Stevenson of South Bend, Indiana, TC, April 24, 1936, Wayne Coy and Hopkins, TC, April 24, 1936, and May 8, 1936, all in Hopkins MSS; memo, Roosevelt to Hopkins, October 6, 1936, Roosevelt MSS, Official File 444-c; Coy to A. Williams, October 12, 1936, Senator Murray to Marvin McIntyre, January 14, 1936, Westbrook to Farley, July 22, 1935, Hopkins to Mrs. Roosevelt, December 13, 1935, Anna M. Brownyard to Farley, January 17, 1936, Hopkins to Farley, November 8, 1935, Westbrook to H. L. Pierson, state administrator of Michigan, October 16, 1935, Lorena Hickok to Hopkins, December 21, 1935, Westbrook to Hopkins, December 21, 1935, Westbrook to Hopkins, March 21, 1936, all in Hopkins MSS.

18. Hopkins and Rotch, TC, May 18, 1935, James Roosevelt to Hopkins, July 26, 1935, and August 26, 1935, Rotch to Westbrook, September 9, 1935, Westbrook to Hopkins, October 3, 1935, Farley to Hopkins, November 12, 1935, all in Hopkins MSS; Rotch to me, February 18, 1952.

19. Hopkins to Roosevelt, January 25, 1936, Paul Edwards and Hopkins, TC, January 31, 1936, both in Hopkins MSS.

20. Ray Branion and Hopkins, TC, March 26, 1936, Hopkins MSS.

21. Olson to A. Williams, August 1, 1935, memo for McIntyre, signed R. B., May 29, 1935, press conference, May 19, 1938, all in Hopkins MSS; Minneapolis *Journal,* January 12, 1939; Baltimore *Sun,* May 31, 1938; New York *Herald Tribune,* May 31, 1938; Christgau to Roosevelt, June 9, 1938, and Roose-

velt to Christgau, June 9, 1938, Hopkins MSS. Newspapers in the area were strong for Christgau. See Scrapbook XVI, WPA, Hopkins MSS.

22. Lorena Hickok to Hopkins, November 3, 1935, Hopkins MSS.

23. Johnstone and Hopkins, TC, Hopkins MSS.

24. *Cong. Record*, 74th Cong., 2nd Sess., Part IV, 80:3668, 3669; report of Alan Johnstone to Hopkins, March 11, 1936, and Hopkins to Senator Rush Holt, March 10, 1936, Hopkins MSS.

25. *Cong. Record*, 74th Cong., 2nd Sess., Part IV, 90:3924.

26. *Ibid.*, 80:3667.

27. *Ibid.*, 80:3657.

28. *Ibid.*, 80:3926, 3668, 3669; Washington *Post*, March 12, 1936.

29. Curtis to Hopkins, May 21, 1936, Matt Murray and Hopkins, TC, May 25, 1936, Hopkins to Curtis, May 27, 1936, all in Hopkins MSS. Also included are copies of the report of the investigations conducted in Missouri.

30. Cited by Clapper, *Forum*, XCVIII (December, 1937), 285; Stark to Roosevelt, June 29, 1938, Stark and Hopkins, TC, July 19, 1938, Hopkins to Stark, July 22, 26, 1938, press conference, July 21, 1938, Harrington to Hopkins, May 31, 1939, Howard Hunter to Hopkins, May 31, 1939, all in Hopkins MSS.

31. A. Williams to me, October 16, 1952; F. C. Schaub to General R. E. Wood, June 21, 1935, Hopkins MSS; Lorena Hickok to Hopkins, July 24, 1935, Hopkins MSS.

32. New York *American*, March 10, 1936; Investigations—Politics, WPA, National Archives.

33. Hopkins to Vandenberg, March 5, 1936, Hopkins MSS.

34. April 29, 1936, Hopkins MSS and October 7, 1936, Hopkins MSS.

35. David Stern and Hopkins, TC, October 7, 1936, press conferences, October 8, 1938, and October 17, 1936, all in Hopkins MSS.

36. Roosevelt MSS, Official File 444.

37. Washington *News*, June 7, 1938; Baltimore *Sun*, June 10, 1938; New York *Times*, July 1, 1938; New York *World Telegram*, June 9, 1938; Washington *Daily News*, July 1, 1938.

38. Louisville *Times*, September 12, 1938; Hopkins to Sena-

tor Sheppard, WPA Release 4-1768, September 21, 1938, Hopkins MSS.

39. Knoxville *News Sentinel,* May 27, 1939; Howard, *The WPA,* pp. 750, 751; Washington *Daily News,* January 16, 1939.

40. July 7, 1935, Roosevelt MSS, Official File 444-c.

41. N. B. Donaher to Farley, September 11, 1936, Hopkins MSS.

42. December 21, 1935, and July 7, 1936, Hopkins MSS; November 8, 1935, Hopkins MSS.

43. Congressman Jerry Voorhis, "Whose Politics in Relief," *Social Work Today* (November, 1939), p. 3. Investigations—Politics, WPA, National Archives.

44. Westbrook to Hopkins, June 23, 1938, Hopkins MSS. This refers particularly to a discussion Westbrook had had with the editor of one of the leading newspapers in Memphis, Tennessee; Washington *News,* May 5, 1938; prepared statement of Hopkins for use in testifying before a House committee, November, 1938, Hopkins MSS.

45. Washington *Daily News,* March 19, 1936.

46. New York *Herald Tribune,* "He'll Boss America's Business," January 22, 1939; Washington *Daily News,* December 24, 1938, and January 16, 1939; Williams to me, October 16, 1952.

47. Interview with Mrs. Eleanor Roosevelt, June 2, 1951; interview with Lorena Hickok, July 16, 1958.

48. Macmahon, Millett, and Ogden, *Federal Work Relief,* pp. 285–88; *Cong. Record,* 76th Cong., 3rd Sess., Part IV, 86:3930; U. S. Congress, House of Representatives, Subcommittee on appropriations, *Investigation and Study of the Works Projects Administration,* 76th Cong., 3rd Sess., Report No. 2187, p. 263.

49. Bakke, *The Unemployed Worker,* p. 405; Howard, *The WPA,* pp. 113, 114, 118, 301, 302; A. Williams to me, October 16, 1952.

50. Williams to me, October 16, 1952.

X. PRESIDENTIAL ASPIRATIONS

1. Press conference, August 29, 1934, Hopkins MSS; Will Ross to Robert Sherwood (n.d.). Cited by Sherwood in *Roosevelt and Hopkins* (2 vols., New York: Bantam Books ed., 1950),

I, 530, 531; *Roosevelt and Hopkins*, pp. 80–88, gives a description of Hopkins' actions and reactions to the presidential campaign of 1936.

2. Lorena Hickok to Hopkins, March 2, 1936, Hopkins MSS.

3. Westbrook to Hopkins, September, 1936[?], Griffith to Farley, September 18, 1936, William Everson to the WPA office in Washington, September 19, 1936, Isidore Dockweiler to Farley, September 22, 1936, Jean Hard, Jr., to Farley (n.d.), all in Hopkins MSS. (The last letter was mailed September 23, 1936.) These letters are typical of many. The few dozen letters and memos in the Hopkins file which refer to Hopkins' activities in the campaign of 1936 left me with one major impression—that Hopkins believed deeply in WPA and therefore wanted to make the people appreciate its value and to combat false stories.

4. Cited in Sherwood, *Roosevelt and Hopkins*, pp. 84, 85.

5. Sherwood, *Roosevelt and Hopkins*, pp. 82, 87, 88; Hopkins, address, March 1, 1937, Hopkins MSS; Hopkins and Jerome Frank, TC, March 1, 1937; memo by Hopkins on the Supreme Court Plan of 1937 written by him in April, 1939, Hopkins MSS; James Farley, *Jim Farley's Story* (New York: Whittlesey House, 1948), p. 92.

6. Eleanor Roosevelt, *This I Remember* (New York: Harper and Brothers, 1949), pp. 167, 168; E. K. Lindley, Washington *Post*, October 26, 1938; Clapper, *Forum*, XCVIII (December, 1937), 286; A. Williams to me, October 16, 1952.

7. Cited in Sherwood, *Roosevelt and Hopkins*, p. 91; see also Will Ross to Robert Sherwood (n.d.), cited in Sherwood, *Roosevelt and Hopkins* (Bantam Books ed.), I, 530, 531.

8. Cited in the Washington *Herald*, May 19, 1936; interview with Mrs. Eleanor Roosevelt, June 2, 1951; St. Louis *Post-Dispatch*, January 22, 1939; Washington *Star*, April 18, 1938; Eleanor Roosevelt, *This I Remember*, p. 213; Marquis Childs, "The President's Best Friend," *The Saturday Evening Post*, CCXIII (April 19, 1941), 128; interview with Lorena Hickok, July 16, 1958.

9. Cited in Sherwood, *Roosevelt and Hopkins*, pp. 91, 92; Swope to Hopkins, December 15, 1938, Coffee to Hopkins, September 27, 1938, Tugwell to Hopkins, June 18, 1938, LaGuardia to Hopkins, August 18, 1938, all in Hopkins MSS.

10. Hopkins MSS.

11. Sherwood, *Roosevelt and Hopkins*, pp. 80, 92, 93; La-

Follette and Hopkins, TC, November 7, 1936, Hopkins MSS; Hopkins' Office Datebook, Hopkins MSS; Dr. George B. Eusterman to Roosevelt, January 15, 1938, Roosevelt MSS, President's Personal File, 4096; Hopkins to Mrs. R. (Dorothy) Stevenson, April 6, 1938, Hopkins MSS.

12. Washington *Post,* January 22, 1939; Washington *Star,* May 26, 1938; Providence *Journal,* May 27, 1938; Pittsburgh *Post-Gazette,* June 9, 1938.

13. New York *Herald Tribune,* July 22, 1938.

14. Washington *Post,* August 30, 1938.

15. September 21, 1938, Hopkins MSS; cited in Sherwood, *Roosevelt and Hopkins,* pp. 102, 103, Harry Hopkins to Lewis Hopkins, April, 1933; cited in Sherwood, *Roosevelt and Hopkins,* pp. 33, 34; address, Conference of State Administrators, October, 1937, Division of Information, WPA-B, National Archives; Washington *Star,* October 30, 1937; Leon Henderson to Hopkins, October 12, 1937, Hopkins MSS; New York *World Telegram,* December 19, 1938.

16. Howard Hunter to Hopkins, November 21, 1938, Hopkins MSS; Sherwood, *Roosevelt and Hopkins,* p. 111; Hunter to Hopkins, December 6, 1938, Hopkins MSS; Senator William Smathers of New Jersey to Hopkins, December 10, 1938, Hopkins MSS.

17. New York *World Telegram,* December 24, 1938; New York *Herald Tribune,* November 24, 1938; Polls by Gallup, *Fortune,* etc., December, 1938, March, 1939, August, 1939, September, 1939, February, 1940; Roper Poll, December, 1938. Cited in Sherwood, *Roosevelt and Hopkins,* p. 105.

18. Sherwood, *Roosevelt and Hopkins,* p. 92; interview with Mrs. Eleanor Roosevelt, June 2, 1951; interview with Lorena Hickok, July 16, 1958.

XI. THE TASK: WELL DONE?

1. Macmahon, Millett, and Ogden, *Federal Work Relief,* pp. 392–95.

2. Cited in the New York *Times,* January 5, 1935.

3. Meriam, *Relief and Social Security,* pp. 364, 365; House Committee on Appropriations, *Hearings on Work Relief and Relief for Fiscal Year,* 1941, p. 442; Macmahon, Millett, and Ogden, *Federal Work Relief,* pp. 132, 133, 224, 225.

4. Meriam, *Relief and Social Security,* pp. 423, 424; Brown, *Public Relief,* p. 325; Dr. Grace Abbott, cited in the Newark *Evening News,* February 18, 1936; New York *Times,* May 20, 1938; *Proceedings,* National Conference of Social Workers (1940), p. 173.

5. Meriam, *Relief and Social Security,* pp. 413, 414, 415.

6. Macmahon, Millett, and Ogden, *Federal Work Relief,* pp. 124–26; WPA, *Our Job With the WPA* (Washington: Government Printing Office, 1936), p. 14; WPA, *Handbook of Procedures,* Chapter 15, Sec. 5, May 15, 1936; Howard, *The WPA,* pp. 232–46, 260; Hopkins, statement to the Committee to Investigate Unemployment and Relief, April 8, 1938, Hopkins MSS; *The Efficiency of Skilled Workmen on Works Progress Administration Projects* (Washington: Government Printing Office, 1937), pp. 1, 2; Bakke, *The Unemployed Worker,* p. 404.

7. National Appraisal Committee Report, p. 23.

8. Cited in Howard, *The WPA,* p. 254.

9. Hearings on Work Relief and Relief for Fiscal Year 1943, 77th Cong., 2nd Sess., p. 40; *Fortune,* XVI (October, 1937), p. 42; R. Post, New York *Times,* June 2, 1935.

10. Cited in the New York *Herald Tribune,* May 23, 1935.

11. Meriam, *Relief and Social Security,* pp. 416–18; Howard, *The WPA,* p. 173.

12. *Cong. Record,* May 16, 1940, p. 6250.

13. File of Polls, Hopkins MSS.

14. National Appraisal Committee Report, p. 7.

15. Howard, *The WPA,* 847.

XII. HOPKINS' IMPRINT

1. Heywood Broun, Washington *Daily News,* December 26, 1938.

2. December 24, 1938.

3. Commencement Address, Babson Institute, June 12, 1937, Hopkins MSS. A. Williams delivered the address for Hopkins.

4. August 16, 1940, Hopkins MSS.

5. May 31, 1939, Hopkins MSS.

6. Walter Davenport to W. H. Matthews of the Community Service Society of New York, May 11, 1939, Hopkins MSS;

Raymond Gram Swing as cited in Howard, *The WPA*, p. 746.

7. Interview with Lorena Hickok, July 16, 1958.

8. Eleanor Roosevelt, *This I Remember*, pp. 167, 168; interview with Benjamin Cohen, December 30, 1958.

9. November 6, 1935, Hopkins MSS.

Bibliography

The most valuable source of information used in the preparation of this book was the Hopkins Manuscript material located in the Franklin D. Roosevelt Library. These materials are rich in information concerning Hopkins and the federal relief agencies. In addition, the reports of Miss Lorena Hickok and the field representatives for the FERA and WPA contain useful social, economic, and political history of the mid-thirties. Other worthwhile resources were the personal interviews, letters to the author, material in the National Archives, the Oral History Research Office, and the various official papers in the Franklin D. Roosevelt manuscripts. Several secondary works contain helpful information. The listing of them is limited to those I found most useful.

MANUSCRIPTS

THE HOPKINS MANUSCRIPTS

Addresses and Speeches
Appointment and Datebooks
Collections of Cartoons
Congressional Hearings at which Hopkins Testified
Executive Orders of the President (related to relief agencies, 1933–1938)
File of Polls (summary), 1935–1940
Files of Correspondence (Individual and Organizations)
Photograph Album
Press Conferences
Proceedings, The Advisory Committee on Allotments, vols. 1–16, May-August, 1935
Proceedings, Staff Meetings and Conferences of State Administrators
Reports of Field Representatives
Scrapbooks: FERA, CWA, FSRC, WPA, vols. 1–18; Commerce, vols. 1–5
Special Reports and Letters of Lorena Hickok
Telephone Conversations
Works Progress Administration, General Letters; Hopkins to State Administrators; Bulletins; Press Releases

THE FRANKLIN D. ROOSEVELT MANUSCRIPTS

President's Official File
President's Personal File
President's Secretary File

NATIONAL ARCHIVES

National Resources Planning Board, General Correspondence, WPA-310
Works Progress Administration, Division of Information, Press Releases and Clippings; Investigations and Politics
———. General Administration (Washington Office), WPA-100
———. State Administration (Washington, Regional, and State Offices), WPA-600

DOCUMENTS

Congressional Record. 73rd Cong., 1st Sess.–76th Cong., 3rd Sess., vols. 77–86. Washington: Government Printing Office, 1932–1940.
U.S. Congress, House of Representatives. Hearings before the Subcommittee of the Committee on Appropriations. *Emergency Relief Appropriations.* 74th Cong., 1st Sess., H. J. Res. 117. Washington: Government Printing Office, 1935.
———. Hearings before the Subcommittee of the Committee on Appropriations. *First Deficiency Appropriations Bill for 1936.* 74th Cong., 2nd Sess., statements of Harry L. Hopkins (extract). Washington: Government Printing Office, 1936.
———. Hearings before the Subcommittee of the House Committee on Appropriations. *First Deficiency Appropriation Bill for 1937.* 75th Cong., 1st Sess. Washington: Government Printing Office, 1937.
———. Hearings before the Subcommittee of the Committee on Appropriations. *Emergency Relief Appropriation Act of 1937.* 75th Cong., 1st Sess. Washington: Government Printing Office, 1937.
———. Hearings before the Subcommittee of the House Committee on Appropriations. *Emergency Relief Appropriation Act of 1938 and Public Works Administration Act of 1938.* 75th Cong., 3rd Sess. Washington: Government Printing Office, 1938.

———. Subcommittee of the Committee on Appropriations. *Investigation and Study of the Works Projects Administration.* 76th Cong., 1st–3rd Sess., H. Res. 130, Report No. 2187. Washington: Government Printing Office, 1939–1940.

———. Hearings before the Committee on Appropriations. *Work Relief and Relief for Fiscal Year 1941.* 76th Cong., 3rd Sess. Washington: Government Printing Office, 1940.

———. Special Committee on Un-American Activities. *Investigation of Un-American Propaganda Activities in the United States.* 75th Cong., 2nd Sess.–77th Cong., 1st Sess., vols. 1–14. Washington: Government Printing Office, 1939–1941.

U.S. Congress, Senate. Subcommittee of the Committee on Manufactures. *Unemployment Relief.* 72nd. Cong., 1st Sess., S. 174 and S. 262. Washington: Government Printing Office, 1932.

———. Committee on Manufactures. *Hearings on Senate Bill No. 4592.* 72nd. Cong., 1st Sess. Washington: Government Printing Office, 1932.

———. Committee on Manufactures. *Federal Aid for Unemployment Relief.* 72nd Cong., 2nd Sess., S. 5125. Washington: Government Printing Office, 1933.

———. Hearings before the Committee on Appropriations. *Federal Emergency Relief and Civil Works Program.* 73rd Cong., 2nd Sess., H. R. 7527. Washington: Government Printing Office, 1934.

———. Committee on Appropriations. *Expenditure of Funds, Federal Emergency Relief Administration.* 74th Cong., 1st Sess., Sen. Doc. No. 56. Washington: Government Printing Office, 1935.

———. Hearings before the Committee on Appropriations. *Emergency Relief Appropriation.* 74th Cong., 1st Sess., H. J. Res. 117. Washington: Government Printing Office, 1935.

———. Committee on Appropriations. *Supplemental Hearings, Emergency Relief Appropriation.* 74th Cong., 1st Sess., H. J. Res. 117. Washington: Government Printing Office, 1935.

———. Hearings before the Subcommittee on Appropriations. *First Deficiency Appropriation Bill for 1936.* 74th Cong., 2nd Sess., H. R. 12624. Washington: Government Printing Office, 1936.

———. Hearings before the Subcommittee of the Committee on Appropriations. *First Deficiency Appropriation Bill for*

1937. 75th Cong., 1st Sess., H. R. 3587. Washington: Government Printing Office, 1937

———. Hearings before the Committee on Appropriations. *Emergency Relief Appropriation.* 75th Cong., 1st Sess. Washington: Government Printing Office, 1937.

———. Committee on Unemployment and Relief. *Preliminary Report.* 75th Cong., 3rd Sess., Report No. 1625. Washington: Government Printing Office, 1938.

———. Hearings before the Committee on Appropriations. *Work Relief and Public Works Appropriation Act of 1938.* 75th Cong., 3rd Sess., H. J. Res. 679. Washington: Government Printing Office, 1938.

———. Hearings before the Committee on Appropriations. *Work Relief and Public Works Appropriation Act of 1938.* 75th Cong., 3rd Sess., H. J. Res. 83. Washington: Government Printing Office, 1938.

———. Special Committee to Investigate Campaign Expenditures and Use of Government Funds. *Investigation of Senatorial Campaign Expenditures and Use of Government Funds.* 76th Cong., 1st Sess., Report No. 1 (Pursuant to S. Res. Nos. 283 and 290). Washington: Government Printing Office, 1939.

———. Hearings before the Committee on Appropriations. *Work Relief and Relief, Fiscal Year 1939.* 76th Cong., 1st Sess., H. J. Res. 83. Washington: Government Printing Office, 1939.

BOOKS, NEWSPAPERS, PERIODICALS

Adams, Grace K. *Workers on Relief.* New Haven: Yale University Press, 1939.

Alsop, Joseph, and Kintner, Robert. *Men Around the President.* New York: Doubleday, Doran and Co., 1939.

Armstrong, Louise. *We Too Are the People.* Boston: Little, Brown and Co., 1938.

Bakke, E. Wight. *The Unemployed Worker.* New Haven: Yale University Press, 1940.

Belair, Felix. "Harry L. Hopkins: Lender and Spender," *Life* (September 22, 1941), 11:88–90.

Blum, John M. *From the Morgenthau Diaries: Years of Crises, 1928–1938.* Boston: Houghton, Mifflin Co., 1959.

Brown, Josephine C. *Public Relief, 1929–1939.* New York: Henry Holt and Co., 1940.

Burns, Arthur E. "The Federal Emergency Relief Administration," *Municipal Year Book.* Chicago: International City Managers Association, 1937.

Carothers, Doris. *Chronology of the Federal Emergency Relief Administration, May 12, 1933 to December 31, 1935.* Washington: Works Progress Administration, 1937.

Carter, John Franklin. *The New Dealers.* New York: Simon and Schuster, 1934.

Childs, Marquis. "The President's Best Friend," *Saturday Evening Post* (April 19, 26, 1941), 213:9–11; 213:29.

Clapper, Raymond. "Who is Hopkins?" *Forum* (December, 1937). 98:283–87.

Clark, Delbert. "The Brain Trust Remolded," New York *Times,* December 29, 1935, VII.

Coyle, David Cushman. "The W. P. A.; Loafers or Workers?" *Forum* (March, 1939), 101:170–74.

Davenport, Walter. "From Whom All Blessings Flow," *Collier's* (July 20, 1935), 96:7, 8.

Dewey, Thomas E. *The Case Against the New Deal.* 2nd ed. New York: Harper and Brothers, 1940.

Farley, James. *Jim Farley's Story: The Roosevelt Years.* New York: Whittlesey House, 1948.

FERA. *The Emergency Work Relief Program of the FERA, April 1, 1934–July 1, 1935.* Federal Emergency Relief Administration, 1935.

Flanagan, Hallie. *Arena.* New York: Russell Sage Foundation, 1940.

Flynn, John T. *Country Squire in the White House.* Garden City: Doubleday, Doran and Co., Inc., 1940.

———. *The Roosevelt Myth.* New York: The Devin-Adair Co., 1948.

Gebhart, John C. "Boon or Bone? But An Expensive One!" *Christian Science Monitor* (Magazine Section), August 19, 1936.

Gill, Corrington. "The Civil Works Administration," *Municipal Year Book* (1937), 4:419–32.

———. *Wasted Manpower.* New York: W. W. Norton Co., 1939.

Hayes, E. P. *Activities of the President's Committee for Employment*. Concord, New Hampshire: The Rumford Press, 1936.

Hellman, G. T. "House Guest: Harry Hopkins," *The Roosevelt Era*, Milton Crane, ed. New York: Boni and Gaer, 1947.

High, Stanley. *Roosevelt—and Then?* New York: Harper and Brothers, 1937.

Hoover, Herbert C. *Memoirs*, Vol. 3, *The Great Depression, 1929–1941*. New York: Macmillan Co., 1952.

———. "My White House Years; The Great Depression," *Collier's* (April 19, 26, May 3, 10, 17, 24, 31, 1952), 129:15–17; 129:26–27; 129:18–19; 129:26–27; 129:22–31; 129:27; 129:30.

Hopkins, Harry L. "Beyond Relief: The Larger Task," New York *Times*, August 19, 1934, VI.

———. "Employment in America," *Vital Speeches* (December, 1936), 3:103–107.

———. "Food for the Hungry," *Collier's* (December 7, 1935), 96:10, 11.

———. "The Future of Relief," *New Republic* (February 10, 1937), 90:7–10.

———. *Spending to Save: The Complete Story of Relief*. New York: W. W. Norton and Co., Inc., 1936.

Howard, Donald S. *The WPA and Federal Relief Policy*. New York: Russell Sage Foundation, 1943.

Ickes, Harold L. *Back to Work: The Story of the PWA*. New York: Macmillan Co., 1935.

———. "My Twelve Years With Roosevelt," *Saturday Evening Post* (June 5, 12, 19, 26, July 3, 10, 17, 24, 1948), 220:15–17; 220:30–31; 220:34–35; 220:36–37; 221:28; 221:30–31; 221:32–33.

———. *The Secret Diary of Harold L. Ickes*. Vol. 1. *The First Thousand Days, 1933–1936*. New York: Simon and Schuster, 1953.

Leuchtenberg, William E. *The Perils of Prosperity, 1914–1932*. Chicago: University of Chicago Press, 1958.

Macmahon, A. W., and Millett, J. D., and Ogden, Gladys. *The Administration of Federal Work Relief*. Chicago: Public Administration Service, 1941.

Meriam, Lewis. *Relief and Social Security*. Washington: The Brookings Institution, 1946.

Millett, John D. *The Works Progress Administration in New York City*. Chicago: Public Administrative Service, 1938.

Myers, William S., ed. *The State Papers and Other Public Writings of Herbert Hoover*. 2 vols. Garden City: Doubleday, Doran and Co., Inc., 1934.

National Conference of Social Work. *Proceedings*. Chicago: University of Chicago Press, 1932–38.

National Youth Administration. *Administrative and Program Operation of the National Youth Administration*. Washington: Government Printing Office, 1937.

Newsweek. Vols. 1–17, 1933–1940.

New York *Times*. 1930–1940.

Rodgers, Cleveland. *Robert Moses*. New York: Henry Holt and Co., 1953.

Schlesinger, Jr., Arthur M. *The Age of Roosevelt*. Vols. I, II, III. Boston: Houghton Mifflin Co., 1957, 1958, 1960.

Sherwood, Robert. *Roosevelt and Hopkins: An Intimate History*. New York: Harper and Brothers, 1948.

Survey Graphic. Vols. 22–26. July, 1932–June, 1937.

Tugwell, Rexford G. *The Democratic Roosevelt*. New York: Doubleday and Co., Inc., 1957.

Whiting, Theodore. *Final Statistical Report of the Federal Emergency Relief Administration*. Washington: Government Printing Office, 1942.

Wilbur, R. L., and Hyde, A. M. *The Hoover Policies*. New York: Charles Scribner's Sons, 1937.

Williams, Edward A. *Federal Aid for Relief*. New York: Columbia University Press, 1939.

Index

Aberdeen (South Dakota) *News*, 212
Acton, Lord, 93
Adams, Alva B., 182
Advisory Committee on Allotments (PWA), 111, 116, 118, 119, 123, 138, 139
Agricultural Adjustment Administration, 69, 82, 86
Agriculture, Department of, 223
Alabama, 84
Allen, C. L., 187
Allotment Board, *see* Advisory Committee on Allotments
Alsop, Joseph, 216
American Association of Social Workers, 61, 66
American Bankers Association, 95, 111
American Farm Bureau, 18
American Federation of Labor, 150
American Liberty League, 49, 99
American Public Welfare Association, 29, 30, 226
Anacostia Flats, *see* Veterans Bonus March (1932)
Anderson, George, 81
Anderson, Sherwood, 14
Arnstein, Daniel, 216
Association for Improving the Condition of the Poor, 227
Atlanta, Georgia, 149, 152

Babson Institute, 241
Bailey, Josiah W., 162, 163
Baker, Jacob: early years, 30; heads Work Division of FERA, 30; role in WPA, 129
Bakke, E. Wight, 23, 148
Baltimore, Maryland, 152
Bane, Frank, 29, 46, 48
Barkley, Alben W., 96, 163, 195–98 *passim*, 211
Bartlett, Joseph W., 48
Baruch, Bernard, 15
Bell, Daniel, 103, 109, 122, 164
Benson, Elmer A., 186
Bilbo, Theodore, 74, 163, 165, 183, 205
Blanket codes (NRA), 52
Bloch, Don, 89
Blue Bonnet, The, 125
Boland, Patrick, 174
Bookman, C. M., 29, 225
Boondoggling, 70, 154
Borah, William E., 8, 9
Bordeaux, University of, 29
Boston, Massachusetts, 11
Boston Council of Social Agencies, 29
Branion, Ray, 55, 56
Broun, Heywood, 217, 239
Brown, Josephine C., 225
Brown, Lewis, 96
Brownlow, Louis, 46–48 *passim*
Bulkley, Robert, 95, 165
Bureau of the Budget, 111, 113
Bureau of Public Roads, Chief of, 111
Burnes, Allen T., 233
Business Advisory and Planning Council, 96, 111
Byrd, H. C., 242
Byrd, Harry F., 205, 206
Byrnes, James F., 106, 107, 161–63 *passim*

California, 51, 55, 182, 184, 199, 207

Caraway, Thaddeus H., 8
Census Bureau, 58
Census of 1940, 168
Chandler, Albert B., 195–98 *passim*
Charleston (S.C.) *Mail*, 240
Chautauqua Institution, 216
Chicago, 57, 217
Chicago *News*, 42
Chicago, University of, 30, 46
Christgau, Victor, 186, 187
Churchill, Winston, 44
Cincinnati, Ohio, 231
Citizens League of Cleveland, 78
Civilian Conservation Corps, 112, 153, 154
Civil Works Administration: well received by public, 48; criticized by Al Smith, 49; organization of, 50; funds for, 50, 51, 60; types of projects, 52; wage scale, 52, 53, 63; staff, 54; politics in, 55–58 *passim*; graft in, 57, 58; curtailed, 61, 62; psychological influence, 63; defects and assets summarized, 62–65; general, 24, 27, 31, 35, 66, 92, 104, 113, 128, 129, 145
Clapper, Raymond, 200, 201, 212
Clark, Bennett Champ, 105, 214
Clark, Delbert, 94
Cleveland, 11
Cleveland *News*, 78
Cleveland (Ohio) *Plain Dealer*, 78
Cleveland Welfare Association, 30
Coffee, John M., 212
Commissioner of Reclamation, 111
Committee on Economic Security, 91
Committee on Procedure (WPA), 130, 131
Committee on Stabilization of Industry, 19
Committee to Investigate Unemployment and Relief, 149
Commons, John R., 47
Commonwealth Club of San Francisco, 208
Communists, 61
Community Chests and Councils, 233
Comptroller General, 139, 222
Congress: aid to drought (1930) victims, 30; provides 345 million dollars for CWA, 50; prevailing wage for WPA, 105; sets WPA administrative costs, 138; earmarks WPA funds, 159–62 *passim;* WPA rolls, 167, 168; general, 14, 90, 94, 100, 103, 151, 157, 173, 182, 187, 200–03 *passim*, 212, 215, 222, 230, 232, 237
Congressional Record, 102
Contract systems, 51, 228
Copeland, Royal S., 164
Corcoran, Thomas G., 215
Costigan, Edward P., 54, 55
Coughlin, Charles E., 99, 100
Council of Social Agencies (Cincinnati, Ohio), 29
Cox, Edward E., 106
Coy, Wayne, 177, 188, 194
Cramford, Fred L., 59, 60
Creel, George, 55, 56
Croxton, Fred, 11, 13
Culkin, Francis D., 106
Curley, James M., 184, 185
Curtis, Arthur M., 190
Cutting, Bronson, 60

Davey, Martin L., 76–80 *passim*, 92, 174
Davey-Roosevelt Clubs, 207
Davies, Joseph E., 24

Democratic National Committee, 56
Depression, impact, 1, 2, 5, 6, 11, 15, 96
Detroit *Free Press*, 89
Dewey, Thomas E., 167
Dickinson, Lester J., 212
Dieterich, William H., 182
District of Columbia, 84
Division of Application and Information, 122, 130, 138
Dolan, Ed, 54
Donahey, Alvin V., 165
Dort, Dallas, 130, 136
Douglas, James M., 191
Douglas, Lewis, 61
Drought: of 1930, 7, 8; of 1934, 82, 86; of 1936, 159
Dunham, Robert, 182

Earle, George, 41, 164, 192, 213
Early, Steve, 105, 108, 126
Edmonds, T. S., 48
Edwards, Paul, 185
Elections: of 1932, 1; of 1934, 98; of 1936, 114, 156, 159, 175, 195, 206–10 *passim*; of 1938, 175, 195, 197; of 1940, 213, 214, 215, 235
Elliott, John B., 56
Emergency and Reconstruction Relief Act of 1932, 16
Emergency Relief Appropriations Act (1935), 101, 102, 103–06 *passim*, 176
Employables, 31
Employment Stabilization Research Institute (University of Minnesota), 13
Evansville, Indiana, 231
Ewing, Sherrard, 30

Fairmont, West Virginia, 230
Farley, James, 53, 74, 75, 92, 96, 97, 126, 142, 185, 187, 199, 205–08 *passim*, 217, 218
Farm Security Administration, 221
Federal Bureau of Investigation, 136
Federal Emergency Relief Act, 5
Federal Emergency Relief Administration (FERA): staff, 28–30; administrative organization, 30, 31; objectives, 30–32 *passim*; major regulations, 32, 33; field representatives, 32, 36; funds, 33–35 *passim*, 39; states told to contribute, 37; encouragement of adequate relief, 37; Municipal Finance Section, 39–41; types of projects, 67; accomplishments of, 67, 68; white-collar projects, 69, 70; mattress-making, 69, 70; politics in, 74–76 *passim*; transient program, 84, 85, 86; rural rehabilitation, 87–89 *passim*; Matanuska Valley Project, 88, 89; to liquidate direct relief, 101; general, 22, 23, 28, 29, 53, 61, 94, 109, 130, 134, 153, 178, 204, 221, 226, 238, 247
Federal Employment Stabilization Board, 29
Federal Housing Administration (FHA), 95, 99
Federal Surplus Relief Corporation (FSRC): formed, 82; products handled, 82; removes surpluses, 84; difficulties handling beef cattle, 83
Federal Work Relief Corporation, 95
Federal Works Agency, 130, 135
Fee, Harry W., 193
First Talbot Act (Pennsylvania), 227
Fish, Hamilton, 174
Fletcher, Henry P., 191

Floods: of 1936, 159; of 1937, 159
Fortune, 236
Frank, Waldo, 17

Gardner, Neil, 75
Garfield, James R., 13
Garner, John N.: supports public works, 14; opposes funds for CWA, 61; and politics in FERA, 75, 76
General Accounting Office, 222, 223
George, Walter F., 206, 215
Gifford, Walter S., 13
Gill, Corrington: background, 29; works on CWA plans, 48; CWA projects, 51; on WPA staff, 129
Gillette, Guy, 165, 214–16 *passim*
Glass, Carter, 38, 105
Glass, Harry, Jr., 198, 199
Gompers, Samuel, 47
Goodman, George H., 196, 197
Gordon, Max, 216
Gore, Thomas P., 183
Governor's Committee on Unemployment (N.Y.), 19
Grand Rapids, Michigan, 140
Grant-in-aid system, 33, 34
Greater Cleveland, 78
Green, William, 12
Griffith, E. J., 207
Grinnell College, 23
Guffey, Joseph F., 74, 192, 194, 205

Haber, William, 199
Hague, Frank, 217
Hall, P. M., 56
Hard, William, 194
Harriman, Henry I., 96
Harrington, F. C., 192, 204, 229, 240
Harrison, Pat (Bryan Patton), 96, 163, 165. 211
Hart, Roy, 182, 184
Hartford, Connecticut, 54
Harvard Law School, 30
Hayden, Carl, 163
Haynes, Rowland, 30
Heinz, Howard, 96
Herring, Clyde L., 165
Hess, William E., 102
Hickok, Lorena, 140, 150, 179, 192, 186, 187, 193, 194, 199, 207
High, Stanley, 174, 244
Hinckley, Robert, 182
Hofstadter, Richard, 45, 99
Hoke, Fred, 51
Holiday Farm Movement, 18
Holt, Rush, 187–90 *passim*, 201
Home Loan Bank Bill, 14
Hoover, Herbert C.: response to 1929 crash, 6, 7; aid to drought victims, 1930, 8–10, *passim*; health of nation better, 12; forms voluntary relief organization, 10, 13; opposed to non-self-liquidating public works, 14; confers with congressional leaders, 15; supports Emergency and Reconstruction Relief Act of 1932, 16; opposes direct federal relief, 16, 18; response to Veterans Bonus March of 1932, 17; pattern of aid to needy, 18, 19, 54
"Hoovervilles," 15
Hope, Grover, 75
Hopkins, Barbara, 174, 202, 214, 239
Hopkins, Harry L.: becomes federal relief administrator, 5; early career, 23; personal traits, 24, 25, 92, 93, 219, 242–46 *passim*; described by Ernie Pyle, 25; faith in unemployed, 28; selects FERA personnel, 29, 30; organizes FERA, 31–33; stresses state

and local contributions, 37–39, 43; accused of coercing state of Illinois, 42; raises quality of relief, 43; seeks to aid recovery, 46, 47; sells CWA to Roosevelt, 47; organizes CWA, 48; replies to criticism by Al Smith, 49, 50; dislikes CWA wage scales, 53; politics in CWA, 54–57 *passim;* graft in CWA, 58, 59; seeks public understanding of CWA, 59, 60; curtails CWA, 61; prefers work relief, 68, 69; defends white-collar projects, 70–73; battles politics in FERA, 74–81 *passim;* named president of FSRC, 82; maintains transient program, 84, 85; for low-cost housing, 90, 91; interest in self-help communities, 87, 90; helps with Social Security Act, 91; to Europe, 91; leading New Dealer, 92, 93; address on economic security, 98; backs security wage, 104, 105; plans for work program, 108, 109; head of WPA, 112; feud with Ickes, 106–27 *passim;* pushes WPA, 120; responsibilities defined, 124; to Cocos Islands, 125; names WPA staff, 129, 130; organizes WPA, 133–38; dislikes red tape, 139, 140; defends WPA workers, 148; opposed to congressional earmarking of funds, 160, 164; comments on unemployment trends, 169–71; curtails WPA, 172; says WPA not a political asset, 174; dislikes senatorial courtesy system, 176; sends directives on political activity in WPA, 180, 181; and politics in WPA, 184–205 *passim;* wants WPA staff on civil service, 200, 201; presidential aspirations, 206–19 *passim;* speech before Commonwealth Club, 208, 209; speech "Jobs vs. Jibes," 209, 210; presidential chances in 1940, 213; health, 213, 214; tax and spend and elect incident, 216; Secretary of Commerce, 216, 218; opposes means tests, 226; hates "dole" relief, 237; evaluation as administrator, 237–48; general, 2, 21, 34, 35, 41, 66, 89, 94, 102, 103, 112, 114, 118, 127, 144, 151, 159, 174, 178, 179, 182, 189, 190, 191, 197, 199, 202, 205, 211, 225, 231, 232, 234, 236, 241

Hopkins, Lewis, 140

Horner, Henry, 42

Howe, Louis, 92, 107, 211, 246

Hull, Cordell, 213

Hundred Days, 5, 44

Hunter, Howard O., 30, 48, 130, 165, 217

Hutchins, Robert, 46

Hyde Park (New York), 97, 121

Hyde Park Conference, 122, 123

Ickes, Harold: develops PWA slowly, 47; confers with FDR, 96; plans public works, 98; Ickes-Hopkins feud, 106–27 *passim;* named head of Advisory Committee on Allotments, 111; and new work organization, 113, 115–27 *passim;* seeks larger role for PWA, 121, 122, 124; dislikes Roosevelt's allotment of funds, 124, 125; to Cocos Islands, 125; general, 49, 92, 102, 103, 143, 159, 206, 213, 215, 221, 240, 242, 245

Illinois, 51, 187

Indiana, 51

Indiana County, Pennsylvania, 192
Iowa, 217

Jackson (Mississippi) *Daily News*, 212
Jenckes, Virginia E., 184
Jersey City, New Jersey, 217
Johnson, Hiram, 164
Johnson, Hugh S., 92, 129, 145, 154–57 *passim*, 201, 212, 217
Johnstone, Alan, 30, 56, 130, 188, 190
Jones, Edward, 192–94 *passim*
Justice, Department of, 58

Kansas, 210
Kansas City, Missouri, 47, 190, 192
Keenan, Joseph, 56
Keller, K. E., 230
Kelley, Ed, 121, 217
Kelly-Nash Machine, 57
Kelso, Robert, 29
Kennedy, Joseph P., 215
Kent, Frank, 216
Kentucky, 187, 195–97 *passim*
King, William H., 183
Kintner, Robert, 216
Krock, Arthur, 165, 216
Kump, Herman Guy, 187

Laffoon, Ruby, 38
La Follette, Robert, Jr., 163, 174, 213
La Guardia, Fiorello, 98, 164, 212, 213
Landon, Alfred, 209, 210, 225
Langer, William, 76
Lehman, Herbert, 38
Lee, John C. H., 64, 65
Lewis, Fulton, Jr., 89
Lewis, Hamilton J., 182
Lippmann, Walter, 44
London Economic Conference, 46
Long, Huey, 98, 177
Long Island, 239
Los Angeles, 208
Ludlow, Louis, 104
Lundeen, Ernest, 164, 186

MacArthur, Douglas, 17
Maine, 183
Maryland, 17
Maryland, University of, 242
Massachusetts, 48, 183, 184
Matthews, William H., 227
Maverick, Maury, 161
Mayo Clinic, 214
McAdoo, William G., 55–57 *passim*, 163
McCarran, Patrick, 75, 105, 106, 183
McCarran Amendment to Work Relief Bill, 105
McCormack, John, 185
McCullough, Wicher, 187, 189
McElroy, J. F., 47
McGrath, Joseph, 185
McIntyre, Marvin H., 58, 75, 105, 108
McKellar, Kenneth, 205
McNutt, Paul, 51, 184, 213
Mexico, 30
Michigan, 13, 51, 184, 198, 199, 217
Minnesota, 41, 184, 217
Mississippi, 183, 187
Missouri, 187, 191, 192
Moffett, James, 95, 96
Moley, Raymond, 92
Morgenthau, Henry, Jr., 96, 107, 120, 126, 127
Morrill Act of 1862, 33
Moser, Guy L., 163, 164
Moses, Robert, 126
Murphy, Frank, 213, 217
Murray, James, 75, 182, 184
Murray, Matt, 191–92 *passim*

National Appraisal Committee, 230, 235

National Association of Manufacturers, 70, 95, 240
National Conference of Social Work, 29
National Conference on Economic Security, 98
National Democratic Committee, 95
National Emergency Council, 111
National Industrial Recovery Act, 45, 48, 52, 95
National Recovery Administration, 95, 154
National Resources Planning Board, 111
National Works Authority, 109, 110
National Youth Administration: objectives, 152; programs, 153; effects, 247
Need: defined, 27; importance in allotting funds, 41
Neely, Matthew M., 187–89 *passim*
Nevada, 183
New Deal, 2, 33, 46, 62, 92, 96, 99, 107, 196, 200, 211
New England, 48
New England hurricane (1938), 168
New Haven, Connecticut, 148
New Jersey, 51, 194
New Republic, The, 187
New York City, 11, 23, 70, 151, 152, 154–57 *passim*, 231
New York *Daily News,* 121
New York State, 38, 51, 172, 207
New York Temporary Relief Administration, 23
New York Temporary Relief Commission, 20
New York *Times,* The, 94, 217
Niles, David K., 130
Norris, George, 9, 163
North Dakota, 217
O'Connor, John, 216
Oglethorpe University, 21
Ohio, 51, 246
Ohio State Legislature, 81
Ohio State University, 246
Olson, Floyd, 41, 76, 186
Omaha, Nebraska, 152
O'Neal, Ed, 18
Orland, Indiana, 230
Osborn, Chase S., 89
Overton, John H., 165

Pendergast political machine, 190, 191
Pennsylvania, 11, 42, 51, 152, 187, 194, 227
Peoples, Christian J., 105, 109
Philadelphia, Pennsylvania, 11, 194
Pierson, H. L., 199
Pinchot, Gifford, 11, 54
Pittman, Key, 75, 183, 184
Pittsburgh, Pennsylvania, 152, 194
Pittsburgh *Post Gazette,* 215
Politics, *see* same topic under FERA, CWA, and WPA
"Poor laws," 25, 26
Portland, Oregon, 207
Portland *Oregonian,* 215
Powell, Hickman, 201
President's Emergency Relief Organization, 10, 11
President's Organization on Unemployment Relief, 13
Production-for-use projects, 68–70
Public Administration Clearing House, 46
Public Administration Service, 130, 141
Public Health Service, 12, 221
Public Service Commission (Kansas City, Missouri), 192
Public Works Administration: objectives, 46; man-year costs, 143; general, 48, 49, 53, 59, 60,

Public Works Adm. (*cont.*) 103, 104, 108, 110, 112, 114, 117–23 *passim*, 138, 142, 153, 223, 228
Pulaski County, Kentucky, 197
Pulliam, Eugene, 242
Purge of 1938, *see* Elections, of 1938
Pyle, Ernie, 24

Rayburn, Sam, 163
Recession of 1937–38, 159, 167, 168
Reconstruction Finance Corporation, 14, 16, 19, 29, 54
Red Cross, 8
Relief: types of relief, 68, 69; funds for in 1933–1935, 73
Republican National Committee, 190
Resettlement Administration, 153, 221, 223
Richberg, Donald, 96, 97
Robinson, Joseph: drought relief, 8; public works, 14, 15; senate majority leader, 163; death, 210
Roosevelt, Eleanor, 179, 202, 211, 239, 243, 246
Roosevelt, Franklin D.: becomes president, 1; sweeping actions, 2; wants adequate relief, 5; relief program as governor, 19, 20; "forgotten man" address, 21; wants experimentation, 21; appoints Hopkins head of FERA, 23; tells states to contribute, 37, 38; conservative course in 1933, 45; London Conference, 46; starts CWA, 47, 50; curtails CWA, 61, 62; directs Hopkins to control relief in Ohio, 79; starts FSRC, 82; sends Hopkins to Europe,, 91; confers with congressional leaders, 96, 97; challenged by demagogues, 99; for low-cost housing, 98, 99; outlines new work program, 100, 101; selects personnel for new work program, 106, 110, 111; divides work relief funds, 123; to Cocos Islands, 125; supports idea of 90 per cent of WPA workers from relief rolls, 145; removes Hugh Johnson, 154; curtails WPA, 172; keeps Hopkins' name in 1940 presidential picture, 216; mentioned, 6, 44, 49, 54, 56, 60, 68, 74, 90, 92, 95, 105, 108, 109, 112, 114, 118, 130, 136, 140, 142, 143, 160–62 *passim*, 163, 182, 183, 184–87 *passim*, 191, 199, 202, 205–09 *passim*, 211, 213, 215–25 *passim*, 234, 237, 239, 243–47 *passim*
Roosevelt, James, 183–85 *passim*
Roosevelt, Theodore, 45
Roper, Daniel, 96, 126
Roper, Richard F., 56
Rotch, Arthur, 184, 185
Rowe, Ernest, 197
Rural Electrification Administration, 109
Rural Rehabilitation Division of FERA, *see* FERA, rural rehabilitation
Russell County, Kentucky, 197

Saratoga Springs, New York, 214
Sault Ste. Marie *Evening News*, 89
Schall, Thomas D., 183
Schlesinger, Arthur, Jr., 108
Schwellenbach, Lewis B., 184
Self-sufficient communities, 88
Senate Committee on Appropriations, 103
Shearer, Mary C., 193
Sheppard Committee, 197, 198

Sherwood, Robert E., 207, 217, 218
Shrivers, Paul, 183
Sinclair, Upton, 95
Sioux City, Iowa, 49
Smith, Al, 15, 49, 54
Smoot, Reed, 11, 12
Social Security Act of 1935, 195
Somervell, Brehon, 203
South Carolina Relief Administration, 30
Spread-the-work program, 13
Stark, Lewis, 95
Stark, Lloyd C., 191, 192
Starnes, Joe, 164
State Board of Social Welfare (New York), 20
State Charities Aid Association (New York), 20
State relief before 1933, 26
Steiver, Frederick, 102, 103, 106, 226
Stevenson, R. A., 13
Stillman, Charles C., 77, 246
Stokes, Thomas L., 195–98 *passim*
Stone, Donald C., 130, 141
Stone, Julius F., 48
Stork, Tom, 208
Straus, Jesse I., 23
Strawn, Silas, 12
St. Louis Community Fund, 29
"Submerged third," 100, 166
Sunday, Billy, 233
Supreme Court, 195, 210
Swope, Herbert, 212, 213

Talmadge, Eugene, 24, 92, 96, 174
Tennessee, 187
Texas, 51
Time, 24, 59
Townsend, Francis E., 98
Trammell, Park, 183
Travelers' Aid Society, 30
Treasury, Department of, 139, 221–23 *passim*
Truman, Harry S., 47, 130
Tugwell, Rexford G., 96, 109, 122, 212
Tydings, Millard, 126

U.S. Army, 17, 111
U.S. Chamber of Commerce, 62, 95, 96
U.S. Employment Bureau, 12
U.S. Employment Service, 62, 188, 189, 221

Vandenburg, Arthur, 103, 105, 106, 192, 193
Vanguard Press, 30
Van Nuys, Frederick, 184
Veterans Bonus March (1932), 17
Vinson, Fred, 195
Voorhis, Horace (Jerry), 199

Wagner, Robert, 14, 16, 60, 174
Waite, Henry M., 97
Walker, Frank, 96, 111–15 *passim*, 119, 122
Wall, Roland, 183
Wallace, Henry A., 82, 92, 126, 213
Warm Springs, Georgia, 96, 97
Warner, Albert, 218
Washington *Post*, 72
Washington Press Service, 29
Washington *Star*, 89
Washington *Times*, 182
Wearin, Otha, 214, 215
Westbrook, Lawrence, 130, 207
West Virginia, 187–90 *passim*
Williams, Aubrey: early years, 30; administrator in FERA and CWA, 31, 47, 75, 76; WPA and NYA activities, 98, 129, 130, 152, 183, 192; comments

Williams, Aubrey (*cont.*)
on Hopkins and WPA, 202, 204, 243
Williams, Pierce, 29, 48, 55, 130
Wisconsin, 51, 217
Wisconsin State Journal, 49
Wisconsin, University of, 29
Woodrum, C. A., 233
Woodrum-Taylor Committee, 203
Woods, Arthur, 10, 11
Woods Committee, *see* President's Emergency Relief Organization
Woodson, Colonel (Kentucky), 197
Woodward, Mrs. Ellen S., 129
Work relief bill, 102–06 *passim*
Work tests, 25, 26
Workers' Alliance, 162
Works Progress Administration: wage policy, 104, 105, 150–52, 232; staff, 129–32; objectives of, 131; administrative organization, 133–37; field representatives, 135; investigative force, 136; administrative costs, 137, 138; expansion and curtailment, 159–73 *passim*; relations with federal agencies, 139, 221–24; red tape in, 139, 140; criteria for selecting projects, 141, 142; project sponsors, 143; man-year costs, 143, 144; types of projects, 144; skills of workers, 144, 170; workers from relief rolls, 145; workers refuse jobs, 146, 147, 148; and labor shortage, 148, 149; strikes, 155; funds for, 161–66 *passim*; politics in, 174–205 *passim*, 226, 227; policy regarding politics, 179, 180; congressional pressures, 181, 182; evaluation of WPA, 220–36 *passim*; relations with states, 184–99, 225; efficiency of, 228, 229; as work agency, 227–29; as relief agency, 231–33; popularity, 235; general, 27, 62, 86, 123, 128, 156, 157, 158, 160, 177, 178, 203, 206–09, 212, 214, 215, 244, 247
World Court, 105, 162
World War I, 7, 29
World War II, 234, 247
Wyllie, J. E., 80

Young, Owen D., 13, 15